Churchyard Shadows

Churchyard Shadows

Tales of Clerical Crime,
Mystery and Suspense

Edited by Kevin Carolan

Hodder & Stoughton
LONDON SYDNEY AUCKLAND

British Library Cataloguing in Publication Data
A record for this book is available from the British Library

ISBN 0 340 74573 8

Typeset by Avon Dataset Ltd, Bidford-on-Avon, Warks

Printed and bound in Great Britain by
the Guernsey Press Co. Ltd, Channel Isles

Hodder & Stoughton Ltd
A Division of Hodder Headline
338 Euston Road
London NW1 3BH

To Elisabeth, Catherine and William
Three joyful mysteries

Contents

Acknowledgments

Every effort has been made to trace the owners of the copyright material in this book. It is the Editor's belief that the necessary permissions from publishers, authors, and authorised agents have been obtained. In the case of any question arising as to the use of any material, the Editor will be pleased to make the necessary corrections in future editions of the book.

The Editor gratefully acknowledges permission to reprint copyright material as follows:

Ms Bella Jones on behalf of the Estate of E. C. Bentley for 'The Genuine Tabard' from *Trent Intervenes*, © 1938 E. C. Bentley.

Penguin Books for 'The Graveyard Sisterhood' from *Guy de Maupassant: Selected Short Stories*, translated by Roger Collet (Penguin Classics, 1971). © 1971 Roger Collet.

The Literary Trustees of Walter de la Mare, and the Society of Authors as their representative, for 'All Hallows' by Walter de la Mare.

'The Yellow Slugs', by H. C. Bailey, copyright © 1935 H. C. Bailey, from *Mr Fortune Objects* by permission of the Tessa Sayle Agency.

Mr Christopher Sinclair-Stevenson for 'The Hunted Beast' by T. F. Powys, copyright in this collection © 1999 by the Estate of T. F. Powys.

Introduction

We live busy lives nowadays. Most of us must have walked around a country church at some time or other, looked at the carefully laid-out gravestones, and felt a sense of peace and order. But there can also be movements in the shadows which make us uncomfortable. The desolation of many churches and cemeteries makes them an ideal spot to commit atrocious crimes. The vicarage can be filled with bitterness and religious frenzy as much as spiritual calm. The vicar can be as tormented a soul as his parishioners, if not more so.

The impact of temptation on a man of God is a recurrent theme in some of the most powerful stories in *Churchyard Shadows*. In 'The Strength of God' the Reverend Hartman accidentally spies upon a beautiful woman, while in the 'The Hunted Beast' the vicar of the village of East Dodder sees children hurting a rabbit – with terrible consequences. On the other hand, the great insight of a spiritual leader can be used as a tool to fight crime. This is true of the shaman of a small Alaskan tribe in Jack London's 'The Master of Mystery', and is a recurring theme of Post's celebrated 'Uncle Abner' stories. Uncle Abner is a farmer in Virginia at the beginning of the nineteenth century who is also a lay preacher. Note the electric tension of the story 'The Angel of the Lord', as well as Abner's voice whose denunciation of evil is like that of an Old Testament prophet.

One of the great battles of the nineteenth century was between the Church of England and the Nonconformist churches, between 'church' and 'chapel'. 'The Narrow Way' depicts this happening in a small Cornish fishing village. Is it great loneliness which drives the Reverend Lascelles to his dreadful crimes, or something more personal? Note the hints in the story of the vicar's intense friendship with young boys. 'The Yellow Slugs' is a story which shows the negative side of the Nonconformist tradition, where anybody could call themselves a 'preacher'. I have always thought that Bailey's detective Reggie Fortune has been unfairly neglected, and the story has a taut intensity as well as a great sense of spiritual evil.

Even the very fabric of a church can be dangerous if we think about it, which is the subject of the opening story in the collection, Aytoun's 'The Man in the Bell', as well as of Herman Melville's mysterious bell-tower. Of course, in the past church buildings were scenes of hideous cruelty, and both Edgar Allan Poe and Viscount de Lisle explore the horror of being a captive of the Spanish Inquisition. 'All Hallows' shows an old cathedral itself under attack, but by whom, or what? On the other hand, Guy de Maupassant finds love in a graveyard, perhaps something only a French writer could do.

The longest story in *Churchyard Shadows* is 'The Young Man in Holy Orders'. Written in Stevenson's breeziest style, it is the account of a young curate who discovers a fabulous stolen diamond, which corrupts him and leads him into great danger. Stevenson's detective, Prince Florizel, does have the great advantage of being King of Bohemia, and the character is believed to have been based upon Bertie, Prince of Wales, later King Edward VII. E. C. Bentley's novel *Trent's Last Case* is one of the classics of detective-story writing. In 'The Genuine Tabard' Trent investigates a church that seems to disappear.

In short, a wide variety of plots, subjects and styles. I enjoyed re-reading them, and I hope they entertain the reader. Can churchyards keep their old magic in the era of the Internet? Well, I have tried to tackle this in my own story 'Churchyard Shadows' which gives the book its title.

The Man in the Bell

W. E. Aytoun

In my younger days bell-ringing was much more in fashion among the young men of – than it is now. Nobody, I believe, practises it there at present except the servants of the church, and the melody has been much injured in consequence. Some fifty years ago about twenty of us who dwelt in the vicinity of the cathedral formed a club, which used to ring every peal that was called for; and from continual practice and a rivalry which arose between us and a club attached to another steeple, and which tended considerably to sharpen our zeal, we became very Mozarts on our favourite instruments. But my bell-ringing practice was shortened by a singular accident, which not only stopped my performance, but made even the sound of a bell terrible to my ears.

One Sunday I went with another into the belfry to ring for noon prayers, but the second stroke we had pulled showed us that the clapper of the bell we were at was muffled. Some one had been buried that morning, and it had been prepared, of course, to ring a mournful note. We did not know of this, but the remedy was easy.

'Jack,' said my companion, 'step up to the loft and cut off the hat;' for the way we had of muffling was by tying a piece of an old hat, or of cloth (the former was preferred), to one side of the clapper, which deadened every second toll.

I complied, and mounting into the belfry, crept as usual into the bell, where I began to cut away. The hat had been tied on in

1

some more complicated manner than usual, and I was perhaps three or four minutes in getting it off, during which time my companion below was hastily called away, by a message from his sweetheart, I believe; but that is not material to my story.

The person who called him was a brother of the club, who, knowing that the time had come for ringing for service, and not thinking that any one was above, began to pull. At this moment I was just getting out, when I felt the bell moving; I guessed the reason at once – it was a moment of terror; but by a hasty, and almost convulsive effort, I succeeded in jumping down, and throwing myself on the flat of my back under the bell.

The room in which it was was little more than sufficient to contain it, the bottom of the bell coming within a couple of feet of the floor of lath. At that time I certainly was not so bulky as I am now, but as I lay it was within an inch of my face. I had not laid myself down a second when the ringing began. It was a dreadful situation. Over me swung an immense mass of metal, one touch of which would have crushed me to pieces; the floor under me was principally composed of crazy laths, and if they gave way, I was precipitated to the distance of about fifty feet upon a loft, which would, in all probability, have sunk under the impulse of my fall, and sent me to be dashed to atoms upon the marble floor of the chancel, a hundred feet below.

I remembered – for fear is quick in recollection – how a common clock-wright, about a month before, had fallen, and bursting through the floors of the steeple, driven in the ceilings of the porch, and even broken into the marble tombstone of a bishop who slept beneath. This was my first terror, but the ringing had not continued a minute before a more awful and immediate dread came on me. The deafening sound of the bell smote into my ears with a thunder which made me fear their drums would crack. There was not a fibre of my body it did not thrill through; it entered my very soul; thought and reflection were almost utterly banished; I only retained the sensation of agonising terror.

Every moment I saw the bell sweep within an inch of my

2

face; and my eyes – I could not close them, though to look at the object was bitter as death – followed it instinctively in its oscillating progress until it came back again. It was in vain I said to myself that it could come no nearer at any future swing than it did at first; every time it descended I endeavoured to shrink into the very floor to avoid being buried under the down-sweeping mass; and then reflecting on the danger of pressing too weightily on my frail support, would cower up again as far as I dared.

At first my fears were mere matter of fact. I was afraid the pulleys above would give way and let the bell plunge on me. At another time the possibility of the clapper being shot out in some sweep, and dashing through my body, as I had seen a ramrod glide through a door, flitted across my mind. The dread also, as I have already mentioned, of the crazy floor, tormented me; but these soon gave way to fears not more unfounded, but more visionary, and of course more tremendous. The roaring of the bell confused my intellect, and my fancy soon began to teem with all sorts of strange and terrifying ideas. The bell pealing above, and opening its jaws with a hideous clamour, seemed to me at one time a ravening monster, raging to devour me; at another, a whirlpool ready to suck me into its bellowing abyss.

As I gazed on it, it assumed all shapes; it was a flying eagle, or rather a roc of the Arabian story-tellers, clapping its wings and screaming over me. As I looked upwards into it, it would appear sometimes to lengthen into indefinite extent, or to be twisted at the end into the spiral folds of the tail of a flying-dragon. Nor was the flaming breath, or fiery glance of that fabled animal, wanting to complete the picture. My eyes, inflamed, bloodshot, and glaring, invested the supposed monster with a full proportion of unholy light.

It would be endless were I to merely hint at all the fancies that possessed my mind. Every object that was hideous and roaring presented itself to my imagination. I often thought that I was in a hurricane at sea, and that the vessel in which I was embarked tossed under me with the most furious vehemence. The air, set in motion by the swinging of the bell, blew over me, nearly with the violence, and more than the thunder of a tempest; and the floor seemed to reel under me, as under a drunken man.

But the most awful of all the ideas that seized on me were drawn from the supernatural. In the vast cavern of the bell hideous faces appeared, and glared down on me with terrifying frowns, or with grinning mockery, still more appalling. At last the devil himself, accoutred, as in the common description of the evil spirit, with hoof, horn and tail, and eyes of infernal lustre, made his appearance, and called on me to curse God and worship him, who was powerful to save me. This dread suggestion he uttered with the full-toned clangour of the bell. I had him within an inch of me and I thought on the fate of the Santon Barsisa. Strenuously and desperately I defied him, and bade him begone.

Reason then, for a moment, resumed her sway, but it was only to fill me with fresh terror, just as the lightning dispels the gloom that surrounds the benighted mariner, but to show him that his vessel is driving on a rock, where she must inevitably be dashed to pieces. I found I was becoming delirious, and trembled lest reason should utterly desert me. This is at all times an agonising thought, but it smote me then with tenfold agony. I feared lest, when utterly deprived of my senses, I should rise, to do which I was every moment tempted by that strange feeling which calls on a man, whose head is dizzy from standing on the battlement of a lofty castle, to precipitate himself from it, and then death would be instant and tremendous.

When I thought of this I became desperate. I caught the floor with a grasp which drove the blood from my nails; and I yelled with the cry of despair. I called for help, I prayed, I shouted, but all the efforts of my voice were, of course, drowned in the bell. As it passed over my mouth it occasionally echoed my cries, which mixed not with its own sound, but preserved their distinct character. Perhaps this was but fancy. To me, I know, they then sounded as if they were the shouting, howling, or laughing of

4

the fiends with which my imagination had peopled the gloomy cave which swung over me.

You may accuse me of exaggerating my feelings; but I am not. Many a scene of dread have I since passed through, but they are nothing to the self-inflicted terrors of this half-hour. The ancients have doomed one of the damned in their Tartarus to lie under a rock, which every moment seems to be descending to annihilate him – and an awful punishment it would be. But if to this you add a clamour as loud as if ten thousand furies were howling about you – a deafening uproar banishing reason, and driving you to madness, you must allow that the bitterness of the pang was rendered more terrible. There is no man, firm as his nerves may be, who could retain his courage in this situation.

In twenty minutes the ringing was done. Half of that time passed over me without power of computation – the other half appeared an age. When it ceased, I became gradually more quiet, but a new fear retained me. I knew that five minutes would elapse without ringing, but at the end of that short time the bell would be rung a second time, for five minutes more. I could not calculate time. A minute and an hour were of equal duration. I feared to rise, lest the five minutes should have elapsed, and the ringing be again commenced, in which case I should be crushed, before I could escape, against the walls or framework of the bell. I therefore still continued to lie down, cautiously shifting myself, however, with a careful gliding, so that my eye no longer looked into the hollow.

This was of itself a considerable relief. The cessation of the noise had, in a great measure, the effect of stupefying me, for my attention, being no longer occupied by the chimeras I had conjured up, began to flag. All that now distressed me was the constant expectation of the second ringing, for which, however, I settled myself with a kind of stupid resolution. I closed my eyes, and clenched my teeth as firmly as if they were screwed in a vice. At last the dreaded moment came, and the first swing of the bell extorted a groan from me, as they say the most resolute

5

victim screams at the sight of the rack, to which he is for a second time destined. After this, however, I lay silent and lethargic, without a thought. Wrapped in the defensive armour of stupidity, I defied the bell and its intonations. When it ceased, I was roused a little by the hope of escape. I did not, however, decide on this step hastily, but, putting up my hand with the utmost caution, I touched the rim.

Though the ringing had ceased, it still was tremulous from the sound, and shook under my hand, which instantly recoiled as from an electric jar. A quarter of an hour probably elapsed before I again dared to make the experiment, and then I found it at rest. I determined to lose no time, fearing that I might have delayed already too long, and that the bell for evening service would catch me. This dread stimulated me, and I slipped out with the utmost rapidity and arose. I stood, I suppose, for a minute, looking with silly wonder on the place of my imprisonment, penetrated with joy of escaping, but then rushed down the stony and irregular stair with the velocity of lightning and arrived in the bell-ringer's room. This was the last act I had power to accomplish. I leaned against the wall, motionless and deprived of thought, in which posture my companions found me, when in the course of a couple of hours, they returned to their occupation.

They were shocked, as well they might, at the figure before them. The wind of the bell had excoriated my face, and my dim and stupefied eyes were fixed with a lack-lustre gaze in my raw eyelids. My hands were torn and bleeding, my hair dishevelled, and my clothes tattered. They spoke to me, but I gave no answer. They shook me, but I remained insensible. They then became alarmed, and hastened to remove me. He who had first gone up with me in the forenoon met them as they carried me through the churchyard, and through him, who was shocked at having, in some measure, occasioned the accident, the cause of my misfortune was discovered. I was put to bed at home, and remained for three days delirious, but gradually recovered my senses.

You may be sure the bell formed a prominent topic of my

ravings, and if I heard a peal, they were instantly increased to the utmost violence. Even when the delirium abated, my sleep was continually disturbed by imagined ringings, and my dreams were haunted by the fancies which almost maddened me while in the steeple. My friends removed me to a house in the country, which was sufficiently distant from any place of worship to save me from the apprehensions of hearing the churchgoing bell; for what Alexander Selkirk, in Cowper's poem, complained of as a misfortune, was then to me as a blessing.

Here I recovered; but, even long after recovery, if a gale wafted the notes of a peal towards me, I started with nervous apprehension. I felt a Mahometan hatred to all the bell tribe, and envied the subjects of the Commander of the Faithful the sonorous voice of their Muezzin. Time cured this, as it does the most of our follies; but, even at the present day, if, by chance, my nerves be unstrung, some particular tones of the cathedral bell have power to surprise me into a momentary start.

The Graveyard Sisterhood

Guy de Maupassant

The five friends had nearly finished their dinner. They were all rich, middle-aged men of the world, two of them bachelors, three married men. They met like this once a month, in memory of their younger days, and after dinner chatted together until two in the morning. These evenings were some of the happiest in their lives, for they had remained close friends and enjoyed one another's company. Their conversation was about anything and everything that interests and amuses Parisians; as in most drawing-rooms, it was a sort of spoken recapitulation of the morning papers.

One of the gayest of the five, Joseph de Bardon, was a bachelor. He lived the Parisian life in the most thorough and whimsical fashion, without being either debauched or depraved. It interested him, and as he was still young, being scarcely forty, he enjoyed it to the full. A man of the world in the widest and best sense of the word, he possessed a great deal of wit without much depth, varied knowledge without real erudition, and quick understanding without serious penetration; and his observations and adventures, his experiences and encounters furnished him with amusing anecdotes of a comical and philosophical nature which earned him a considerable reputation in society as an intelligent man.

He was the after-dinner speaker of the group, always having a story to tell which the others looked forward to hearing. He began telling one now without being asked.

Smoking a cigar, with his elbows on the table and a half-full glass of liqueur brandy in front of his plate, lulled by the smoky atmosphere filled with the fragrance of hot coffee, he seemed completely at ease, just as certain beings are perfectly at ease in certain places and at certain times – a nun in a chapel, for instance, or a goldfish in its bowl.

Between two puffs of his cigar, he said: 'I had a strange adventure a little while ago.'

The others said with almost a single voice: 'Tell us about it.'

'Gladly,' he replied. 'You know that I love wandering round Paris, like a collector peering into shop windows. I for my part enjoy watching people and things, everything that's happening and everything that's passing by.

'Well, about the middle of September, when we were having a spell of very fine weather, I went out one afternoon without knowing where I was going. We men always have a vague desire to call on some pretty woman. We review our gallery of acquaintances, we compare them in our mind, we gauge their relative charms and the interest they arouse in us, and we finally choose the one who attracts us most. But when the sun is shining brightly and the air is warm, we often lose all desire to pay calls.

'That day the sun was shining brightly and the air was warm, so I just lit a cigar and went for a stroll along the outer boulevard. Then, as I was sauntering along, the idea occurred to me of going to have a look round the Montmartre Cemetery.

'I like cemeteries, you know. They sadden me and soothe my nerves, and I need something to do that. Besides, there are some good friends of mine there, friends nobody goes to see any more, so I go to see them now and then.

'As it happens, in that very cemetery, I once buried an old romance, a mistress of mine to whom I was greatly attached, a charming little woman whose memory not only grieves me deeply but awakens regrets in my heart . . . all kinds of regret . . . I go and dream beside her grave . . . It's all over for her.

'I like cemeteries too because they are huge, densely populated

9

cities. Just think of all the bodies in that small space, of all the generations of Parisians lodged there for ever, troglodytes eternally imprisoned in their little vaults, in little holes covered with a stone or marked by a cross, while the living, fools that they are, take up so much room and make so much noise.

'Again, in cemeteries you can find monuments that are almost as interesting as those you find in museums. Though I wouldn't compare the two works, Cavaignac's tomb reminded me of that masterpiece of Jean Goujon's, the statue of Louis de Brézé in the underground chapel in Rouen Cathedral. Gentlemen, all so-called modern, realistic art started there. That statue of the dead Louis de Brézé is more convincing, more terrible, more suggestive of inanimate flesh still convulsed by the death-agony, than any of the tortured corpses you see on modern tombs.

'But in the Montmartre Cemetery you can still admire the monument to Baudin, which is quite impressive, Gautier's tomb, and Murger's – where the other day I saw a poor, solitary wreath of yellow immortelles. Who do you think laid it there? Perhaps the last of the *grisettes*, an old woman who has become a concierge in the neighbourhood. It's a pretty little statue by Millet, but spoilt by dirt and neglect. Sing the joys of youth, Murger!

'So there I was, going into the Montmartre Cemetery, and suddenly filled with sadness, a sadness which didn't hurt too much, as it happened, the sort of sadness which makes a healthy man think: This isn't a very cheerful place, but at least it isn't time yet for me to come here . . .

'The feeling of autumn, that warm dampness which evokes the idea of dead leaves and tired, anaemic sunshine, intensified and poeticized the sense of solitude and finality surrounding that place, which evokes the idea of dead men.

'I wandered slowly along those streets of tombs where the neighbours never call on each other, no longer sleep together, and don't read the papers. And I started reading the epitaphs. Let me assure you that nothing in the whole world could be more amusing. Labiche and Meilhac have never made me laugh as much as that tombstone prose. Those crosses and marble slabs on which the relatives of the dead have poured out their grief, their wishes for the happiness of the departed in the next world, and their longing to rejoin their loved one – the hypocrites! – make funnier reading than any book by Paul de Kock.

'But what I love most of all in that cemetery is the deserted, lonely part planted with great yew trees and cypresses, the old district inhabited by those who died long ago. For soon it will once again become a new district, and the green trees nourished by human corpses will be felled to make room for the recently departed to be lined up under little marble slabs.

'After I had wandered about long enough to refresh my mind I realized that I was in danger of getting bored and that it was time for me to go to the last bed of my sometime mistress and pay her the faithful tribute of my memory. My heart was heavy as I reached her grave. The poor darling was so sweet and loving, so fair and lovely . . . and now . . . if her grave were opened . . .

'Bending over the iron railing I whispered a few sorrowful words to her which she probably never heard, and I was about to walk away when I saw a woman in deep mourning kneeling down in front of the next grave. Her crape veil had been thrown back to reveal a pretty head of fair hair which looked like a bright dawn under the dark night of her head-dress. I stayed where I was.

'She was obviously in the grip of profound sorrow. She had buried her face in her hands and was deep in meditation, holding herself as rigid as a statue. Absorbed in her grief, and telling the painful beads of memory behind her closed and hidden eyes, she seemed herself like a corpse mourning a corpse. Then, all of a sudden, from a slight movement of her back like a willow stirring in the wind, I guessed that she was going to cry. She wept gently at first, then more violently, her neck and shoulders shaking. Suddenly she uncovered her eyes. They were full of tears and quite charming. She looked around her frantically, as if awakening from a nightmare. She saw me gazing at her, looked embarrassed, and hid her face again in her hands. Then she burst into convulsive sobs and her head slowly bent towards the marble tombstone. She rested her forehead on it and her veil, falling around her, covered the white corners of the beloved sepulchre like a new mourning-cloth. I heard her moan, and then she collapsed with her cheek against the tombstone and lay there motionless and unconscious.

'I rushed over to her, slapped her hands and breathed on her eyelids, at the same time reading the simple epitaph on the tombstone:

HERE LIES LOUIS-THÉODORE CARREL,
Captain in the Marine Light Infantry,
killed by the enemy in Tonkin.
PRAY FOR HIS SOUL.

This death had occurred only a few months earlier. I was moved to tears, and I redoubled my efforts to revive her. At last they succeeded and she came to. I am not a bad-looking fellow – I'm not forty yet – and at that moment I looked extremely upset. I realized from her first glance that she was likely to be polite and grateful. I was not disappointed, and between further tears and sobs she told me about the officer who had been killed in Tonkin after they had been married only a year. He had married her for love, as she was an orphan and possessed nothing but her dowry.

'I consoled her, comforted her, lifted her up, and helped her to her feet. Then I said: "You can't stay here. Come along."

' "I'm incapable of walking," she murmured.

' "Let me help you."

' "Thank you, Monsieur, you are very kind. Did you come here to mourn someone?"

' "Yes, Madame."

' "Your wife?"

' "A mistress."

' "A man may love a mistress as much as a wife, for passion knows no law."

' "Yes, Madame," I replied.

'And we walked away together, she leaning on me and I almost carrying her along the alleys. As we left the cemetery she murmured: "I think I'm going to faint."

' "Would you like to go somewhere and take something to revive you?"

' "Yes, Monsieur."

'I noticed a restaurant nearby, one of those restaurants where the friends of the dead go to celebrate the end of their mournful duty. We went in and I made her drink a cup of hot tea which seemed to restore her strength. A faint smile came to her lips, and she started telling me about herself. It was so sad, she said, to be all alone in the world, to be alone at home day and night, to have nobody any more to whom she could give her love, trust and intimacy.

'This all seemed sincere and sounded well on her lips. I felt my heart softening. She was very young, perhaps twenty. I paid her a few compliments which she accepted gracefully. Then, as it was getting late, I offered to take her home in a cab. She accepted. In the cab we were so close to each other that we could feel the warmth of our bodies through our clothes, which is really the most disturbing thing in the world.

'When the cab drew up in front of her house she murmured: "I don't feel capable of walking upstairs by myself, for I live on the fourth floor. You have already been so kind to me: will you give me your arm as far as my apartment?"

'I gladly agreed. She walked up slowly, breathing hard. Then, outside her door, she added: "Do come in for a few minutes so that I can thank you."

'And I went in.

'Her apartment was modest, even rather poor, but simply and tastefully furnished.

'We sat down side by side on a little sofa, and she began

13

talking to me again about her loneliness.

'She rang for her maid, to offer me a drink, but the girl didn't come. I was delighted, concluding that this maid probably came only in the morning and was really just a cleaning-woman.

'She had taken off her hat. She was so charming with her limpid eyes fixed upon me, so clear and steady, that I was seized by a terrible temptation to which I succumbed. I clasped her in my arms and kissed her again and again on her eyelids, which she had promptly lowered.

'She struggled to free herself, pushing me away and repeating: "Please . . . please . . . please . . ."

'What did she mean by that word? In such circumstances "please" could have at least two meanings. To silence her I passed from her eyes to her lips and gave the word "please" the conclusion I preferred. She didn't resist over-much, and when we looked at each other again after this insult to the memory of the captain killed in Tonkin, she had a languorous expression of tender resignation which dispelled my misgivings.

'I showed my gratitude by being gallant and attentive. After further conversation lasting about an hour I asked her: "Where do you usually dine?"

' "In a little restaurant near here."

' "All alone?"

' "Why, yes."

' "Will you have dinner with me?"

' "Where?"

' "In a good restaurant on the boulevard."

'She demurred, but I insisted, and she finally gave way, consoling herself with the argument that she was bored and lonely. Then she added: "I must put on a dress that isn't so dark."

'She went into her bedroom, and when she came out she was in half-mourning, wearing a very simple grey dress which made her look slim and charming. She obviously had different outfits for town and cemetery.

'Dinner was very pleasant. She drank some champagne and

14

became very animated and lively. I went back to her apartment with her.

'This liaison begun among the tombstones lasted about three weeks. But men grow tired of everything, and especially of women. I left her on the pretext of an unavoidable journey. I was very generous when we parted, and she was very grateful. She made me promise and even swear that I would come back on my return to Paris, for she really seemed to care for me a little.

'I lost no time in forming other attachments and about a month went by without the temptation to resume that funereal affair becoming strong enough for me to yield to it. However, I had not forgotten her. The memory of her haunted me like a mystery, a psychological problem, one of those inexplicable questions which nag at you for an answer.

'I don't know why, but one day it occurred to me that I might find her in the Montmartre Cemetery, so I went back there.

'I walked around for a long time without meeting anyone but the usual visitors to the place, mourners who had not yet broken off all relations with their dead. The tomb of the captain killed in Tonkin had no weeping woman kneeling beside it and no flowers or wreaths on the marble slab.

'But as I was walking through another district of that great city of the dead I suddenly saw a couple in deep mourning coming towards me down a narrow avenue lined with crosses. To my amazement, when they drew near, I recognized . . . her!

'She saw me and blushed. As I brushed past her she gave me a little signal, a little glance which meant: "Don't recognize me," but which also seemed to say: "Come back and see me, darling."

'The man with her was about fifty years old, distinguished and well-dressed, with the rosette of an officer of the Legion of Honour. And he was supporting her, just as I had supported her when we had left the cemetery together.

'I went off dumbfounded, puzzling over what I had just seen, and wondering to what race of creatures that graveyard huntress belonged. Was she just an ordinary whore, an inspired prostitute

15

who visited graveyards to pick up unhappy men haunted by the loss of a wife or mistress and troubled by the memory of past caresses? Was she unique? Or were there several like her? Was it a profession – a graveyard sisterhood who walked the cemeteries as others walk the streets? Or had she alone hit upon that admirable idea, that profoundly philosophical notion, of exploiting the amorous regrets awakened in those mournful places?

'I would have dearly loved to know whose widow she had chosen to be that day . . .'

The Pit and the Pendulum

Edgar Allan Poe

Impia tortorum longas hic turba furores
Sanguinis innocui, non satiata, aluit.
Sospite nunc patria, fracto nunc funeris antro,
Mors ubi dira fuit vita salusque patent.
*Quatrain composed for the gates of a market
to be erected upon the site of the
Jacobin Club House at Paris*

I was sick – sick unto death with that long agony; and when they
at length unbound me, and I was permitted to sit, I felt that my
senses were leaving me. The sentence – the dread sentence of
death – was the last of distinct accentuation which reached my
ears. After that the sound of the inquisitorial voices seemed
merged in one dreamy indeterminate hum. It conveyed to my
soul the idea of *revolution* – perhaps from its association in fancy
with the burr of a mill-wheel. This only for a brief period, for
presently I heard no more. Yet, for a while, I saw – but with how
terrible an exaggeration! I saw the lips of the black-robed judges.
They appeared to me white – whiter than the sheet upon which I
trace these words – and thin even to grotesqueness; thin with the
intensity of their expression of firmness – of immovable resolution – of stern contempt of human torture. I saw that the decrees
of what to me was Fate were still issuing from those lips. I
saw them writhe with a deadly locution. I saw them fashion
the syllables of my name; and I shuddered because no sound

succeeded. I saw, too, for a few moments of delirious horror, the soft and nearly imperceptible waving of the sable draperies which enwrapped the walls of the apartment. And then my vision fell upon the seven tall candles upon the table. At first they wore the aspect of charity, and seemed white slender angels who would save me; but then, all at once, there came a most deadly nausea over my spirit, and I felt every fibre in my frame thrill as if I had touched the wire of a galvanic battery, while the angel forms became meaningless spectres, with heads of flame, and I saw that from them there would be no help. And then there stole into my fancy, like a rich musical note, the thought of what sweet rest there must be in the grave. The thought came gently and stealthily, and it seemed long before it attained full appreciation; but just as my spirit came at length properly to feel and entertain it, the figures of the judges vanished, as if magically, from before me; the tall candles sank into nothingness; their flames went out utterly; the blackness of darkness supervened; all sensations appeared swallowed up in a mad rushing descent as of the soul into Hades. Then silence, and stillness, and night were the universe.

I had swooned; but still will not say that all of consciousness was lost. What of it remained I will not attempt to define, or even to describe; yet all was not lost. In the deepest slumber – no! In delirium – no! In a swoon – no! In death – no! even in the grave all *is not* lost. Else there is no immortality for man. Arousing from the most profound of slumbers, we break the gossamer web of *some* dream. Yet in a second afterward (so frail may that web have been) we remember not that we have dreamed. In the return to life from the swoon there are two stages: first, that of the sense of mental or spiritual; secondly, that of the sense of physical, existence. It seems probable that if, upon reaching the second stage, we could recall the impressions of the first, we should find these impressions eloquent in memories of the gulf beyond. And that gulf is – what? How at least shall we distinguish its shadows from those of the tomb? But if the

18

impressions of what I have termed the first stage, are not at will, recalled, yet, after long interval, do they not come unbidden, while we marvel whence they come? He who has never swooned, is not he who finds strange palaces and wildly familiar faces in coals that glow; is not he who beholds floating in mid-air the sad visions that the many may not view; is not he who ponders over the perfume of some novel flower; is not he whose brain grows bewildered with the meaning of some musical cadence which has never before arrested his attention.

Amid frequent and thoughtful endeavours to remember, amid earnest struggles to regather some token of the state of seeming nothingness into which my soul had lapsed, there have been moments when I have dreamed of success; there have been brief, very brief periods when I conjured up remembrances which the lucid reason of a later epoch assures me could have had reference only to that condition of seeming unconsciousness. These shadows of memory tell, indistinctly, of tall figures that lifted and bore me in silence down – down – still down – till a hideous dizziness oppressed me at the mere idea of the interminableness of the descent. They tell also of a vague horror at my heart, on account of that heart's unnatural stillness. Then comes a sense of sudden motionlessness throughout all things; as if those who bore me (a ghastly train!) had outrun, in their descent, the limits of the limitless, and paused from the wearisomeness of their toil. After this I call to mind flatness and dampness; and then all is *madness* – the madness of a memory which busies itself among forbidden things.

Very suddenly there came back to my soul motion and sound – the tumultuous motion of my heart, and, in my ears, the sound of its beating. Then a pause in which all is blank. Then again sound, and motion, and touch – a tingling sensation pervading my frame. Then the mere consciousness of existence, without thought – a condition which lasted long. Then very suddenly, *thought*, and shuddering terror, and earnest endeavour to comprehend my true state. Then a strong desire to lapse into insensibility. Then a rushing revival of soul and a successful effort to move. And now a full memory of the trial, of the judges, of the sable draperies, of the sentence, of the sickness, of the swoon. Then entire forgetfulness of all that followed; of all that a later day and much earnestness of endeavour have enabled me vaguely to recall.

So far, I had not opened my eyes. I felt that I lay upon my back, unbound. I reached out my hand, and it fell heavily upon something damp and hard. There I suffered it to remain for many minutes, while I strove to imagine where and *what* I could be. I longed, yet dared not, to employ my vision. I dreaded the first glance at objects around me. It was not that I feared to look upon things horrible, but that I grew aghast lest there should be *nothing* to see. At length, with a wild desperation at heart, I quickly unclosed my eyes. My worst thoughts, then, were confirmed. The blackness of eternal night encompassed me. I struggled for breath. The intensity of the darkness seemed to oppress and stifle me. The atmosphere was intolerably close. I still lay quietly, and made effort to exercise my reason. I brought to mind the inquisitorial proceedings, and attempted from that point to deduce my real condition. The sentence had passed; and it appeared to me that a very long interval of time had since elapsed. Yet not for a moment did I suppose myself actually dead. Such a supposition, notwithstanding what we read in fiction, is altogether inconsistent with real existence; – but where and in what state was I? The condemned to death, I knew, perished usually at the *autos-da-fé*, and one of these had been held on the very night of the day of my trial. Had I been remanded to my dungeon, to await the next sacrifice, which would not take place for many months? This I at once saw could not be. Victims had been in immediate demand. Moreover, my dungeon, as well as all the condemned cells at Toledo, had stone floors, and light was not altogether excluded.

A fearful idea now suddenly drove the blood in torrents upon my heart, and for a brief period I once more relapsed into insensibility. Upon recovering, I at once started to my feet, trembling convulsively in every fibre. I thrust my arms wildly above and around me in all directions. I felt nothing; yet dreaded to move a step, lest I should be impeded by the walls of a *tomb*. Perspiration burst from every pore, and stood in cold big beads upon my forehead. The agony of suspense grew at length intolerable, and I cautiously moved forward, with my arms extended, and my eyes straining from their sockets in the hope of catching some faint ray of light. I proceeded for many paces; but still all was blackness and vacancy. I breathed more freely. It seemed evident that mine was not, at least, the most hideous of fates.

And now, as I still continued to step cautiously onward, there came thronging upon my recollection a thousand vague rumours of the horrors of Toledo. Of the dungeons there had been strange things narrated – fables I had always deemed them – but yet strange, and too ghastly to repeat, save in a whisper. Was I left to perish of starvation in this subterranean world of darkness; or what fate, perhaps even more fearful, awaited me? That the result would be death, and a death of more than customary bitterness, I knew too well the character of my judges to doubt. The mode and the hour were all that occupied or distracted me.

My outstretched hands at length encountered some solid obstruction. It was a wall, seemingly of stone masonry – very smooth, slimy, and cold. I followed it up; stepping with all the careful distrust with which certain antique narratives had inspired me. This process, however, afforded me no means of ascertaining the dimensions of my dungeon, as I might make its circuit and return to the point whence I set out without being aware of the fact, so perfectly uniform seemed the wall. I therefore sought the knife which had been in my pocket when led into the inquisitorial chamber; but it was gone; my clothes had been exchanged for a wrapper of coarse serge. I had thought of forcing the blade in some minute crevice of the masonry, so as to identify my point of departure. The difficulty, nevertheless, was but trivial; although, in the disorder of my fancy, it seemed at first insuperable. I tore a part of the hem from the robe and placed the fragment at full length, and at right angles to the wall. In groping my way around the prison, I could not fail to encounter this rag upon completing the circuit. So, at least, I thought; but I had not counted upon the extent of the dungeon, or upon my own weakness. The ground was moist and slippery. I staggered onward for some time, when I stumbled and fell. My excessive fatigue induced me to remain prostrate; and sleep soon overtook me as I lay.

Upon awaking, and stretching forth an arm, I found beside me a loaf and a pitcher with water. I was too much exhausted to reflect upon this circumstance, but ate and drank with avidity. Shortly afterward, I resumed my tour around the prison, and with much toil, came at last upon the fragment of the serge. Up to the period when I fell, I had counted fifty-two paces, and, upon resuming my walk, I had counted forty-eight more – when I arrived at the rag. There were in all, then, a hundred paces; and, admitting two paces to the yard, I presumed the dungeon to be fifty yards in circuit. I had met, however, with many angles in the wall, and thus I could form no guess at the shape of the vault, for vault I could not help supposing it to be.

I had little object – certainly no hope – in these researches; but a vague curiosity prompted me to continue them. Quitting the wall, I resolved to cross the area of the enclosure. At first, I proceeded with extreme caution, for the floor, although seemingly of solid material, was treacherous with slime. At length, however, I took courage, and did not hesitate to step firmly – endeavouring to cross in as direct a line as possible. I had advanced some ten or twelve paces in this manner, when the remnant of the torn hem of my robe became entangled between my legs. I stepped on it, and fell violently on my face.

In the confusion attending my fall, I did not immediately apprehend a somewhat startling circumstance, which yet, in a few seconds afterward, and while I still lay prostrate, arrested my attention. It was this: my chin rested upon the floor of the prison, but my lips, and the upper portion of my head, although seemingly at a less elevation than the chin, touched nothing. At the same time, my forehead seemed bathed in a clammy vapour, and the peculiar smell of decayed fungus arose to my nostrils. I put forward my arm, and shuddered to find that I had fallen at the very brink of a circular pit, whose extent, of course, I had no means of ascertaining at the moment. Groping about the masonry just below the margin, I succeeded in dislodging a small fragment, and let it fall into the abyss. For many seconds I harkened to its reverberations as it dashed against the sides of the chasm in its descent; at length, there was a sullen plunge into water, succeeded by loud echoes. At the same moment, there came a sound resembling the quick opening and as rapid closing of a door overhead, while a faint gleam of light flashed suddenly through the gloom, and as suddenly faded away.

I saw clearly the doom which had been prepared for me, and congratulated myself upon the timely accident by which I had escaped. Another step before my fall, and the world had seen me no more. And the death just avoided was of that very character which I had regarded as fabulous and frivolous in the tales respecting the Inquisition. To the victims of its tyranny, there was the choice of death with its direst physical agonies, or death with its most hideous moral horrors. I had been reserved for the latter. By long suffering my nerves had been unstrung, until I trembled at the sound of my own voice, and had become in every respect a fitting subject for the species of torture which awaited me.

Shaking in every limb, I groped my way back to the wall – resolving there to perish rather than risk the terrors of the wells, of which my imagination now pictured many in various positions about the dungeon. In other conditions of mind, I might have had courage to end my misery at once, by a plunge into one of these abysses; but now I was the veriest of cowards. Neither could I forget what I had read of these pits – that the *sudden* extinction of life formed no part of their most horrible plan.

Agitation of spirit kept me awake for many long hours, but at length I again slumbered. Upon arousing, I found by my side, as before, a loaf and a pitcher of water. A burning thirst consumed me, and I emptied the vessel at a draught. It must have been drugged – for scarcely had I drunk, before I became irresistibly drowsy. A deep sleep fell upon me – a sleep like that of death. How long it lasted, of course I know not; but when, once again, I unclosed my eyes, the objects around me were visible. By a wild, sulphurous lustre, the origin of which I could not at first determine, I was enabled to see the extent and aspect of the prison.

In its size I had been greatly mistaken. The whole circuit of its walls did not exceed twenty-five yards. For some minutes this fact occasioned me a world of vain trouble; vain indeed – for what could be of less importance, under the terrible circumstances which environed me, than the mere dimensions of my dungeon? But my soul took a wild interest in trifles, and I busied myself in endeavours to account for the error I had committed in my measurement. The truth at length flashed upon me. In my first attempt at exploration I had counted fifty-two paces, up to the period when I fell: I must then have been within a pace or two of the fragment of serge; in fact, I had nearly performed the circuit of the vault. I then slept – and upon awaking, I must have turned upon my steps – thus supposing the circuit nearly double what it actually was. My confusion of mind prevented me from observing that I began my tour with the wall to the left, and ended with the wall to the right.

I had been deceived, too, in respect to the shape of the enclosure. In feeling my way I had found many angles, and thus deduced an idea of great irregularity; so potent is the effect of total darkness upon one arousing from lethargy or sleep! The angles were simply those of a few slight depressions, or niches at odd intervals. The general shape of the prison was square. What I had taken for masonry seemed now to be iron, or some other metal, in huge plates, whose sutures or joints occasioned the depression. The entire surface of this metallic enclosure was rudely daubed in all the hideous and repulsive devices to which the charnel superstition of the monks has given rise. The figures of fiends in aspects of menace, with skeleton forms, and other more really fearful images, overspread and disfigured the walls. I observed that the outlines of these monstrosities were sufficiently distinct, but that the colours seemed faded and blurred, as if from the effects of a damp atmosphere. I now noticed the floor, too, which was of stone. In the centre yawned the circular pit from whose jaws I had escaped; but it was the only one in the dungeon.

All this I saw indistinctly and by much effort – for my personal condition had been greatly changed during slumber. I now lay upon my back, and at full length, on a species of low framework of wood. To this I was securely bound by a long strap resembling a surcingle. It passed in many convolutions about my limbs and body, leaving at liberty only my head, and my left arm to such extent, that I could, by dint of much exertion, supply myself with food from an earthen dish which lay by my side on the floor. I saw, to my horror, that the pitcher had been removed. I say to my horror – for I was consumed with intolerable thirst. This thirst it appeared to be the design of my persecutors to stimulate – for the food in the dish was meat pungently seasoned.

Looking upward, I surveyed the ceiling of my prison. It was some thirty or forty feet overhead, and constructed much as the side walls. In one of its panels a very singular figure riveted my whole attention. It was the painted figure of Time as he is commonly represented, save that, in lieu of a scythe, he held what, at a casual glance, I supposed to be the pictured image of a huge pendulum, such as we see on antique clocks. There was something, however, in the appearance of this machine which caused me to regard it more attentively. While I gazed directly upward at it (for its position was immediately over my own) I fancied that I saw it in motion. In an instant afterward the fancy was confirmed. Its sweep was brief, and of course slow. I watched it for some minutes somewhat in fear, but more in wonder.

Wearied at length with observing its dull movement, I turned my eyes upon the other objects in the cell.

A slight noise attracted my notice, and, looking to the floor, I saw several enormous rats traversing it. They had issued from the well which lay just within view to my right. Even then, while I gazed, they came up in troops, hurriedly, with ravenous eyes, allured by the scent of the meat. From this it required much effort and attention to scare them away.

It might have been half an hour, perhaps even an hour (for I could take but imperfect note of time), before I again cast my eyes upward. What I then saw confounded and amazed me. The sweep of the pendulum had increased in extent by nearly a yard. As a natural consequence its velocity was also much greater. But what mainly disturbed me was the idea that it had perceptibly *descended*. I now observed – with what horror it is needless to say – that its nether extremity was formed of a crescent of glittering steel, about a foot in length from horn to horn; the horns upward, and the under edge evidently as keen as that of a razor. Like a razor also, it seemed massive and heavy, tapering from the edge into a solid and broad structure above. It was appended to a weighty rod of brass, and the whole *hissed* as it swung through the air.

I could no longer doubt the doom prepared for me by monkish ingenuity in torture. My cognizance of the pit had become known to the inquisitorial agents – *the pit*, whose horrors had been destined for so bold a recusant as myself – *the pit*, typical of hell and regarded by rumour as the Ultima Thule of all their punishments. The plunge into this pit I had avoided by the merest of accidents, and I knew that surprise, or entrapment into torment, formed an important portion of all the grotesquerie of these dungeon deaths. Having failed to fall, it was no part of their demon plan to hurl me into the abyss; and thus (there being no alternative) a different and a milder destruction awaited me. Milder! I half smiled in my agony as I thought of such application of such a term.

What boots it to tell of the long, long hours of horror more than mortal, during which I counted the rushing oscillations of the steel! Inch by inch – line by line – with a descent only appreciable at intervals that seemed ages – down and still down it came! Days passed – it might have been that many days passed – ere it swept so closely over me as to fan me with its acrid breath. The odour of the sharp steel forced itself into my nostrils. I prayed – I wearied heaven with my prayer for its more speedy descent. I grew frantically mad, and struggled to force myself upward against the sweep of the fearful scimitar. And then I fell suddenly calm, and lay smiling at the glittering death, as a child at some rare bauble.

There was another interval of utter insensibility; it was brief; for upon again lapsing into life, there had been no perceptible descent in the pendulum. But it might have been long – for I knew there were demons who took note of my swoon, and who could have arrested the vibration at pleasure. Upon my recovery, too, I felt very – oh! inexpressibly – sick and weak, as if through long inanition. Even amid the agonies of that period the human nature craved food. With painful effort I outstretched my left arm as far as my bonds permitted, and took possession of the small remnant which had been spared me by the rats. As I put a portion of it within my lips, there rushed to my mind a half-formed thought of joy – of hope. Yet what business had *I* with hope? It was, as I say, a half-formed thought – man has many such, which are never completed. I felt that it was of joy – of hope; but I felt also that it had perished in its formation. In vain I struggled to perfect – to regain it. Long suffering had nearly annihilated all my ordinary powers of mind. I was an imbecile – an idiot.

The vibration of the pendulum was at right angles to my length. I saw that the crescent was designed to cross the region of the heart. It would fray the serge of my robe – it would return and repeat its operations – again – and again. Notwithstanding its terrifically wide sweep (some thirty feet or more), and the hissing vigour of its descent, sufficient to sunder these very walls of iron, still the fraying of my robe would be all that, for several minutes, it would accomplish. And at this thought I paused. I dared not go further than this reflection. I dwelt upon it with a pertinacity of attention – as if, in so dwelling, I could arrest *here* the descent of the steel. I forced myself to ponder upon the sound of the crescent as it should pass across the garment – upon the peculiar thrilling sensation which the friction of cloth produces on the nerves. I pondered over all this frivolity until my teeth were on edge.

Down – steadily down it crept. I took a frenzied pleasure in contrasting its downward with its lateral velocity. To the right – to the left – far and wide – with the shriek of a damned spirit! To my heart, with the stealthy pace of the tiger! I alternately laughed and howled, as the one or the other idea grew predominant.

Down – certainly, relentlessly down! It vibrated within three inches of my bosom! I struggled violently – furiously – to free my left arm. This was free only from the elbow to the hand. I could reach the latter, from the platter beside me, to my mouth, with great effort, but no farther. Could I have broken the fastenings above the elbow, I would have seized and attempted to arrest the pendulum. I might as well have attempted to arrest an avalanche!

Down – still unceasingly – still inevitably down! I gasped and struggled at each vibration. I shrunk convulsively at its every sweep. My eyes followed its outward or upward whirls with the eagerness of the most unmeaning despair; they closed themselves spasmodically at the descent, although death would have been a relief, oh, how unspeakable! Still I quivered in every nerve to think how slight a sinking of the machinery would precipitate that keen, glistening axe upon my bosom. It was *hope* that prompted the nerve to quiver – the frame to shrink. It was *hope* – the hope that triumphs on the rack – that whispers to the death-condemned even in the dungeons of the Inquisition.

I saw that some ten or twelve vibrations would bring the steel in actual contact with my robe – and with this observation there suddenly came over my spirit all the keen, collected calmness of despair. For the first time during many hours – or perhaps days – I *thought*. It now occurred to me, that the bandage, or surcingle, which enveloped me, was *unique*. I was tied by no separate cord. The first stroke of the razor-like crescent athwart any portion of the band would so detach it that it might be unwound from my person by means of my left hand. But how fearful, in that case, the proximity of the steel! The result of the slightest struggle, how deadly! Was it likely, moreover, that the minions of the torturer had not foreseen and provided for this possibility? Was it probable that the bandage crossed my bosom in the track of the pendulum? Dreading to find my faint and, as it seemed, my last hope frustrated, I so far elevated my head as to obtain a distinct view of my breast. The surcingle enveloped my limbs and body close in all directions – *save in the path of the destroying crescent.*

Scarcely had I dropped my head back into its original position, when there flashed upon my mind what I cannot better describe than as the unformed half of that idea of deliverance to which I have previously alluded, and of which a moiety only floated indeterminately through my brain when I raised food to my burning lips. The whole thought was now present – feeble, scarcely sane, scarcely definite – but still entire. I proceeded at once, with the nervous energy of despair, to attempt its execution.

For many hours the immediate vicinity of the low framework upon which I lay had been literally swarming with rats. They were wild, bold, ravenous – their red eyes glaring upon me as if they waited but for motionlessness on my part to make me their prey. 'To what food,' I thought, 'have they been accustomed in the well?'

They had devoured, in spite of all my efforts to prevent them, all but a small remnant of the contents of the dish. I had fallen into an habitual see-saw or wave of the hand about the platter; and, at length, the unconscious uniformity of the movement deprived it of effect. In their voracity, the vermin frequently fastened their sharp fangs in my fingers. With the particles of the oily and spicy viand which now remained, I thoroughly rubbed the bandage wherever I could reach it; then, raising my hand from the floor, I lay breathlessly still.

At first, the ravenous animals were startled and terrified at the change – at the cessation of movement. They shrank alarmedly back; many sought the well. But this was only for a moment. I had not counted in vain upon their voracity. Observing that I remained without motion, one or two of the boldest leaped upon the framework, and smelt at the surcingle. This seemed the signal for a general rush. Forth from the well they hurried in fresh troops. They clung to the wood – they overran it, and leaped in hundreds upon my person. The measured movement of the pendulum disturbed them not at all. Avoiding its strokes, they busied themselves with the anointed bandage. They pressed – they swarmed upon me in ever accumulating heaps. They writhed upon my throat; their cold lips sought my own; I was half stifled by their thronging pressure; disgust, for which the world has no name, swelled my bosom, and chilled, with a heavy clamminess, my heart. Yet one minute, and I felt that the struggle would be over. Plainly I perceived the loosening of the bandage. I knew that in more than one place it must be already severed. With a more than human resolution I lay *still*.

Nor had I erred in my calculations – nor had I endured in vain. I at length felt that I was *free*. The surcingle hung in ribands from my body. But the stroke of the pendulum already pressed upon my bosom. It had divided the serge of the robe. It had cut through the linen beneath. Twice again it swung, and a sharp sense of pain shot through every nerve. But the moment of escape had arrived. At a wave of my hand my deliverers hurried tumultuously away. With a steady movement – cautious, sidelong, shrinking, and slow – I slid from the embrace of the bandage and beyond the reach of the scimitar. For the moment, at least, *I was free*.

Free! – and in the grasp of the Inquisition! I had scarcely stepped from my wooden bed of horror upon the stone floor of the prison, when the motion of the hellish machine ceased, and I beheld it drawn up, by some invisible force, through the ceiling. This was a lesson which I took desperately to heart. My every motion was undoubtedly watched. Free! – I had but escaped death in one form of agony, to be delivered unto worse than death in some other. With that thought I rolled my eyes nervously around on the barriers of iron that hemmed me in. Something unusual – some change, which, at first, I could not appreciate distinctly – it was obvious, had taken place in the apartment. For many minutes of a dreamy and trembling abstraction, I busied myself in vain, unconnected conjecture. During this period, I became aware, for the first time, of the origin of the sulphurous light which illumined the cell. It proceeded from a fissure, about half an inch in width, extending entirely around the prison at the base of the walls, which thus appeared, and were completely separated from the floor. I endeavoured, but of course in vain, to look through the aperture.

As I arose from the attempt, the mystery of the alteration in the chamber broke at once upon my understanding. I have observed that, although the outlines of the figures upon the walls were sufficiently distinct, yet the colours seemed blurred and indefinite. These colours had now assumed, and were momentarily assuming, a startling and most intense brilliancy, that gave to the spectral and fiendish portraitures an aspect that might have thrilled even firmer nerves than my own. Demon eyes, of a wild and ghastly vivacity, glared upon me in a thousand directions, where none had been visible before, and gleamed with the lurid lustre of a fire that I could not force my imagination to regard as unreal.

Unreal! – Even while I breathed there came to my nostrils the breath of the vapour of heated iron! A suffocating odour pervaded the prison! A deeper glow settled each moment in the eyes that glared at my agonies! A richer tint of crimson diffused itself over the pictured horrors of blood. I panted! I gasped for breath! There could be no doubt of the design of my tormentors – oh! most unrelenting! oh! most demoniac of men! I shrank from the glowing metal to the centre of the cell. Amid the thought of the fiery destruction that impended, the idea of the coolness of the well came over my soul like balm. I rushed to its deadly brink. I threw my straining vision below. The glare from the enkindled roof illumined its inmost recesses. Yet, for a wild moment, did my spirit refuse to comprehend the meaning of what I saw. At length it forced – it wrestled its way into my soul – it burned itself in upon my shuddering reason. Oh! for a voice to speak! – oh! horror! – oh! any horror but this! With a shriek, I rushed from the margin, and buried my face in my hands – weeping bitterly.

The heat rapidly increased, and once again I looked up, shuddering as with a fit of the ague. There had been a second change in the cell – and now the change was obviously in the *form*. As before, it was in vain that I at first endeavoured to appreciate or understand what was taking place. But not long was I left in doubt. The Inquisitorial vengeance had been hurried by my two-fold escape, and there was to be no more dallying with the King of Terrors. The room had been square. I saw that two of its iron angles were now acute – two, consequently, obtuse. The fearful difference quickly increased with a low rumbling or moaning sound. In an instant the apartment had shifted its form into that of a lozenge. But the alteration stopped not here – I neither hoped nor desired it to stop. I could have clasped the red walls to my bosom as a garment of eternal peace. 'Death,' I said, 'any death but that of the pit!' Fool! might I not have known that *into the pit* it was the object of the burning iron to urge me? Could I resist its glow? or if even that, could I withstand its pressure? And now, flatter and flatter grew the lozenge, with a rapidity that left me no time for contemplation. Its centre, and of course its greatest width, came just over the yawning gulf. I shrank back – but the closing walls pressed me resistlessly onward. At length for my seared and writhing body there was no longer an inch of foothold on the firm floor of the prison. I struggled no more, but the agony of my soul found vent in one loud, long, and final scream of despair. I felt that I tottered upon the brink – I averted my eyes –

There was a discordant hum of human voices! There was a loud blast as of many trumpets! There was a harsh grating as of a thousand thunders! The fiery walls rushed back! An outstretched arm caught my own as I fell, fainting, into the abyss. It was that of General Lasalle. The French army had entered Toledo. The Inquisition was in the hands of its enemies.

A Torture by Hope

Villiers de l'Isle-Adam

Below the vaults of the *Oficial* of Saragossa one nightfall long ago, the venerable Pedro Arbuez d'Espila, sixth Prior of the Dominicans of Segovia, third Grand Inquisitor of Spain – followed by a *fra redemptor* (master-torturer), and preceded by two familiars of the Holy Office holding lanterns – descended towards a secret dungeon. The lock of a massive door creaked; they entered a stifling *in pace*, where the little light that came from above revealed an instrument of torture blackened with blood, a chafing-dish, and a pitcher. Fastened to the wall by heavy iron rings, on a mass of filthy straw, secured by fetters, an iron circlet about his neck, sat a man in rags: it was impossible to guess at his age.

This prisoner was no other than Rabbi Aser Abarbanel, a Jew of Aragon, who, on an accusation of usury and pitiless contempt of the poor, had for more than a year undergone daily torture. In spite of all, 'his blind obstinacy being as tough as his skin', he had refused to abjure.

Proud of his descent and his ancestors – for all Jews worthy of the name are jealous of their race – he was descended, according to the Talmud, from Othoniel, and consequently from Ipsiboe, wife of this last Judge of Israel, a circumstance which had sustained his courage under the severest of the incessant tortures.

It was, then, with tears in his eyes at the thought that so steadfast a soul was excluded from salvation, that the venerable

Pedro Arbuez d'Espila, approaching the quivering Rabbi, pronounced the following words:

'My son, be of good cheer; your trials here below are about to cease. If, in presence of such obstinacy, I have had to permit, though with sighs, the employment of severe measures, my task of paternal correction has its limits. You are the barren fig-tree, that, found so oft without fruit, incurs the danger of being dried up by the roots . . . but it is for God alone to decree concerning your soul. Perhaps the Infinite Mercy will shine upon you at the last moment! Let us hope so. There *are* instances. May it be so! Sleep, then, this evening in peace. Tomorrow you will take part in the *auto da fé*, that is to say, you will be exposed to the *quemadero*, the brazier premonitory of the eternal flame. It burns, you are aware, at a certain distance, my son; and death takes, in coming, two hours at least, often three, thanks to the moistened and frozen clothes with which we take care to preserve the forehead and the heart of the holocausts. You will be only forty-three. Consider, then, that, placed in the last rank, you will have the time needful to invoke God, to offer unto Him that baptism of fire which is of the Holy Spirit. Hope, then, in the Light, and sleep.'

As he ended this discourse, Dom Arbuez – who had motioned the wretched man's fetters to be removed – embraced him tenderly. Then came the turn of the *fra redemptor*, who, in a low voice, prayed the Jew to pardon what he had made him endure in the effort to redeem him; then the two familiars clasped him in their arms: their kiss, through their cowls, was unheard. The ceremony at an end, the captive was left alone in the darkness.

Rabbi Aser Abarbanel, his lips parched, his face stupefied by suffering, stared, without any particular attention, at the closed door. Closed? The word, half unknown to himself, awoke a strange delusion in his confused thoughts. He fancied he had seen, for one second, the light of the lanterns through the fissure between the sides of this door. A morbid idea of hope, due to the enfeeblement of his brain, took hold on him. He dragged himself towards this strange thing he had seen; and, slowly inserting a finger, with infinite precautions, into the crack, he pulled the door towards him. Wonder of wonders! By some extraordinary chance the familiar who had closed it had turned the great key a little before it had closed upon its jambs of stone. So, the rusty bolt not having entered its socket, the door rolled back into the cell.

The Rabbi ventured to look out.

By means of a sort of livid obscurity he distinguished, first of all, a half-circle of earthy walls, pierced by spiral stairways, and, opposite to him, five or six stone steps, dominated by a sort of black porch, giving access to a vast corridor, of which he could only see, from below, the nearest arches.

Stretching himself along, he crawled to the level of this threshold. Yes, it was indeed a corridor, but of boundless length. A faint light – a sort of dream-light – was cast over it; lamps suspended to the arched roof, turned, by intervals, the wan air blue; the far distance was lost in shadow. Not a door visible along all this length! On one side only, to the left, small holes, covered with a network of bars, let a feeble twilight through the depths of the wall – the light of sunset apparently, for red gleams fell at long intervals on the flagstones. And how fearful a silence! . . . Yet there – there in the depths of the dim distance – the way might lead to liberty! The wavering hope of the Jew was dogged, for it was the last.

Without hesitation he ventured forth, keeping close to the side of the light-holes, hoping to render himself indistinguishable from the darksome colour of the long walls. He advanced slowly, dragging himself along the ground, forcing himself not to cry out when one of his wounds, recently opened, sent a sharp pang through him.

All of a sudden the beat of a sandal, coming in his direction, echoed along the stone passage. A trembling fit seized him, he choked with anguish, his sight grew dim. So this, no doubt, was to be the end! He squeezed himself, doubled up on his hands and knees, into a recess, and, half dead with terror, waited.

It was a familiar hurrying along. He passed rapidly, carrying an instrument for tearing out the muscles, his cowl lowered; he disappeared. The violent shock which the Rabbi had received had half suspended the functions of life; he remained for nearly an hour unable to make a single movement. In the fear of an increase of torments if he were caught, the idea came to him of returning to his cell. But the old hope chirped in his soul – the divine 'Perhaps', the comforter in the worst of distresses. A miracle had taken place! There was no more room for doubt. He began again to crawl towards the possible escape. Worn out with suffering and with hunger, trembling with anguish, he advanced. The sepulchral corridor seemed to lengthen out mysteriously. And he, never ceasing his slow advance, gazed forward through the darkness, on, on, where there *must* be an outlet that should save him.

But, oh! steps sounding again; steps, this time, slower, more sombre. The forms of two Inquisitors, robed in black and white, and wearing their large hats with rounded brims, emerged into the faint light. They talked in low voices, and seemed to be in controversy on some important point, for their hands gesticulated.

At this sight Rabbi Aser Abarbanel closed his eyes, his heart beat as if it would kill him, his rags were drenched with the cold sweat of agony; motionless, gasping, he lay stretched along the wall, under the light of one of the lamps – motionless, imploring the God of David.

As they came opposite to him the two Inquisitors stopped under the light of the lamp, through a mere chance, no doubt, in their discussion. One of them, listening to his interlocutor, looked straight at the Rabbi. Under this gaze – of which he did not at first notice the vacant expression – the wretched man seemed to feel the hot pincers biting into his poor flesh; so he was again to become a living wound, a living woe! Fainting, scarce able to breathe, his eyelids quivering, he shuddered as the robe grazed him. But – strange at once and natural – the eyes of the Inquisitor were evidently the eyes of a man profoundly preoccupied with what he was going to say in reply, absorbed by what he was listening to; they were fixed, and seemed to look at the Jew *without seeing him*.

And, indeed, in a few minutes, the two sinister talkers went on their way, slowly, still speaking in low voices, in the direction from which the prisoner had come. They had not seen him! And it was so, that, in the horrible disarray of his sensations, his brain was traversed by this thought: 'Am I already dead, so that no one sees me?' A hideous impression drew him from his lethargy. On gazing at the wall, exactly opposite to his face, he fancied he saw, over against his, two ferocious eyes observing him! He flung back his head in a blind and sudden terror; the hair started upright upon his head. But no, no. He put out his hand, and felt along the stones. What he saw was the *reflection* of the eyes of the Inquisitor still left upon his pupils, and which he had refracted upon two spots of the wall.

Forward! He must hasten towards that end that he imagined (fondly, no doubt) to mean deliverance; towards those shadows from which he was no more than thirty paces, or so, distant. He started once more – crawling on hands and knees and stomach – upon his dolorous way, and he was soon within the dark part of the fearful corridor.

All at once the wretched man felt the sensation of cold *upon* his hands that he placed on the flagstones; it was a strong current which came from under a little door at the end of the passage. O God, if this door opened on the outer world! The whole being of the poor prisoner was overcome by a sort of vertigo of hope. He examined the door from top to bottom without being able to distinguish it completely on account of the dimness around him. He felt over it. No lock, not a bolt! A latch! He rose to his feet: the latch yielded beneath his finger; the silent door opened before him.

'Hallelujah!' murmured the Rabbi, in an immense sigh, as he

gazed at what stood revealed to him from the threshold.

The door opened upon gardens, under a night of stars – upon spring, liberty, life! The gardens gave access to the neighbouring country that stretched away to the sierras, whose sinuous white lines stood out in profile on the horizon. There lay liberty! Oh, to fly! He would run all night under those woods of citrons, whose perfume intoxicated him. Once among the mountains, he would be saved. He breathed the dear, holy air: the wind reanimated him, his lungs found free play. He heard, in his expanding heart, the 'Lazarus, come forth!' And, to give thanks to God who had granted him this mercy, he stretched forth his arms before him, lifting his eyes to the firmament in an ecstasy.

And then he seemed to see the shadow of his arms returning upon himself; he seemed to feel those shadow-arms surround, enlace him, and himself pressed tenderly against some breast. A tall figure, indeed, was opposite to him. Confidently he lowered his eyes upon this figure, and remained gasping, stupefied, with staring eyes and mouth drivelling with fright.

Horror! He was in the arms of the Grand Inquisitor himself, the venerable Pedro Arbuez d'Espila, who gazed at him with eyes full of tears, like a good shepherd who has found the lost sheep.

The sombre priest clasped the wretched Jew against his heart with so fervent a transport of charity that the points of the monacal hair-cloth rasped against the chest of the Dominican. And, while the Rabbi Aser Abarbanel, his eyes convulsed beneath his eyelids, choked with anguish between the arms of the ascetic Dom Arbuez, realizing confusedly *that all the phases of the fatal evening had been only a calculated torture, that of Hope!* the Grand Inquisitor, with a look of distress, an accent of poignant reproach, murmured in his ear, with the burning breath of much fasting: 'What! my child! on the eve, perhaps, of salvation . . . you would then leave us?'

The Bell-tower

Herman Melville

In the south of Europe, nigh a once frescoed capital, now with dank mold cankering its bloom, central in a plain, stands what, at distance, seems the black mossed stump of some immeasurable pine, fallen, in forgotten days, with Anak and the Titan.

As all along where the pine tree falls, its dissolution leaves a mossy mound – last-flung shadow of the perished trunk; never lengthening, never lessening; unsubject to the fleet falsities of the sun; shade immutable, and true gauge which cometh by prostration – so westward from what seems the stump, one steadfast spear of lichened ruin veins the plain.

From that treetop, what birded chimes of silver throats had rung. A stone pine, a metallic aviary in its crown: the Bell-Tower, built by the great mechanician, the unblest foundling, Bannadonna.

Like Babel's, its base was laid in a high hour of renovated earth, following the second deluge, when the waters of the Dark Ages had dried up and once more the green appeared. No wonder that, after so long and deep submersion, the jubilant expectation of the race should, as with Noah's sons, soar into Shinar aspiration.

In firm resolve, no man in Europe at that period went beyond Bannadonna. Enriched through commerce with the Levant, the state in which he lived voted to have the noblest Bell-Tower in Italy. His repute assigned him to be architect.

Stone by stone, month by month, the tower rose. Higher,

higher, snail-like in pace, but torch or rocket in its pride.

After the masons would depart, the builder, standing alone upon its ever-ascending summit at close of every day, saw that he overtopped still higher walls and trees. He would tarry till a late hour there, wrapped in schemes of other and still loftier piles. Those who of saints' days thronged the spot – hanging to the rude poles of scaffolding like sailors on yards or bees on boughs, unmindful of lime and dust, and falling chips of stone – their homage not the less inspired him to self-esteem.

At length the holiday of the Tower came. To the sound of viols, the climax-stone slowly rose in air, and, amid the firing of ordnance, was laid by Bannadonna's hands upon the final course. Then mounting it, he stood erect, alone, with folded arms, gazing upon the white summits of blue inland Alps, and whiter crests of bluer Alps offshore – sights invisible from the plain. Invisible, too, from thence was that eye he turned below, when, like the cannon booms, came up to him the people's combustions of applause.

That which stirred them so was seeing with what serenity the builder stood three hundred feet in air, upon an unrailed perch. This none but he durst do. But his periodic standing upon the pile, in each stage of its growth – such discipline had its last result.

Little remained now but the bells. These, in all respects, must correspond with their receptacle.

The minor ones were prosperously cast. A highly enriched one followed, of a singular make, intended for suspension in a manner before unknown. The purpose of this bell, its rotary motion and connection with the clockwork, also executed at the time, will, in the sequel, receive mention.

In the one erection, bell-tower and clock-tower were united, though, before that period, such structures had commonly been built distinct; as the Campanile and Torre del Orologio of St Mark to this day attest.

But it was upon the great state bell that the founder lavished his more daring skill. In vain did some of the less elated magistrates here caution him, saying that though truly the tower was titanic, yet limit should be set to the dependent weight of its swaying masses. But, undeterred, he prepared his mammoth mold, dented with mythological devices; kindled his fires of balsamic firs; melted his tin and copper, and, throwing in much plate contributed by the public spirit of the nobles, let loose the tide.

The unleashed metals bayed like hounds. The workmen shrunk. Through their fright, fatal harm to the bell was dreaded. Fearless as Shadrach, Bannadonna, rushing through the glow, smote the chief culprit with his ponderous ladle. From the smitten part, a splinter was dashed into the seething mass, and at once was melted in.

Next day a portion of the work was heedfully uncovered. All seemed right. Upon the third morning, with equal satisfaction, it was bared still lower. At length, like some old Theban king, the whole cooled casting was disinterred. All was fair except in one strange spot. But as he suffered no one to attend him in these inspections, he concealed the blemish by some preparation which none knew better to devise.

The casting of such a mass was deemed no small triumph for the caster; one, too, in which the state might not scorn to share. The homicide was overlooked. By the charitable that deed was but imputed to sudden transports of esthetic passion, not to any flagitious quality. A kick from an Arabian charger; not sign of vice, but blood.

His felony remitted by the judge, absolution given him by the priest, what more could even a sickly conscience have desired.

Honoring the tower and its builder with another holiday, the republic witnessed the hoisting of the bells and clockwork amid shows and pomps superior to the former.

Some months of more than usual solitude on Bannadonna's part ensued. It was not unknown that he was engaged upon something for the belfry, intended to complete it and surpass all that had gone before. Most people imagined that the design would involve a casting like the bells. But those who thought they had some further insight would shake their heads, with hints that not for nothing did the mechanician keep so secret. Meantime, his seclusion failed not to invest his work with more or less of that sort of mystery pertaining to the forbidden.

Erelong he had a heavy object hoisted to the belfry, wrapped in a dark sack or cloak – a procedure sometimes had in the case of an elaborate piece of sculpture, or statue, which being intended to grace the front of a new edifice, the architect does not desire exposed to critical eyes till set up, finished, in its appointed place. Such was the impression now. But, as the object rose, a statuary present observed, or thought he did, that it was not entirely rigid, but was, in a manner, pliant. At last, when the hidden thing had attained its final height, and, obscurely seen from below, seemed almost of itself to step into the belfry, as if with little assistance from the crane, a shrewd old blacksmith present ventured the suspicion that it was but a living man. This surmise was thought a foolish one, while the general interest failed not to augment.

Not without demur from Bannadonna, the chief magistrate of the town, with an associate – both elderly men – followed what seemed the image up the tower. But, arrived at the belfry, they had little recompense. Plausibly entrenching himself behind the conceded mysteries of his art, the mechanician withheld present explanation. The magistrates glanced toward the cloaked object, which, to their surprise, seemed now to have changed its attitude, or else had before been more perplexingly concealed by the violent muffling action of the wind without. It seemed now seated upon some sort of frame, or chair, contained within the domino. They observed that nigh the top, in a sort of square, the web of the cloth, either from accident or design, had its warp partly withdrawn, and the cross threads plucked out here and there, so as to form a sort of woven grating. Whether it were the low wind or no, stealing through the stone latticework, or only their own perturbed imaginations, is uncertain, but they thought they discerned a slight sort of fitful, springlike motion in the domino. Nothing, however incidental or insignificant, escaped their uneasy eyes. Among other things, they pried out, in a corner, an earthen cup, partly corroded and partly encrusted, and one whispered to the other that this cup was just such a one as might, in mockery, be offered to the lips of some brazen statue, or, perhaps, still worse.

But, being questioned, the mechanician said that the cup was simply used in his founder's business, and described the purpose – in short, a cup to test the condition of metals in fusion. He added that it had got into the belfry by the merest chance.

Again and again they gazed at the domino, as at some suspicious incognito at a Venetian mask. All sorts of vague apprehensions stirred them. They even dreaded lest, when they should descend, the mechanician, though without a flesh-and-blood companion, for all that, would not be left alone.

Affecting some merriment at their disquietude, he begged to relieve them, by extending a coarse sheet of workman's canvas between them and the object.

Meantime he sought to interest them in his other work, nor, now that the domino was out of sight, did they long remain insensible to the artistic wonders lying round them – wonders hitherto beheld but in their unfinished state, because, since hoisting the bells, none but the caster had entered within the belfry. It was one trait of his, that, even in details, he would not let another do what he could, without too great loss of time, accomplish for himself. So, for several preceding weeks, whatever hours were unemployed in his secret design had been devoted to elaborating the figures on the bells.

The clock bell, in particular, now drew attention. Under a patient chisel, the latent beauty of its enrichments, before obscured by the cloudings incident to casting, that beauty in its shyest grace, was now revealed. Round and round the bell, twelve figures of gay girls, garlanded, hand-in-hand, danced in a choral ring – the embodied hours.

'Bannadonna,' said the chief, 'This bell excels all else. No added touch could here improve. Hark!' hearing a sound, 'was that the wind?'

'The wind, Excellenza,' was the light response. 'But the figures, they are not yet without their faults. They need some touches yet. When those are given, and the – block yonder,' pointing towards the canvas screen, 'when Haman there, as I merrily call him – him? *it*, I mean – when Haman is fixed on this, his lofty tree, then, gentlemen, will I be most happy to receive you here again.'

The equivocal reference to the object caused some return of restlessness. However, on their part, the visitors forbore further allusion to it, unwilling, perhaps, to let the foundling see how easily it lay within his plebeian art to stir the placid dignity of nobles.

'Well, Bannadonna,' said the chief, 'how long ere you are ready to set the clock going, so that the hour shall be sounded? Our interest in you, not less than in the work itself, makes us anxious to be assured of your success. The people, too – why, they are shouting now. Say the exact hour when you will be ready.'

'Tomorrow, Excellenza, if you listen for it – or should you not, all the same – strange music will be heard. The stroke of one shall be the first from yonder bell,' pointing to the bell adorned with girls and garlands, 'that stroke shall fall there, where the hand of Una clasps Dua's. The stroke of one shall sever that loved clasp. Tomorrow, then, at one o'clock, as struck here, precisely here,' advancing and placing his finger upon the clasp, 'the poor mechanic will be most happy once more to give you liege audience, in this his littered shop. Farewell till then, illustrious magnificoes, and hark ye for your vassal's stroke.'

His still, Vulcanic face hiding its burning brightness like a forge, he moved with ostentatious deference towards the scuttle, as if so far to escort their exit. But the junior magistrate, a kind-hearted man, troubled at what seemed to him a certain sardonical disdain lurking beneath the foundling's humble mien, and in Christian sympathy more distressed at it on his account than on his own, dimly surmising what might be the final fate of such a cynic solitaire, nor perhaps uninfluenced by the general strangeness of surrounding things, this good magistrate had glanced sadly, sideways from the speaker, and thereupon his foreboding eye had started at the expression of the unchanging face of the Hour Una.

'How is this, Bannadonna,' he lowly asked, 'Una looks unlike her sisters.'

'In Christ's name, Bannadonna,' impulsively broke in the chief, his attention for the first attracted to the figure by his associate's remark. 'Una's face looks just like that of Deborah, the prophetess, as painted by the Florentine, Del Fonca.'

'Surely, Bannadonna,' lowly resumed the milder magistrate, 'you meant the twelve should wear the same jocundly abandoned air. But see, the smile of Una seems but a fatal one. 'Tis different.'

While his mild associate was speaking, the chief glanced inquiringly from him to the caster, as if anxious to mark how the discrepancy would be accounted for. As the chief stood, his advanced foot was on the scuttle's curb.

Bannadonna spoke:

'Excellenza, now that, following your keener eye, I glance upon the face of Una, I do, indeed perceive some little variance. But look all round the bell, and you will find no two faces entirely correspond. Because there is a law in art – but the cold wind is rising more; these lattices are but a poor defense. Suffer me, magnificoes, to conduct you at least partly on your way. Those in whose well-being there is a public stake, should be heedfully attended.'

'Touching the look of Una, you were saying, Bannadonna, that there was a certain law in art,' observed the chief, as the three now descended the stone shaft, 'pray, tell me, then—'

'Pardon; another time, Excellenza – the tower is damp.'

46

'Nay, I must rest, and hear it now. Here, – here is a wide landing, and through this leeward slit, no wind, but ample light. Tell us of your law, and at large.'

'Since, Excellenza, you insist, know that there is a law in art which bars the possibility of duplicates. Some years ago, you may remember, I graved a small seal for your republic, bearing, for its chief device, the head of your own ancestor, its illustrious founder. It becoming necessary, for the customs' use, to have innumerable impressions for bales and boxes, I graved an entire plate, containing one hundred of the seals. Now, though, indeed, my object was to have those hundred heads identical, and though, I dare say, people think them so, yet, upon closely scanning an uncut impression from the plate, no two of those five-score faces, side by side, will be found alike. Gravity is the air of all, but diversified in all. In some, benevolent; in some, ambiguous; in two or three, to a close scrutiny, all but incipiently malign, the variation of less than a hair's breadth in the linear shadings round the mouth sufficing to all this. Now, Excellenza, transmute that general gravity into joyousness, and subject it to twelve of those variations I have described, and tell me, will you not have my hours here, and Una one of them? But I like—'

'Hark! is that – a footfall above?'

'Mortar, Excellenza; sometimes it drops to the belfry floor from the arch where the stonework was left undressed. I must have it seen to. As I was about to say: for one, I like this law forbidding duplicates. It evokes fine personalities. Yes, Excellenza, that strange, and – to you – uncertain smile, and those forelooking eyes of Una, suit Bannadonna very well.'

'Hark! – sure we left no soul above?'

'No soul, Excellenza; rest assured, no *soul*. – Again the mortar.'

'It fell not while we were there.'

'Ah, in your presence, it better knew its place, Excellenza,' blandly bowed Bannadonna.

47

'But Una,' said the milder magistrate, 'she seemed intently gazing on you; one would have almost sworn that she picked you out from among us three.'

'If she did, possibly it might have been her finer apprehension, Excellenza.'

'How, Bannadonna? I do not understand you.'

'No consequence, no consequence, Excellenza – but the shifted wind is blowing through the slit. Suffer me to escort you on, and then, pardon, but the toiler must to his tools.'

'It may be foolish, signor,' and the milder magistrate, as, from the third landing, the two now went down unescorted, 'but, somehow, our great mechanician moves me strangely. Why, just now, when he so superciliously replied, his walk seemed Sisera's, God's vain foe, in Del Fonca's painting. And that young, sculptured Deborah, too. Aye, and that –'

'Tush, tush, signor!' returned the chief. 'A passing whim. Deborah? – Where's Jael, pray?'

'Ah,' said the other, as they now stepped upon the sod, 'ah, signor, I see you leave your fears behind you with the chill and gloom; but mine, even in this sunny air, remain. Hark!'

It was a sound from just within the tower door, whence they had emerged. Turning, they saw it closed.

'He has slipped down and barred us out,' smiled the chief; 'but it is his custom.'

Proclamation was now made that the next day, at one hour after meridian, the clock would strike, and – thanks to the mechanician's powerful art – with unusual accompaniments. But what those should be, none as yet could say. The announcement was received with cheers.

By the looser sort, who encamped about the tower all night, lights were seen gleaming through the topmost blindwork, only disappearing with the morning sun. Strange sounds, too, were heard, or were thought to be, by those whom anxious watching might not have left mentally undisturbed – sounds, not only of some ringing implement, but also, so they said, half-suppressed screams and plainings, such as might have issued from some ghostly engine overplied.

Slowly the day drew on, part of the concourse chasing the weary time with songs and games, till, at last, the great blurred sun rolled, like a football, against the plain.

At noon, the nobility and principal citizens came from the town in cavalcade, a guard of soldiers, also, with music, the more to honor the occasion.

Only one hour more. Impatience grew. Watches were held in hands of feverish men, who stood, now scrutinizing their small dial-plates, and then, with neck thrown back, gazing toward the belfry, as if the eye might foretell that which could only be made sensible to the ear, for, as yet, there was no dial to the tower clock.

The hour hands of a thousand watches now verged within a hair's breadth of the figure 1. A silence, as of the expectations of some Shiloh, pervaded the swarming plain. Suddenly a dull, mangled sound, naught ringing in it, scarcely audible, indeed, to the outer circles of the people – that dull sound dropped heavily from the belfry. At the same moment, each man stared at his neighbor blankly. All watches were upheld. All hour hands were at – had passed – the figure 1. No bell stroke from the tower. The multitude became tumultuous.

Waiting a few moments, the chief magistrate, commanding silence, hailed the belfry to know what thing unforeseen had happened there.

No response.

He hailed again and yet again.

All continued hushed.

By his order, the soldiers burst in the tower door, when, stationing guards to defend it from the now surging mob, the chief, accompanied by his former associate, climbed the winding stairs. Halfway up, they stopped to listen. No sound. Mounting faster, they reached the belfry, but, at the threshold, started at the spectacle disclosed. A spaniel, which, unbeknown to them, had followed them thus far, stood shivering as before some unknown monster in a brake, or, rather, as if it snuffed footsteps leading to some other world.

Bannadonna lay, prostrate and bleeding, at the base of the bell which was adorned with girls and garlands. He lay at the feet of the hour Una; his head coinciding, in a vertical line, with her left hand, clasped by the hour Dua. With downcast face impending over him, like Jael over nailed Sisera in the tent, was the domino; now no more becloaked.

It had limbs, and seemed clad in a scaly mail; lustrous as a dragon-beetle's. It was manacled, and its clubbed arms were uplifted, as if, with its manacles, once more to smite its already smitten victim. One advanced foot of it was inserted beneath the dead body, as if in the act of spurning it.

Uncertainty falls on what now followed.

It were but natural to suppose that the magistrates would, at first, shrink from immediate personal contact with what they saw. At the least, for a time, they would stand in involuntary doubt, it may be, in more or less of horrified alarm. Certain it is that an arquebuss was called for from below. And some add that its report, followed by a fierce whiz, as of the sudden snapping of a mainspring, with a steely din, as if a stack of sword blades should be dashed upon a pavement; these blended sounds came ringing to the plain, attracting every eye far upward to the belfry, whence, through the latticework, thin wreaths of smoke were curling.

Some averred that it was the spaniel, gone mad by fear, which was shot. This, others denied. True it was, the spaniel never more was seen; and, probably for some unknown reason, it shared the burial now to be related of the domino. For, whatever the preceding circumstances may have been, the first instinctive panic over, or else all ground of reasonable fear removed, the two magistrates, by themselves, quickly rehooded the figure in the dropped cloak wherein it had been hoisted. The same night, it was secretly lowered to the ground, smuggled to the beach, pulled far out to sea, and sunk. Nor to any after urgency, even in free convivial hours, would the twain ever disclose the full secrets of the belfry.

From the mystery unavoidably investing it, the popular solution of the foundling's fate involved more or less of supernatural agency. But some few less unscientific minds pretended to find little difficulty in otherwise accounting for it. In the chain of circumstantial inferences drawn, there may or may not have been some absent or defective links. But, as the explanation in question is the only one which tradition has explicitly preserved, in dearth of better, it will here be given. But, in the first place, it is requisite to present the supposition entertained as to the entire motive and mode, with their origin, of the secret design of Bannadonna, the minds above-mentioned assuming to penetrate as well into his soul as into the event. The disclosure will indirectly involve reference to peculiar matters, none of the clearest, beyond the immediate subject.

At that period, no large bell was made to sound otherwise than as at present, by agitation of a tongue within by means of ropes, or percussion from without, either from cumbrous machinery, or stalwart watchmen, armed with heavy hammers, stationed in the belfry or in sentry boxes on the open roof, according as the bell was sheltered or exposed.

It was from observing these exposed bells, with their watchmen, that the foundling, as was opined, derived the first suggestion of his scheme. Perched on a great mast or spire, the human figure, viewed from below, undergoes such a reduction in its apparent size as to obliterate its intelligent features. It evinces no personality. Instead of be-speaking volition, its gestures rather resemble the automatic ones of the arms of a telegraph.

Musing, therefore, upon the purely Punchinello aspect of the human figure thus beheld, it had indirectly occurred to Bannadonna to devise some metallic agent which should strike the hour with its mechanic hand, with even greater precision than the vital one. And, moreover, as the vital watchman on the roof, sallying from his retreat at the given periods, walked to the bell with uplifted mace to smite it, Bannadonna had resolved that his invention should likewise possess the power of locomotion, and, along with that, the appearance, at least, of intelligence and will.

If the conjectures of those who claimed acquaintance with the intent of Bannadonna be thus far correct, no unenterprising spirit could have been his. But they stopped not here; intimating that though, indeed, his design had, in the first place, been prompted by the sight of the watchman, and confined to the devising of a subtle substitute for him, yet, as is not seldom the case with projectors, by insensible gradations proceeding from comparatively pigmy aims to titanic ones, the original scheme had, in its anticipated eventualities, at last attained to an unheard-of degree of daring. He still bent his efforts upon the locomotive figure for the belfry, but only as a partial type of an ulterior creature, a sort of elephantine helot, adapted to further, in a degree scarcely to be imagined, the universal conveniences and glories of humanity; supplying nothing less than a supplement to the Six Days' Work; stocking the earth with a new serf, more useful than the ox, swifter than the dolphin, stronger than the lion, more cunning than the ape, for industry an ant, more fiery than serpents, and yet, in patience, another ass. All excellences of all God-made creatures which served man were here to receive advancement, and then to be combined in one. Talus was to have been the all-accomplished helot's name. Talus, iron slave to Bannadonna, and, through him, to man.

Here, it might well be thought that, were these last conjectures as to the foundling's secrets not erroneous, then must he have been hopelessly infected with the craziest chimeras of his age; far outgoing Albert Magus and Cornelius Agrippa. But the contrary was averred. However marvelous his design, however apparently transcending not alone the bounds of human invention, but those of divine creation, yet the proposed means to be employed were alleged to have been confined within the sober forms of sober reason. It was affirmed that, to a degree of more than skeptic scorn, Bannadonna had been without sympathy for any of the vainglorious irrationalities of his time. For example, he had not concluded, with the visionaries among the metaphysicians, that between the finer mechanic forces and the ruder animal vitality some germ of correspondence might prove discoverable. As little did his scheme partake of the enthusiasm of some natural philosophers, who hoped, by physiological and chemical inductions, to arrive at a knowledge of the source of life, and so qualify themselves to manufacture and improve upon it. Much less had he aught in common with the tribe of alchemists, who sought by a species of incantations to evoke some surprising vitality from the laboratory. Neither had he imagined, with certain sanguine theosophists, that, by faithful adoration of the Highest, unheard-of powers would be vouchsafed to man. A practical materialist, what Bannadonna had aimed at was to have been reached, not by logic, not by crucible, not by conjuration, not by altars, but by plain vise-bench and hammer. In short, to solve nature, to steal into her, to intrigue beyond her, to procure someone else to bind her to his hand – these, one and all, had not been his objects, but, asking no favors from any element or any being, of himself to rival her, outstrip her, and rule her. He stooped to conquer. With him, common sense was theurgy; machinery, miracle; Prometheus, the heroic name for machinist; man, the true God.

Nevertheless, in his initial step, so far as the experimental automaton for the belfry was concerned, he allowed fancy some little play, or, perhaps, what seemed his fancifulness was but his utilitarian ambition collaterally extended. In figure, the creature for the belfry should not be likened after the human pattern, nor any animal one, nor after the ideals, however wild, of ancient fable, but equally in aspect as in organism be an original production – the more terrible to behold, the better.

Such, then, were the suppositions as to the present scheme,

and the reserved intent. How, at the very threshold, so unlooked-for a catastrophe overturned all, or rather, what was the conjecture here, is now to be set forth.

It was thought that on the day preceding the fatality, his visitors having left him, Bannadonna had unpacked the belfry image, adjusted it, and placed it in the retreat provided – a sort of sentry box in one corner of the belfry; in short, throughout the night, and for some part of the ensuing morning, he had been engaged in arranging everything connected with the domino: the issuing from the sentry box each sixty minutes; sliding along a grooved way, like a railway; advancing to the clock bell with uplifted manacles; striking it at one of the twelve junctions of the four-and-twenty hands; then wheeling, circling the bell, and retiring to its post, there to bide for another sixty minutes, when the same process was to be repeated; the bell, by a cunning mechanism, meantime turning on its vertical axis, so as to present, to the descending mace, the clasped hands of the next two figures, when it would strike two, three, and so on, to the end. The musical metal in this time bell being so managed in the fusion, by some art perishing with its originator, that each of the clasps of the four-and-twenty hands should give forth its own peculiar resonance when parted.

But on the magic metal, the magic and metallic stranger never struck but that one stroke, drove but that one nail, served but that one clasp, by which Bannadonna clung to his ambitious life. For, after winding up the creature in the sentry box, so that, for the present, skipping the intervening hours, it should not emerge till the hour of one, but should then infallibly emerge, and, after deftly oiling the grooves whereon it was to slide, it was surmised that the mechanician must then have hurried to the bell, to give his final touches to its sculpture. True artist, he here became absorbed, and absorption still further intensified, it may be, by his striving to abate that strange look of Una, which, though, before others, he had treated with such unconcern, might not, in secret, have been without its thorn.

And so, for the interval, he was oblivious of his creature, which, not oblivious of him, and true to its creation, and true to its heedful winding up, left its post precisely at the given moment, along its well-oiled route, slid noiselessly towards its mark, and, aiming at the hand of Una to ring one clangorous note, dully smote the intervening brain of Bannadonna, turned backwards to it, the manacled arms then instantly upspringing to their hovering poise. The falling body clogged the thing's return, so there it stood, still impending over Bannadonna, as if whispering some post-mortem terror. The chisel lay dropped from the hand, but beside the hand; the oil-flask spilled across the iron track.

In his unhappy end, not unmindful of the rare genius of the mechanician, the republic decreed him a stately funeral. It was resolved that the great bell – the one whose casting had been jeopardized through the timidity of the ill-starred workman – should be rung upon the entrance of the bier into the cathedral. The most robust man of the country round was assigned the office of bell ringer.

But as the pallbearers entered the cathedral porch, naught but a broken and disastrous sound, like that of some lone Alpine landslide, fell from the tower upon their ears. And then all was hushed.

Glancing backwards, they saw the groined belfry crashed sideways in. It afterwards appeared that the powerful peasant who had the bell rope in charge, wishing to test at once the full glory of the bell, had swayed down upon the rope with one concentrate jerk. The mass of quaking metal, too ponderous for its frame, and strangely feeble somewhere at its top, loosed from its fastening, tore sideways down, and, tumbling in one sheer fall three hundred feet to the soft sward below, buried itself inverted and half out of sight.

Upon its disinterment, the main fracture was found to have started from a small spot in the ear, which, being scraped, revealed a defect, deceptively minute, in the casting, which defect must subsequently have been pasted over with some unknown compound.

The remolten metal soon reassumed its place in the tower's repaired superstructure. For one year the metallic choir of birds sang musically in its belfry boughwork of sculptured blinds and traceries. But on the first anniversary of the tower's completion – at early dawn, before the concourse had surrounded it – an earthquake came; one loud crash was heard. The stone pine, with all its bower of songsters, lay overthrown upon the plain.

So the blind slave obeyed its blinder lord, but, in obedience, slew him. So the creator was killed by the creature. So the bell was too heavy for the tower. So the bell's main weakness was where man's blood had flawed it. And so pride went before the fall.

All Hallows

Walter de la Mare

And because time in itselfe ... can receive no alteration, the
hallowing ... must consist in the shape or countenance which
we put upon the affaires that are incident in these days.

Richard Hooker

It was about half-past three on an August afternoon when I found
myself for the first time looking down upon All Hallows. And at
glimpse of it, fatigue and vexation passed away. I stood 'at gaze,'
as the old phrase goes – like the two children of Israel sent in to
spy out the Promised Land. How often the imagined transcends
the real. Not so All Hallows. Having at last reached the end of
my journey – flies, dust, heat, wind – having at last come limping
out upon the green sea-bluff beneath which lay its walls – I
confess the actuality excelled my feeble dreams of it.

What most astonished me, perhaps, was the sense not so much
of its age, its austerity, or even its solitude, but its air of abandonment. It lay couched there as if in hiding in its narrow sea-bay.
Not a sound was in the air; not a jackdaw clapped its wings
among its turrets. No other roof, not even a chimney, was in
sight; only the dark-blue arch of the sky; the narrow snow-line
of the ebbing tide; and the gaunt coast fading away into the haze
of a West over which were already gathering the veils of sunset.

We had met, then, at an appropriate hour and season. And yet
– I wonder. For it was certainly not the 'beauty' of All Hallows,
lulled as if into a dream in this serenity of air and heavens, which

was to leave the sharpest impression upon me. And what kind of first showing would it have made, I speculated, if an autumnal gale had been shrilling and trumpeting across its narrow bay – clots of wind-borne spume floating among its dusky pinnacles – and the roar of the sea echoing against its walls! Imagine it frozen stark in winter, icy hoar-frost edging its every boss, moulding, finial, crocket, cusp!

Indeed, are there not works of man, legacies of a half-forgotten past, scattered across this human world of ours from China to Peru, which seem to daunt the imagination with their incomprehensibility? Incomprehensible, I mean in the sense that the passion that inspired and conceived them is incomprehensible. Viewed in the light of the passing day, they might be the monuments of a race of demigods. And yet, if we could but free ourselves from our timidities and follies, we might realize that even we ourselves have an obligation to leave behind us similar memorials – testaments to the creative and faithful genius not so much of the individual as of Humanity itself.

However that may be, it was my own personal fortune to see All Hallows for the first time in the heat of the dog days, after a journey which could hardly be justified except by its end. At this moment of the afternoon the great church almost cheated one into the belief that it was possessed of a life of its own. It lay, as I say, couched in its natural hollow, basking under the dark dome of the heavens like some half-fossilized monster that might at any moment stir and awaken out of the swoon to which the wand of the enchanter had committed it. And with every inch of the sun's descending journey it changed its appearance.

That is the charm of such things. Man himself, says the philosopher, is the sport of change. His life and the life around him are but the flotsam of a perpetual flux. Yet, haunted by ideals, egged on by impossibilities, he builds his vision of the changeless; and time diversifies it with its colours and its 'effects' at leisure. It was drawing near to harvest now; the summer was nearly over; the corn would soon be in stook; the season of silence had come, not even the robins had yet begun to practise their autumnal lament, I should have come earlier.

The distance was of little account. But nine flinty hills in seven miles is certainly hard commons. To plod (the occupant of a cloud of dust) up one steep incline and to see another; to plod up that and to see a third; to surmount that and, half choked, half roasted, to see (as if in unbelievable mirage) a fourth – and always stone walls, discoloured grass, no flower but ragged ragwort, whited fleabane, moody nettle, and the exquisite stubborn bind-weed with its almond-burdened censers, and always the glitter and dazzle of the sun – well, the experience grows irksome. And then that endless flint erection with which some jealous Lord of the Manor had barricaded his verdurous estate! A fly-infested mile of the company of that wall was tantamount to making one's way into the infernal regions – with Tantalus for fellow-pilgrim. And when a solitary and empty dung wagon had lumb-ered by, lifting the dumb dust out of the road in swirling clouds into the heat-quivering air, I had all but wept aloud.

No, I shall not easily forget that walk – or the conclusion of it – when footsore, all but dead beat – dust all over me, cheeks, lips, eyelids, in my hair, dust in drifts even between my naked body and my clothes – I stretched my aching limbs on the turf under the straggle of trees which crowned the bluff of that last hill still blessedly green and verdant, and feasted my eyes on the cathedral beneath me. How odd Memory is – in her sorting arrangements. How perverse her pigeon-holes.

It had reminded me of a drizzling evening many years ago. I had stayed a moment to listen to an old Salvation Army officer preaching at a street corner. The sopped and squalid houses echoed with his harangue. His penitents' drum resembled the block of the executioner. His goatish beard wagged at every word he uttered. 'My brothers and sisters,' he was saying, 'the very instant our fleshly bodies are born they begin to perish; the moment the Lord has put them together, time begins to take them to pieces again. *Now* at this very instant, if you listen close, you can hear the nibblings and frettings of the moth and rust within – the worm that never dies. It's the same with human causes and creeds and institutions – just the same. O then for that Strand of Beauty where all that is mortal shall be shed away and we shall appear in the likeness and verisimilitude of what in sober and awful truth we are.'

The light striking out of an oil and colourman's shop at the street corner lay across his cheek and beard and glassed his eye. The soaked circle of humanity in which he was gesticulating stood staring and motionless – the lassies, the probationers, the melancholy idlers. I had had enough. I went away. But it is odd that so utterly inappropriate a recollection should have edged back into my mind at this moment. There was, as I have said, not a living soul in sight. Only a few sea-birds – oyster catchers maybe – were jangling on the distant beach.

It was now a quarter to four by my watch, and the usual pensive 'lin-lan-lone' from the belfry beneath me would soon no doubt be ringing to evensong. But if at that moment a triple bob-major had suddenly clanged its alarm over sea and shore, I shouldn't have stirred a finger's breadth. Scanty though the shade afforded by the wind-shorn tuft of trees under which I lay might be – I was ineffably at peace.

No bell, as a matter of fact, loosed its tongue that stagnant half-hour. Unless then the walls beneath me already concealed a few such chance visitors as myself, All Hallows would be empty. A cathedral not only without a close but without a congregation – yet another romantic charm. The Deanery and the residences of its clergy, my old guide-book had long since informed me, were a full mile or more away. I determined in due time, first to make sure of an entry, and then having quenched my thirst, to bathe.

How inhuman any extremity – hunger, fatigue, pain, desire – makes us poor humans. Thirst and drouth so haunted my mind that again and again as I glanced towards it I supped up at one long draught that complete blue sea. But meanwhile, too, my eyes had been steadily exploring and searching out this monument of the bygone centuries beneath me.

The headland faced approximately due west. The windows of the Lady Chapel therefore lay immediately beneath me, their fourteenth-century glass showing flatly dark amid their traceries. Above it, the shallow V-shaped, leaden-ribbed roof of the chancel converged towards the unfinished tower, then broke away at right angles – for the cathedral was cruciform. Walls so ancient and so sparsely adorned and decorated could not but be inhospitable in effect. Their stone was of a bleached bone-grey; a grey that none the less seemed to be as immaterial as flame – as incandescent ash. They were substantial enough, however, to cast a marvellously lucent shadow, of a blue no less vivid but paler than that of the sea, on the shelving sward beneath them. And that shadow was steadily shifting as I watched. But even if the complete edifice had vanished into the void, the scene would still have been of an incredible loveliness. The colours in air and sky on this dangerous coast seemed to shed a peculiar unreality even on the rocks of its own outworks.

So, from my vantage place on the hill that dominates it, I continued for a while to watch All Hallows; to spy upon it; and no less intently than a sentry who, not quite trusting his own eyes, has seen a dubious shape approaching him in the dusk. It may sound absurd, but I felt that at any moment I too might surprise All Hallows in the act of revealing what in very truth it looked like – and *was*, when no human witness was there to share its solitude.

Those gigantic statues, for example, which flanked the base of the unfinished tower – an intense bluish-white in the sunlight and a bluish-purple in shadow – images of angels and of saints, as I had learned of old from my guidebook. Only six of them at most could be visible, of course, from where I sat. And yet I found myself counting them again and yet again, as if doubting my own arithmetic. For my first impression had been that seven were in view – though the figure farthest from me at the western angle showed little more than a jutting fragment of stone which might perhaps be only part and parcel of the fabric itself.

But then the lights even of day may be deceitful, and fantasy plays strange tricks with one's eyes. With exercise, none the less, the mind is enabled to detect minute details which the unaided eye is incapable of particularizing. Given the imagination, man himself indeed may some day be able to distinguish what shapes are walking during our own terrestrial midnight amid the black shadows of the craters in the noonday of the moon. At any rate, I could trace at last frets of carving, minute weather marks, crookednesses, incrustations, repairings, that had before passed unnoticed. These walls, indeed, like human faces, were maps and charts of their own long past.

In the midst of this prolonged scrutiny, the hypnotic air, the heat, must suddenly have overcome me. I fell asleep up there in my grove's scanty shade; and remained asleep, too, long enough (as time is measured by the clocks of sleep), to dream an immense panoramic dream. On waking, I could recall only the faintest vestiges of it, and found that the hand of my watch had crept on but a few minutes in the interval. It was eight minutes past four.

I scrambled up – numbed and inert – with that peculiar sense of panic which sometimes follows an uneasy sleep. What folly to have been frittering time away within sight of my goal at an hour when no doubt the cathedral would soon be closed to visitors, and abandoned for the night to its own secret ruminations. I hastened down the steep rounded incline of the hill, and having skirted under the sunlit expanse of the walls, came presently to the south door, only to discover that my expectations had been justified, and that it was already barred and bolted. The discovery seemed to increase my fatigue fourfold. How foolish it is to obey mere caprices. What a straw is a man!

I glanced up into the beautiful shell of masonry above my head. Shapes and figures in stone it showed in plenty – symbols of an imagination that had flamed and faded, leaving this signature for sole witness – but not a living bird or butterfly. There was but one faint chance left of making an entry. Hunted now, rather than the hunter, I hastened out again into the full blazing flood of sunshine – and once more came within sight of the sea; a sea so near at last that I could hear its enormous sallies and murmurings. Indeed I had not realized until that moment how closely the great western door of the cathedral abutted on the beach.

It was as if its hospitality had been deliberately designed, not for a people to whom the faith of which it was the shrine had become a weariness and a commonplace, but for the solace of pilgrims from over the ocean. I could see them tumbling into their cockle-boats out of their great hollow ships – sails idle, anchors down; see them leaping ashore and straggling up across the sands to these all-welcoming portals – 'Parthians and Medes and Elamites; dwellers in Mesopotamia and in the parts of Egypt about Cyrene; strangers of Rome, Jews, and proselytes – we do hear them speak in our own tongue the wonderful works of God.'

And so at last I found my way into All Hallows – entering by a rounded dwarfish side-door with zigzag mouldings. There hung for corbel to its dripstone a curious leering face, with its forked tongue out, to give me welcome. And an appropriate one, too, for the figure I made!

But once beneath that prodigious roof-tree, I forgot myself and everything that was mine. The hush, the coolness, the unfathomable twilight drifted in on my small human consciousness. Not even the ocean itself is able so completely to receive one into its solacing bosom. Except for the windows over my head, filtering with their stained glass the last western radiance of the sun, there was but little visible colour in those great spaces, and a severe economy of decoration. The stone piers carried their round arches with an almost intimidating impassivity.

By deliberate design, too, or by some illusion of perspective, the whole floor of the building appeared steadily to ascend towards the east, where a dark wooden multitudinously-figured rood-screen shut off the choir and the high altar from the nave. I seemed to have exchanged one universal actuality for another: the burning world of nature for this oasis of quiet. Here, the wings of the imagination need never rest in their flight out of the wilderness into the unknown.

Thus resting, I must again have fallen asleep. And so swiftly can even the merest freshet of sleep affect the mind, that when my eyes opened I was completely at a loss.

Where was I? What demon of what romantic chasm had decoyed my poor drowsy body into this stony solitude? The din and clamour of an horrific dream whose fainting rumours were still in my ear became suddenly stilled. Then at one and the same moment, a sense of utter dismay at earthly surroundings no longer serene and peaceful, but grim and forbidding, flooded my mind, and I became aware that I was no longer alone. Twenty or thirty paces away, and a little this side of the rood-screen, an old man was standing.

To judge from the black and purple velvet and tassel-tagged gown he wore, he was a verger. He had not yet realized, it seemed, that a visitor shared his solitude. And yet he was listening. His head was craned forward and leaned sideways on his rusty shoulders. As I steadily watched him, he raised his eyes, and with a peculiar stealthy deliberation scanned the complete upper regions of the northern transept. Not the faintest rumour of any sound that may have attracted his attention reached me where I sat. Possibly a wild bird had made its entry through a broken pane of glass and with its cry had at the same moment awakened me and caught his attention. Or possibly the old man was waiting for some fellow-occupant to join him from above.

I continued to watch him. Even at this distance, the silvery twilight cast by the clerestory windows was sufficient to show me, though vaguely, his face: the high sloping nose, the lean cheekbones and protruding chin. He continued so long in the same position that at last I determined to break in on his reverie.

At sound of my footsteps his head sunk cautiously back upon

his shoulders; and he turned; and then motionlessly surveyed me as I drew near. He resembled one of those old men whom Rembrandt delighted in drawing: the knotted hands, the black drooping eyebrows, the wide thin-lipped ecclesiastical mouth, the intent cavernous dark eyes beneath the heavy folds of their lids. White as a miller with dust, hot and bedraggled, I was hardly the kind of visitor that any self-respecting custodian would warmly welcome, but he greeted me none the less with every mark of courtesy.

I apologized for the lateness of my arrival, and explained it as best I could. 'Until I caught sight of you,' I concluded lamely, 'I hadn't ventured very far in: otherwise I might have found myself a prisoner for the night. It must be dark in here when there is no moon.'

The old man smiled – but wryly. 'As a matter of fact, sir,' he replied, 'the cathedral is closed to visitors at four – at such times, that is, when there is no afternoon service. Services are not as frequent as they were. But visitors are rare too. In winter, in particular, you notice the gloom – as you say, sir. Not that I ever spend the night here: though I am usually last to leave. There's the risk of fire to be thought of and . . . I think I should soon have detected your presence here, sir. One becomes accustomed after many years.'

There was the usual trace of official pedantry in his voice, but it was more pleasing than otherwise. Nor did he show any wish to be rid of me. He continued his survey, although his eye was a little absent and his attention seemed to be divided.

'I thought perhaps I might be able to find a room for the night and really explore the cathedral to-morrow morning. It has been a tiring journey; I come from B—'

'Ah, from B—; it *is* a fatiguing journey, sir, taken on foot. I used to walk in there to see a sick daughter of mine. Carriage parties occasionally make their way here, but not so much as once. We are too far out of the hurly-burly to be much intruded on. Not that those who come to make their worship here are intruders. Far from it. But most that come are mere sightseers. And the fewer of them, I say, in the circumstances, the better.'

Something in what I had said or in my appearance seemed to have reassured him. 'Well, I cannot claim to be a regular church-goer,' I said. 'I am myself a mere sightseer. And yet – even to sit here for a few minutes is to be reconciled.'

'Ah, reconciled, sir,' the old man repeated, turning away. 'I can well imagine it after that journey on such a day as this. But to live here is another matter.'

'I was thinking of that,' I replied, in a foolish attempt to retrieve the situation. 'It must, as you say, be desolate enough in the winter – for two-thirds of the year, indeed.'

'We have our storms, sir – the bad with the good,' he agreed, 'and our position is specially prolific of what they call sea-fog. It comes driving in from the sea for days and nights together – gale and mist, so that you can scarcely see your open hand in front of your eyes even in broad daylight. And the noise of it, sir, sweeping across overhead in that woolliness of mist, if you take me, is most peculiar. It's shocking to a stranger. No, sir, we are left pretty much to ourselves when the fine-weather birds are flown . . . You'd be astonished at the power of the winds here. There was a mason – a local man too – not above two or three years ago, was blown clean off the roof from under the tower – tossed up in the air like an empty sack. But' – and the old man at last allowed his eyes to stray upwards to the roof again – 'but there's not much doing now.' He seemed to be pondering. 'Nothing open.'

'I mustn't detain you,' I said, 'but you were saying that services are infrequent now. Why is that? When one thinks of –' But tact restrained me.

'Pray don't think of keeping me, sir. It's a part of my duties. But from a remark you let fall I was supposing you may have seen something that appeared, I understand, not many months ago in the newspapers. We lost our Dean – Dean Pomfrey – last November. To all intents and purposes, I mean; and his office has not yet been filled. Between you and me, sir, there's a hitch – though I should wish it to go no further. They are greedy monsters – those newspapers: no respect, no discretion, no decency, in my view. And they copy each other like cats in a chorus.

'We have never wanted to be a notoriety here, sir: and not of late of all time. We must face our own troubles. You'd be astonished how callous the mere sightseer can be. And not only them from over the water, whom our particular troubles cannot concern – but far worse – parties as English as you or me. They ask you questions you wouldn't believe possible in a civilized country. Not that they care what becomes of us – not one iota, sir. We talk of them masked-up Inquisitors in olden times, but there's many a human being in our own would enjoy seeing a fellow-creature on the rack if he could get the opportunity. It's a heartless age, sir.'

This was queerish talk in the circumstances: and, after all, I myself was of the glorious company of the sightseers. I held my peace. And the old man, as if to make amends, asked me if I would care to see any particular part of the building. 'The light is smalling,' he explained, 'but still if we keep to the ground level there'll be a few minutes to spare; and we shall not be interrupted if we go quietly on our way.'

For the moment the reference eluded me: I could only thank him for the suggestion and once more beg him not to put himself to any inconvenience. I explained, too, that though I had no personal acquaintance with Dr Pomfrey, I had read of his illness in the newspapers. 'Isn't he,' I added a little dubiously, 'the author of *The Church and the Folk*? If so, he must be an exceedingly learned and delightful man.'

'Aye, sir' – the old verger put up a hand towards me – 'you may well say it: a saint, if ever there was one. But it's worse than "illness," sir – it's oblivion. And, thank God, the newspapers didn't get hold of more than a bare outline.'

He dropped his voice. 'This way, if you please'; and he led

me off gently down the aisle, once more coming to a standstill beneath the roof of the tower. 'What I mean, sir, is that there's very few left in this world who have any place in their minds for a sacred confidence – no reverence, sir. They would as lief All Hallows and all it stands for were swept away to-morrow, demolished to the dust. And that gives me the greatest caution with whom I speak. But sharing one's troubles is sometimes a relief. If it weren't so, why do those Catholics have their wooden boxes all built for the purpose? What else, I ask you, is the meaning of their fasts and penances?

'You see, sir, I am myself, and have been for upwards of twelve years now, the Dean's verger. In the sight of no respecter of persons – of offices and dignities, that is, I take it – I might claim to be even an elder brother. And our Dean, sir, was a man who was all things to all men. No pride of place, no vauntingness, none of your apron-and-gaiter high-and-mightiness whatsoever, sir. And then that! And to come on us without warning; or at least without any warning that could be taken as *such*.' I followed his eyes into the darkening stony spaces above us; a light like tarnished silver lay over the soundless vaultings. But so, of course, dusk, either of evening or daybreak, would affect the ancient stones. Nothing moved there.

'You must understand, sir,' the old man was continuing, 'the procession for divine service proceeds from the vestry over yonder out through those wrought-iron gates and so under the rood-screen and into the chancel there. Visitors are admitted on showing a card or a word to the verger in charge: but not otherwise. If you stand a pace or two to the right, you will catch a glimpse of the altar-screen – fourteenth-century work. Bishop Robert de Beaufort – and a unique example of the age. But what I was saying is that when we proceed for the services *out* of here *into* there, it has always been our custom to keep pretty close together; more seemly and decent, sir, than straggling in like so many sheep.

'Besides, sir, aren't we at such times in the manner of an *array*; "marching as to war," if you take me: it's a lesson in objects. The third verger leading: then the choristers, boys and men, though sadly depleted; then the minor canons; then any other dignitaries who may happen to be present, with the canon in residence; then myself, sir, followed by the Dean.

'There hadn't been much amiss up to then, and on that afternoon, I can vouch – and I've repeated it *ad naushum* – there was not a single stranger out in this beyond here, sir – nave or transepts. Not within view, that is: one can't be expected to see through four feet of Norman stone. Well, sir, we had gone on our way, and I had actually turned about as usual to bow Dr Pomfrey into his stall, when I found to my consternation, to my consternation, I say, he wasn't there! It alarmed me, sir, as you might well believe if you knew the full circumstances.

'Not that I lost my presence of mind. My first duty was to see all things to be in order and nothing unseemly to occur. My feelings were another matter. The old gentleman had left the vestry with us: that I knew: I had myself robed 'im as usual, and he in his own manner, smiling with his "Well, Jones, another day gone; another day gone." He was always an anxious gentleman for *time*, sir. How we spend it and all.

'As I say, then, he was behind me when we swept out of the gates. I saw him coming on out of the tail of my eye – we grow accustomed to it, to see with the whole of the eye, I mean. And then – not a vestige; and me – well, sir, nonplussed, as you may imagine. I gave a look and sign at Canon Ockham, and the service proceeded as usual, while I hurried back to the vestry thinking the poor gentleman must have been taken suddenly ill. And yet, sir, I was not surprised to find the vestry vacant, and him not there. I had been expecting matters to come to what you might call a head.

'As best I could I held my tongue, and a fortunate thing it was that Canon Ockham was then in residence, and not Canon Leigh Shougar, though perhaps I am not the one to say it. No, sir, our beloved Dean – as pious and harmless a gentleman as ever graced the Church – was gone for ever. He was not to appear in our midst again. He had been' – and the old man with elevated eyebrows and long lean mouth nearly whispered the words into my ear – 'he had been absconded – abducted, sir.'

'Abducted!' I murmured.

The old man closed his eyes, and with trembling lids added, 'He was found, sir, late that night up there in what they call the Trophy Room – sitting in a corner there, weeping. A child. Not a word of what had persuaded him to go or misled him there, not a word of sorrow or sadness, thank God. He didn't know us, sir – he didn't know *me*. Just simple; harmless; memory all gone. Simple, sir.'

It was foolish to be whispering together like this beneath these enormous spaces with not so much as a clothes-moth for sign of life within view. None the less I lowered my voice still further: 'Were there no premonitory symptoms? Had he been failing for long?'

The spectacle of grief in any human face is afflicting, but in a face as aged and resigned as this old man's – I turned away in remorse the moment the question was out of my lips; emotion is a human solvent and a sort of friendliness had sprung up between us.

'If you will just follow me,' he whispered, 'there's a little place where I make my ablutions that might be of service, sir. We could converse there in better comfort. I am sometimes reminded of those words in Ecclesiastes: "And a bird of the air shall tell of the matter." There is not much in our poor human affairs, sir, that was not known to the writer of that book.'

He turned and led the way with surprising celerity, gliding along in his thin-soled, square-toed, clerical spring-side boots; and came to a pause outside a nail-studded door. He opened it with a huge key, and admitted me into a recess under the central tower. We mounted a spiral staircase and passed along a corridor hardly more than two feet wide, and so dark that now and again I thrust out my finger-tips in search of his black velvet gown to make sure of my guide.

The corridor at length conducted us into a little room whose only illumination I gathered was that of the ebbing dusk from within the cathedral. The old man with trembling rheumatic fingers lit a candle, and thrusting its stick into the middle of an old oak table, pushed open yet another thick oaken door. 'You will find a basin and a towel in there, sir, if you will be so kind.'

I entered. A print of the Crucifixion was tin-tacked to the panelled wall, and beneath it stood a tin basin and jug on a stand. Never was water sweeter. I laved my face and hands, and drank deep – my throat like a parched-up gully after a drought. What appeared to be a tarnished censer lay in one corner of the room; a pair of seven-branched candlesticks shared a recess with a mouse-trap and a book. My eyes passed wearily yet gratefully from one to another of these mute discarded objects while I stood drying my hands.

When I returned, the old man was standing motionless before the spike-barred grill of the window, peering out and down.

'You asked me, sir,' he said, turning his lank waxen face into the feeble rays of the candle, 'you asked me, sir, a question which, if I understand you aright, was this: Was there anything that had occurred *previous* that would explain what I have been telling you? Well, sir, it's a long story, and one best restricted to them perhaps that have the goodwill of things at heart. All Hallows, I might say, sir, is my second home. I have been here, boy and man, for close on fifty-five years – have seen four bishops pass away and have served under no less than five several deans, Dr Pomfrey, poor gentleman, being the last of the five.

'If such a word could be excused, sir, it's no exaggeration to say that Canon Leigh Shougar is a greenhorn by comparison: which may in part be why he has never quite hit it off, as they say, with Canon Ockham. Or even with Archbishop Trafford, though he's another kind of gentleman altogether. And *he* is at present abroad. He had what they call a breakdown in health, sir.

'Now in my humble opinion, what was required was not only wisdom and knowledge but simple common sense. In the circumstances I am about to mention, it serves no purpose for any of us to be talking too much; to be for ever sitting at a table with shut doors and finger on lip, and discussing what to most intents and purposes would hardly be called evidence at all, sir. What is the use of argufying, splitting hairs, objurgating about trifles, when matters are sweeping rapidly on from bad to worse. I say it with all due respect and not, I hope, thrusting myself into what doesn't concern me: Dr Pomfrey might be with us now in his own self and reason if only common caution had been observed.

'But now that the poor gentleman is gone beyond all that, there is no hope of action or agreement left, none whatsoever. They meet and they meet, and they have now one expert now another down from London, and even from the Continent. And I don't say they are not knowledgeable gentlemen either, nor a pride to their profession. But why not tell *all*? Why keep back the very secret of what we know? That's what I am asking. And, what's the answer? Why, simply that what they don't want to believe, what runs counter to their hopes and wishes and credibilities – and comfort – in this world, that's what they keep out of sight as long as decency permits.

'Canon Leigh Shougar *knows*, sir, what *I* know. And how, I ask, is he going to get to grips with it at this late day if he refuses to acknowledge that such things are what every fragment of evidence goes to prove that they are. It's *we*, sir, and not the rest of the heedless world outside, who in the long and the short of it are responsible. And what I say is: no power or principality here or hereunder can take possession of a place while those inside have faith enough to keep them out. But once let that falter – the seas are in. And when I say no power, sir, I mean – with all deference – even Satan himself.' The lean lank face had set at the word like a wax mask. The black eyes beneath the heavy lids were fixed on mine with an acute intensity and – though more inscrutable things haunted them – with an unfaltering courage. So dense a hush hung about us that the very stones of the walls seemed to be of silence solidified. It is curious what a refreshment of spirit a mere tin basinful of water may be. I stood leaning against the edge of the table so that the candlelight still rested on my companion.

'What is *wrong* here?' I asked him baldly.

He seemed not to have expected so direct an inquiry. 'Wrong, sir? Why, if I might make so bold,' he replied with a wan, far-away smile, and gently drawing his hand down one of the velvet lapels of his gown, 'if I might make so bold, sir, I take it that you have come as a direct answer to prayer.'

His voice faltered. 'I am an old man now, and nearly at the end of my tether. You must realize, if you please, that I can't get any help that I can understand. I am not doubting that the gentlemen I have mentioned have only the salvation of the cathedral at heart – the cause, sir; and a graver responsibility yet. But they refuse to see how close to the edge of things we are: and how we are drifting.

'Take mere situation. So far as my knowledge tells me, there is no sacred edifice in the whole kingdom – of a piece, that is, with All Hallows, not only in mere size and age, but in what I might call sanctity and tradition – that is so open – open, I mean, sir, to attacks of this peculiar and terrifying nature.'

'Terrifying?'

'*Terrifying*, sir; though I hold fast to what wits my Maker has bestowed on me. Where else, may I ask, would you expect the powers of darkness to congregate in open besiegement than in this narrow valley? First, the sea out there. Are you aware, sir, that ever since living remembrance flood-tide has been gnawing and mumbling its way into this bay to the extent of three or four feet per annum? Forty inches, and forty inches, and forty inches corroding on and on: watch it, sir, man and boy as I have these sixty years past and then make a century of it.

'And now, think a moment of the floods and gales that fall upon us autumn and winter through and even in spring, when this valley is liker paradise to young eyes than any place on earth. They make the roads from the nearest towns wellnigh impassable; which means that for seven months of the year we are to all intents and purposes clean cut off from the rest of the world – as the Schindels out there are from the mainland. Are you aware, sir, I continue, that as we stand now we are all but a mile from traces of the nearest human habitation, and them merely the relics of a burnt-out old farmstead? I warrant that if (and which God forbid) you had been shut up here during the coming night, and it was a near thing but what you weren't – I warrant you might have shouted yourself dumb out of the nearest window – if window you could reach – and not a human soul to heed or help you.'

I shifted my hands on the table. It was tedious to be asking questions that received only such vague and evasive replies: and it is always a little disconcerting in the presence of a stranger to be spoken to so close, and with such positiveness.

'Well,' I smiled, 'I hope I should not have disgraced my nerves to such an extreme as that. As a small boy, one of my particular fancies was to spend a night in a pulpit. There's a cushion, you know!'

The old man's solemn glance never swerved from my eyes. 'But I take it, sir,' he said, 'if you had ventured to give out a text up there in the dark hours, your innocent young mind would not have been prepared for any kind of a congregation?'

'You mean,' I said a little sharply, 'that the place is haunted?' The absurd notion had flitted across my mind of some wandering tribe of gipsies chancing on a refuge so ample and isolated as this, and taking up its quarters in its secret parts. The old church must be honeycombed with corridors and passages and chambers pretty much like the one in which we were now concealed: and what does 'catholic' imply but an infinite hospitality within prescribed limits? But the old man had taken me at my word.

'I mean, sir,' he said firmly, shutting his eyes, 'that there are devilish agencies at work here.' He raised his hand. 'Don't, I entreat you, dismiss what I am saying as the wanderings of a foolish old man.' He drew a little nearer. 'I have heard them with these ears; I have seen them with these eyes; though whether they have any positive substance, sir, is beyond my small knowledge to declare. But what indeed might we expect their substance to *be*? First: "I take it," says the Book, "to be such as no man can by learning define, nor by wisdom search out." Is that so? Then I go by the Book. And next: what does the same Word or very near it (I speak of the Apocrypha) say of their *purpose*? It says – and correct me if I go astray – "Devils are creatures made by God, and *that for vengeance*."

'So far, so good, sir. We stop when we can go no further. Vengeance. But of their power, of what they can *do*, I can give you definite evidences. It would be a byword if once the rumour was spread abroad. And if it is *not* so, why, I ask, does every expert that comes here leave us in haste and in dismay? They go off with their tails between their legs. They see, they grope in, but they don't believe. They *invent* reasons. And they *hasten* to leave us!' His face shook with the emphasis he laid upon the word. 'Why? Why, because the experience is beyond their knowledge, sir.' He drew back breathless and, as I could see, profoundly moved.

'But surely,' I said, 'every old building is bound in time to show symptoms of decay. Half the cathedrals in England, half its churches, even, of any age, have been "restored" – and in many cases with ghastly results. This new grouting and so on. Why, only the other day . . . All I mean is, why should you suppose mere wear and tear should be caused by any other agency than –'

The old man turned away. 'I must apologize,' he interrupted me with his inimitable admixture of modesty and dignity, 'I am a poor mouth at explanations, sir. Decay – stress – strain – settling – dissolution: I have heard those words bandied from lip to lip like a game at cup and ball. They fill me with nausea. Why, I am speaking not of dissolution, sir, but of *repairs, restorations*. Not decay, *strengthening*. Not a corroding loss, an awful *progress*. I could show you places – and chiefly obscured from direct view and difficult of a close examination, sir, where stones lately as rotten as pumice and as fretted as a sponge have been replaced by others fresh-quarried – and nothing of their kind within twenty miles.

'There are spots where massive blocks a yard or more square have been *pushed* into place by sheer force. All Hallows is safer at this moment than it has been for three hundred years. They meant well – them who came to see, full of talk and fine language, and went dumb away. I grant you they meant well. I allow that. They hummed and they hawed. They smirked this and they shrugged that. But at heart, sir, they were cowed – horrified: all at a loss. Their very faces showed it. But if you ask me for what purpose doings are afoot – I have no answer, none.

'But now, supposing you yourself, sir, were one of them, with *your* repute at stake, and you were called in to look at a house which the owners of it and them who had it in trust were disturbed by its being re-edificated and restored by some agency unknown to them. Supposing that! *Why,*' and he rapped with his knuckles on the table, 'being human *and not one of us*, mustn't you be going away too with mouth shut, because you didn't want to get talked about to your disadvantage? And wouldn't you at last dismiss the whole thing as a foolish delusion, in the belief that living in out-of-the-way parts like these cuts a man off from the world, breeds maggots in the mind?

'I assure you, sir, they don't – not even Canon Ockham himself to the full – they don't believe even me. And yet, when they have their meetings of the Chapter, they talk and wrangle round and round about nothing else. I can bear the other without a murmur. What God sends, I say, we humans deserve. We have laid ourselves open to it. But when you buttress up blindness and wickedness with downright folly, why then, sir, I sometimes fear for my own reason.'

He set his shoulders as square as his aged frame would permit, and with fingers clutching the lapels beneath his chin, he stood gazing out into the darkness through that narrow inward window.

'Ah, sir,' he began again, 'I have not spent sixty years in this solitary place without paying heed to my own small wandering thoughts and instincts. Look at your newspapers, sir. What they call the Great War is over – and he'd be a brave man who would take an oath before heaven that *that* was only of human designing – and yet what do we see around us? Nothing but strife and juggleries and hatred and contempt and discord wherever you look. I am no scholar, sir, but so far as my knowledge and experience carry me, we human beings are living to-day merely from hand to mouth. We learn to-day what ought to have been done yesterday, and yet are at a loss to know what's to be done to-morrow.

'And the Church, sir. God forbid I should push my way into what does not concern me; and if you had told me half an hour gone by that you were a regular churchman, I shouldn't be pouring out all this to you now. It wouldn't be seemly. But your being not so gives me confidence. By merely listening you can help me, sir; though you can't help *us*. Centuries ago – and in my humble judgment, rightly – we broke away from the parent stem and rooted ourselves in our own soil. But, right or wrong, doesn't that of itself, I ask you, make us all the more open to attack from him who never wearies in going to and fro in the world seeking whom he may devour?

'I am not wishing you to take sides. But a gentleman doesn't scoff; you don't find him jeering at what he doesn't rightly understand. He keeps his own counsel, sir. And that's where, as I say, Canon Leigh Shougar sets me doubting. He refuses to make allowances; though up there in London things may look different. He gets his company there; and then for him the whole kallyidoscope changes, if you take me.'

The old man scanned me an instant as if inquiring within himself whether, after all, I too might not be one of the outcasts. 'You see, sir,' he went on dejectedly, 'I can bear what may be to come. I can, if need be, live on through what few years may yet remain to me, and keep going, as they say. But only if I can be assured that my own inmost senses are not cheating and misleading me. Tell me the worst, and you will have done an old man a service he can never repay. Tell me, on the other hand, that I am merely groping along in a network of devilish *delusion*, sir – well, in that case I hope to be with my master, with Dr Pomfrey, as soon as possible. We were all children once; and now there's nothing worse in this world for him to come into, in a manner of speaking.

'Oh, sir, I sometimes wonder if what we call childhood and growing up isn't a copy of the fate of our ancient forefathers. In the beginning of time there were Fallen Angels, we are told; but even if it weren't there in Holy Writ, we might have learnt it of our own fears and misgivings. I sometimes find myself looking at a young child with little short of awe, sir, knowing that within its mind is a scene of peace and paradise of which we older folk have no notion, and which will fade away out of it, as life wears in, like the mere tabernacling of a dream.'

There was no trace of unction in his speech, though the phraseology might suggest it, and he smiled at me as if in reassurance. 'You see, sir – if I have any true notion of the matter – then I say, heaven is dealing very gently with Dr Pomfrey. He has gone back, and, I take it, his soul is elsewhere and at rest.'

He had come a pace or two nearer, and the candlelight now cast grotesque shadows in the hollows of his brows and cheekbones, silvering his long scanty hair. The eyes, dimming with age, were fixed on mine as if in incommunicable entreaty. I was at a loss to answer him.

He dropped his hands to his sides. 'The fact is,' he looked cautiously about him, 'what I am now being so bold as to suggest, though it's a familiar enough experience to me, may put you in actual physical danger. But then, duty's duty, and a deed of kindness from stranger to stranger quite another matter. You seem to have come, if I may say so, in the nick of time: that was all. On the other hand, we can leave the building at once if you are so minded. In any case, we must be gone well before dark sets in; even mere human beings are best not disturbed at any night-work they may be after. The dark brings recklessness: conscience cannot see as clear in the dark. Besides, I once delayed too long myself. There is not much of day left even now, though I see by the almanac there should be a slip of moon to-night – unless the sky is overclouded. All that I'm meaning is that our all-in-all, so to speak, is the calm untrammelled evidence of the outer senses, sir. And there comes a time when – well, when one hesitates to trust one's own.'

I have read somewhere that it is only its setting – the shape, the line, the fold, the angle of the lid and so on – that gives its finer shades of meaning and significance to the human eye. Looking into his, even in that narrow and melancholy illumina-tion, was like pondering over a grey, salt, desolate pool – such as sometimes neighbours the sea on a flat and dangerous coast.

Perhaps if I had been a little less credulous, or less exhausted, I should by now have begun to doubt this old creature's sanity. And yet, surely, at even the faintest contact with the insane, a sentinel in the mind sends up flares and warnings; the very landscape changes; there is a sense of insecurity. If, too, the characters inscribed by age and experience on a man's face can be evidence of goodness and simplicity, then my companion was safe enough. To trust in his sagacity was another matter.

But then, there was All Hallows itself to take into account. That first glimpse from my green headland of its louring yet lovely walls had been strangely moving. There are buildings (almost as though they were once copies of originals now half-forgotten in the human mind) that have a singular influence on the imagination. Even now in this remote candlelit room, immured between its massive stones, the vast edifice seemed to be gently and furtively fretting its impression on my mind.

I glanced again at the old man: he had turned aside as if to leave me, unbiased, to my own decision. How would a lifetime spent between these sombre walls have affected *me*, I wondered? Surely it would be an act of mere decency to indulge their worn-out hermit! He had appealed to me. If I were ten times more reluctant to follow him, I could hardly refuse. Not, at any rate, without risking a retreat as humiliating as that of the architectural experts he had referred to – with my tail between my legs.

'I only wish I could hope to be of any real help.'

He turned about; his expression changed, as if at the coming of a light. 'Why, then, sir, let us be gone at once. You are with me, sir: that was all I hoped and asked. And now there's no time to waste.'

He tilted his head to listen a moment – with that large, flat, shell-like ear of his which age alone seems to produce. 'Matches and candle, sir,' he had lowered his voice to a whisper, 'but – though we mustn't lose each other; you and me, I mean – not, I think, a naked light. What I would suggest, if you have no objection, is your kindly grasping my gown. There is a kind of streamer here, you see – as if made for the purpose. There will be a good deal of up-and-downing, but I know the building blindfold and, as you might say, inch by inch. And now that the bell-ringers have given up ringing it is more in my charge than ever.'

He stood back and looked at me with folded hands, a whimsical childlike smile on his aged face. 'I sometimes think to myself I'm like the sentry, sir, in that play of William Shakespeare's. I saw it, sir, years ago, on my only visit to London – when I was a boy. If ever there was a villain, for all his fine talk and all, commend me to that ghost. I see him yet.'

Whisper though it was, a sort of chirrup had come into his voice, like that of a cricket in a baker's shop. I took tight hold of the velveted tag of his gown. He opened the door, pressed the box of safety matches into my hand, himself grasped the candlestick, and then blew out the light. We were instantly marooned in an impenetrable darkness. 'Now, sir, if you would kindly remove your walking shoes,' he muttered close in my ear, 'we should proceed with less noise. I shan't hurry you. And please to tug at the streamer if you need attention. In a few minutes the blackness will be less intense.'

As I stooped down to loose my shoe-laces I heard my heart thumping merrily away. It had been listening to our conversation apparently! I slung my shoes round my neck – as I had often done as a boy when going paddling – and we set out on our expedition.

I have endured too often the nightmare of being lost and abandoned in the stony bowels of some strange and prodigious building to take such an adventure lightly. I clung, I confess, desperately tight to my life-line, and we groped steadily onward – my guide ever and again turning back to mutter warning or encouragement in my ear.

Now I found myself steadily ascending; and then in a while, feeling my way down flights of hollowly worn stone steps, and anon brushing along a gallery or corkscrewing up a newel staircase so narrow that my shoulders all but touched the walls on either side. In spite of the sepulchral chill in these bowels of the cathedral, I was soon suffocatingly hot, and the effort to see became intolerably fatiguing. Once, to recover our breath, we paused opposite a slit in the thickness of the masonry, at which to breathe the tepid sweetness of the outer air. It was faint with the scent of wild flowers and cool of the sea. And presently after, at a barred window, high overhead, I caught a glimpse of the night's first stars.

We then turned inward once more, ascending yet another spiral staircase. And now the intense darkness thinned a little, the groined roof above us becoming faintly discernible. A fresher air softly fanned my cheek; and then trembling fingers groped over my breast, and, cold and bony, clutched my own.

'Dead still here, sir, if you please.' So close sounded the whispered syllables the voice might have been a messenger's within my own consciousness. 'Dead still, here. There's a drop of some sixty or seventy feet a few paces on.'

I peered out across the abyss, conscious, as it seemed, of the huge superincumbent weight of the noble fretted roof only a small space now immediately above our heads. As we approached the edge of this stony precipice, the gloom paled a little, and I guessed that we must be standing in some coign of the southern transept, for what light the evening skies now afforded was clearer towards the right. On the other hand, it seemed the northern windows opposite us were most of them boarded up, or obscured in some fashion. Gazing out, I could detect scaffolding poles – like knitting needles – thrust out from the walls and a balloon-like spread of canvas above them. For the moment my ear was haunted by what appeared to be the droning of an immense insect. But this presently ceased. I fancy it was internal only.

'You will understand, sir,' breathed the old man close beside me – and we still stood, grotesquely enough, hand in hand – 'the scaffolding over there has been in position a good many months now. It was put up when the last gentleman came down from London to inspect the fabric. And there it's been left ever since. Now, sir! – though I implore you to be cautious.'

I hardly needed the warning. With one hand clutching my box of matches, the fingers of the other interlaced with my companion's, I strained every sense. And yet I could detect not the faintest stir or murmur under that wide-spreading roof. Only a hush as profound as that which must reign in the Royal Chamber of the pyramid of Cheops faintly swirled in the labyrinths of my ear.

How long we stayed in this position I cannot say; but minutes sometimes seem like hours. And then, without the slightest warning, I became aware of a peculiar and incessant vibration. It is impossible to give a name to it. It suggested the remote whirring of an enormous millstone, or that – though without definite pulsation – of revolving wings, or even the spinning of an immense top.

In spite of his age, my companion apparently had ears as acute as mine. He had clutched me tighter a full ten seconds before I myself became aware of this disturbance of the air. He pressed closer. 'Do you see that, sir?'

I gazed and gazed, and saw nothing. Indeed even in what I had seemed to *hear* I might have been deceived. Nothing is more treacherous in certain circumstances – except possibly the eye – than the ear. It magnifies, distorts, and may even invent. As instantaneously as I had become aware of it, the murmur had ceased. And then – though I cannot be certain – it seemed the dingy and voluminous spread of canvas over there had perceptibly trembled, as if a huge cautious hand had been thrust out to draw it aside. No time was given me to make sure. The old man had hastily withdrawn me into the opening of the wall through which we had issued; and we made no pause in our retreat until we had come again to the narrow slit of window which I have spoken of and could refresh ourselves with a less stagnant air. We stood here resting awhile.

'Well, sir?' he inquired at last, in the same flat muffled tones.

'Do you ever come along here alone?' I whispered.

'Oh, yes, sir. I make it a habit to be the last to leave – and often the first to come; but I am usually gone by this hour.'

I looked close at the dim face in profile against that narrow oblong of night. 'It is so difficult to be sure of oneself,' I said. 'Have you ever actually *encountered* anything – near at hand, I mean?'

'I keep a sharp look-out, sir. Maybe they don't think me of enough importance to molest – the last rat, as they say.'

'But *have* you?' – I might myself have been communicating with the phantasmal *genius loci* of All Hallows – our muffled voices; this intense caution and secret listening; the slight breathlessness, as if at any instant one's heart were ready for flight: 'But *have* you?'

'Well, yes, sir,' he said. 'And in this very gallery. They nearly had me, sir. But by good fortune there's a recess a little farther on – stored up with some old fragments of carving, from the original building, sixth century, so it's said: stone capitals, heads and hands, and suchlike. I had my warning, and managed to leap in there and conceal myself. But only just in time. Indeed, sir, I confess I was in such a condition of terror and horror I turned my back.'

'You mean you heard, but didn't look? And – something came?'

'Yes, sir, I seemed to be reduced to no bigger than a child, huddled up there in that corner. There was a sound like clanging metal – but I don't think it was metal. It drew near at a furious speed, then passed me, making a filthy gust of wind. For some instants I couldn't breathe; the air was gone.'

'And no other sound?'

'No other, sir, except out of the distance a noise like the sounding of a stupendous kind of gibberish. A calling; or so it seemed – no human sound. The air shook with it. You see, sir, I myself wasn't of any consequence, I take it – unless a mere obstruction in the way. But – I have heard it said somewhere that the rarity of these happenings is only because it's a pain and torment and not any sort of pleasure for such beings, such apparitions, sir, good or bad, to visit our outward world. That's what I have heard said; though I can go no further.

'The time I'm telling you of was in the early winter – November. There was a dense sea-fog over the valley, I remember. It eddied through that opening there into the candlelight like flowing milk. I never light up now: and, if I may be forgiven the boast, sir, I seem to have almost forgotten how to be afraid. After all, in any walk of life a man can only do his best, and if there weren't such opposition and hindrances in high places, I should have nothing to complain of. What is anybody's life, sir (come past the gaiety of youth), but marking time? . . . Did you hear anything *then*, sir?'

His gentle monotonous mumbling ceased and we listened together. But every ancient edifice has voices and soundings of its own: there was nothing audible that I could put a name to, only what seemed to be a faint perpetual stir or whir of grinding such as (to one's over-stimulated senses) the stablest stones, set one on top of the other with an ever slightly varying weight and stress, might be likely to make perceptible in a world of matter. A world which, after all, they say, is itself in unimaginably rapid rotation, and under the tyranny of time.

'No, I hear nothing,' I answered; 'but please don't think I am doubting what you say. Far from it. You must remember I am a stranger, and that therefore the influence of the place cannot but be less apparent to me. And you have no help in this now?'

'No, sir. Not now. But even at the best of times we had small company hereabouts, and no money. Not for any substantial outlay, I mean. And not even the boldest suggests making what's called a public appeal. It's a strange thing to me, sir, but whenever the newspapers get hold of anything they turn it into a byword and a sham. Yet how can they help themselves? – with no beliefs to guide them and nothing to stay their mouths except about what for sheer human decency's sake they daren't talk about. But then, who am I to complain? And now, sir,' he continued with a sigh of utter weariness, 'if you are sufficiently rested, would you perhaps follow me on to the roof? It is the last visit I make – though by rights perhaps I should take in what there is of the tower. But I'm too old now for that – clambering and climbing over naked beams; and the ladders are not so safe as they were.'

We had not far to go. The old man drew open a squat, heavily-ironed door at the head of a flight of wooden stairs. It was latched but not bolted, and admitted us at once to the leaden roof of the building and to the immense amphitheatre of evening. The last faint hues of sunset were fading in the west; and silver-bright Spica shared with the tilted crescent of the moon the serene lagoon-like expanse of sky above the sea. Even at this height, the air was audibly stirred with the low lullaby of the tide.

The staircase by which we had come out was surmounted by a flat penthouse roof about seven feet high. We edged softly along, then paused once more; to find ourselves now all but *tête-*

à-tête with the gigantic figures that stood sentinel at the base of the buttresses to the unfinished tower.

The tower was so far unfinished, indeed, as to wear the appearance of the ruinous; besides which, what appeared to be scars and stains as if of fire were detectable on some of its stones, reminding me of the legend which years before I had chanced upon, that this stretch of coast had more than once been visited centuries ago by pillaging Norsemen.

The night was unfathomably clear and still. On our left rose the conical bluff of the headland, crowned with the solitary grove of trees beneath which I had taken refuge from the blinding sunshine that very afternoon. Its grasses were now hoary with faintest moonlight. Far to the right stretched the flat cold plain of the Atlantic – that enormous darkened looking-glass of space; only a distant lightship ever and again stealthily signalling to us with a lean phosphoric finger from its outermost reaches.

The mere sense of that abysm of space – its waste powdered with the stars of the Milky Way; the mere presence of the stony leviathan on whose back we two humans now stood, dwarfed into insignificance beside these gesturing images of stone, were enough of themselves to excite the imagination. And – whether matter-of-fact or pure delusion – this old verger's insinuations that the cathedral was now menaced by some inconceivable danger and assault had set my nerves on edge. My feet were numb as the lead they stood upon; while the tips of my fingers tingled as if a powerful electric discharge were coursing through my body.

We moved gently on – the spare shape of the old man a few steps ahead, peering cautiously to right and left of him as we advanced. Once with a hasty gesture he drew me back and fixed his eyes for a full minute on a figure – at two removes – which was silhouetted at that moment against the starry emptiness: a forbidding thing enough, viewed in this vague luminosity, which seemed in spite of the unmoving stare that I fixed on it to be perceptibly stirring on its wind-worn pedestal.

But no; 'All's well!' the old man had mutely signalled to me, and we pushed on. Slowly and cautiously; indeed I had not time to notice in passing that this particular figure held stretched in its right hand a bent bow, and was crowned with a high weather-worn stone coronet. One and all were frigid company. At last we completed our circuit of the tower, had come back to the place we had set out from, and stood eyeing one another like two conspirators in the clear dusk. Maybe there was a tinge of incredulity on my face.

'No, sir,' murmured the old man, 'I expected no other. The night is uncommonly quiet. I've noticed that before. They seem to leave us at peace on nights of quiet. We must turn in again and be getting home.'

Until that moment I had thought no more of where I was to sleep or to get food, nor had even realized how famished with hunger I was. Nevertheless, the notion of fumbling down again out of the open air into the narrow inward blackness of the walls from which we had just issued was singularly uninviting. Across these wide flat stretches of roof there was at least space for flight, and there were recesses for concealment. To gain a moment's respite, I inquired if I should have much difficulty in getting a bed in the village. And as I had hoped, the old man himself offered me hospitality.

I thanked him; but still hesitated to follow, for at that moment I was trying to discover what peculiar effect of dusk and darkness a moment before had deceived me into the belief that some small animal – a dog, a spaniel, I should have guessed – had suddenly and surreptitiously taken cover behind the stone buttress near by. But that apparently had been a mere illusion. The creature, whatever it might be, was no barker at any rate. Nothing stirred now; and my companion seemed to have noticed nothing amiss.

'You were saying,' I pressed him, 'that when repairs – restora-tions – of the building were in contemplation, even the experts were perplexed by what they discovered? What did they actually say?'

'Say, sir!' Our voices sounded as small and meaningless up here as those of grasshoppers in a noonday meadow. 'Examine that balustrade which you are leaning against at this minute. Look at that gnawing and fretting – that furrowing above the lead. All that is honest wear and tear – constant weathering of the mere elements, sir – rain and wind and snow and frost. That's honest *nature*-work, sir. But now compare it, if you please, with this St Mark here; and remember, sir, these images were intended to be part and parcel of the fabric, as you might say, sentries on a castle – symbols, you understand.'

I stooped close under the huge grey creature of stone until my eyes were scarcely more than six inches from its pedestal. And, unless the moon deceived me, I confess I could find not the slightest trace of fret or friction. Far from it. The stone had been grotesquely decorated in low relief with a gaping crocodile – a two-headed crocodile; and the angles, knubs, and undulations of the creature were cut as sharp as with a knife in cheese. I drew back.

'Now cast your glance upwards, sir. Is that what you would call a saintly shape and gesture?'

What I took to represent an eagle was perched on the image's lifted wrist – but louring and vulture-like. The head of the figure was poised at an angle of defiance – the ears unnaturally high up on the skull; the lean right forearm extended with pointing forefinger as if in derision. Its stony gaze was fixed upon the stars; its whole aspect was undeniably sinister and intimidating. The faintest puff of milk-warm air from over the sea stirred on my cheek. I drew aside.

'Aye, sir, and so with one or two of the rest of them,' the old man commented, as he watched me; 'there are other wills than the Almighty's.'

At this, the pent-up excitement within me broke bounds. This nebulous insinuatory talk! – I all but lost my temper. 'I can't, for the life of me, understand what you are saying,' I exclaimed in a voice that astonished me with its shrill volume of sound in that intense lofty quiet. 'One doesn't *repair* in order to destroy.'

The old man met me without flinching. 'No, sir? Say you so? And why not? Are there not two kinds of change in this world? – a building-up and a breaking-down? To give strength and endurance for evil or misguided purposes, would that be time wasted, if such was your aim? Why, sir, isn't that true even of the human mind and heart? We here are on the outskirts, I grant, but where would you expect the activity to show itself unless in the outer defences? An institution may be beyond dying, sir: it may be being restored for a worse destruction. And a hundred trumpeting voices would make no difference when the faith and life within is tottering to its fall.'

Somehow, this muddle of metaphors reassured me. Obviously the old man's wits had worn a little thin: he was the victim of an intelligible but monstrous hallucination.

'And yet you are taking it for granted,' I expostulated, 'that, if what you say is true, a stranger could be of the slightest help. A visitor – mind you – who hasn't been inside the doors of a church, except in search of what is old and gone, for years.'

The old man laid a trembling hand upon my sleeve. The folly of it – with my shoes hanging like ludicrous millstones round my neck!

'If you please, sir,' he pleaded, 'have a little patience with me. I'm preaching at nobody. I'm not even hinting that them outside the fold, circumstantially speaking, aren't of the flock. All in good time, sir; the Almighty's time. Maybe – with all due respect – it's from them within we have most to fear. And indeed, sir, believe an old man: I could never express the gratitude I feel. You have given me the occasion to unbosom myself, to make a clean breast, as they say. All Hallows is my earthly home, and – well, there, let us say no more. You couldn't *help me* – except only by your presence here. God alone knows who can!'

At that instant, a dull enormous rumble reverberated from within the building – as if a huge boulder or block of stone had been shifted or dislodged in the fabric; a peculiar grinding nerve-racking sound. And for the fraction of a second the flags on which we stood seemed to tremble beneath our feet.

The fingers tightened on my arm. 'Come, sir; keep close; we must be gone at once,' the quavering old voice whispered; 'we have stayed too long.'

But we emerged into the night at last without mishap. The little western door, above which the grinning head had welcomed me on my arrival, admitted us to terra firma again, and we made our way up a deep sandy track, bordered by clumps of herb agrimony, and fennel, and hemlock, with viper's bugloss and sea-poppy blooming in the gentle dusk of night at our feet. We turned when we reached the summit of this sandy incline and looked back. All Hallows, vague and enormous, lay beneath us in its hollow, resembling some natural prehistoric outcrop of that sea-worn rockbound coast; but strangely human and saturnine.

The air was mild as milk – a pool of faintest sweetness – gorse, bracken, heather; and not a rumour disturbed its calm, except only the furtive and stertorous sighings of the tide. But far out to sea and beneath the horizon summer lightnings were now in idle play – flickering into the sky like the unfolding of a signal, planet to planet – then gone. That alone, and perhaps too this feeble moonlight glinting on the ancient glass, may have accounted for the faint vitreous glare that seemed ever and again to glitter across the windows of the northern transept far beneath. And yet how easily deceived is the imagination. This old man's talk still echoing in my ear, I could have vowed this was no reflection but the glow of some light shining fitfully from within outwards.

The old man paused beside a flowering bush of fuchsia at the wicket gate leading into his small square of country garden. 'You'll forgive me, sir, for mentioning it; but I make it a rule as far as possible to leave all my troubles and misgivings outside when I come home. My daughter is a widow, and not long in that sad condition, so I keep as happy a face as I can on things. And yet: well, sir, I wonder at times if – if a personal sacrifice isn't incumbent on them that have their object most at heart. I'd go out myself very willingly, sir, I can assure you, if there was any certainty in my mind that it would serve the cause. It would be little to me if—' He made no attempt to complete the sentence.

On my way to bed, that night, the old man led me in on tiptoe to show me his grandson. His daughter watched me intently as I stooped over the child's cot – with that bird-like solicitude which all mothers show in the presence of a stranger.

Her small son was of that fairness which almost suggests the unreal. He had flung back his bedclothes – as if innocence in this world needed no covering or defence – and lay at ease, the dews of sleep on lip, cheek, and forehead. He was breathing so quietly that not the least movement of shoulder or narrow breast was perceptible.

'The lovely thing!' I muttered, staring at him. 'Where is he now, I wonder?' His mother lifted her face and smiled at me with a drowsy ecstatic happiness, then sighed.

And from out of the distance there came the first prolonged whisper of a wind from over the sea. It was eleven by my watch, the storm after the long heat of the day seemed to be drifting inland; but All Hallows, apparently, had forgotten to wind its clock.

The Cop and the Anthem

O. Henry

On his bench in Madison Square Soapy moved uneasily. When wild goose honk high of nights, and when women without sealskin coats grow kind to their husbands, and when Soapy moves uneasily on his bench in the park, you may know that winter is near at hand.

A dead leaf fell in Soapy's lap. That was Jack Frost's card. Jack is kind to the regular denizens of Madison Square, and gives fair warning of his annual call. At the corners of four streets he hands his pasteboard to the North Wind, footman of the mansion of All Outdoors, so that the inhabitants thereof may make ready.

Soapy's mind became cognizant of the fact that the time had come for him to resolve himself into a singular Committee of Ways and Means to provide against the coming rigor. And therefore he moved uneasily on his bench.

The hibernatorial ambitions of Soapy were not of the highest. In them were no considerations of Mediterranean cruises, of soporific Southern skies or drifting in the Vesuvian Bay. Three months on the Island was what his soul craved. Three months of assured board and bed and congenial company, safe from Boreas and bluecoats, seemed to Soapy the essence of things desirable.

For years the hospitable Blackwell's had been his winter quarters. Just as his more fortunate fellow New Yorkers had bought their tickets to Palm Beach and the Riviera each winter, so Soapy had made his humble arrangements for his annual hegira to the Island. And now the time was come. On the previous night three Sabbath newspapers, distributed beneath his coat, about his ankles and over his lap, had failed to repulse the cold as he slept on his bench near the spurting fountain in the ancient square. So the Island loomed large and timely in Soapy's mind. He scorned the provisions made in the name of charity for the city's dependents. In Soapy's opinion the Law was more benign than Philanthropy. There was an endless round of institutions, municipal and eleemosynary, on which he might set out and receive lodging and food accordant with the simple life. But to one of Soapy's proud spirit the gifts of charity are encumbered. If not in coin you must pay in humiliation of spirit for every benefit received at the hands of philanthropy. As Caesar had his Brutus, every bed of charity must have its toll of a bath, every loaf of bread its compensation of a private and personal inquisition. Wherefore it is better to be a guest of the law, which, though conducted by rules, does not meddle unduly with a gentleman's private affairs.

Soapy, having decided to go to the Island, at once set about accomplishing his desire. There were many easy ways of doing this. The pleasantest was to dine luxuriously at some expensive restaurant; and then, after declaring insolvency, be handed over quietly and without uproar to a policeman. An accommodating magistrate would do the rest.

Soapy left his bench and strolled out of the square and across the level sea of asphalt, where Broadway and Fifth Avenue flow together. Up Broadway he turned, and halted at a glittering café, where are gathered together nightly the choicest products of the grape, the silkworm and the protoplasm.

Soapy had confidence in himself from the lowest button of his vest upward. He was shaven, and his coat was decent and his neat black, ready-tied four-in-hand had been presented to him by a lady missionary on Thanksgiving Day. If he could reach a table in the restaurant unsuspected success would be his. The portion of him that would show above the table would raise no doubt in the waiter's mind. A roasted mallard duck, thought Soapy, would be about the thing – with a bottle of Chablis, and then Camembert, a demi-tasse and a cigar. One dollar for the cigar would be enough. The total would not be so high as to call forth any supreme manifestation of revenge from the café management; and yet the meat would leave him filled and happy for the journey to his winter refuge.

But as Soapy set foot inside the restaurant door the head waiter's eye fell upon his frayed trousers and decadent shoes. Strong and ready hands turned him about and conveyed him in silence and haste to the sidewalk and averted the ignoble fate of the menaced mallard.

Soapy turned off Broadway. It seemed that his route to the coveted island was not to be an epicurean one. Some other way of entering limbo must be thought of.

At a corner of Sixth Avenue electric lights and cunningly displayed wares behind plate-glass made a shop window conspicuous. Soapy took a cobblestone and dashed it through the glass. People came running round the corner, a policeman in the lead. Soapy stood still, with his hands in his pockets, and smiled at the sight of brass buttons.

'Where's the man that done that?' inquired the officer excitedly.

'Don't you figure out that I might have had something to do with it?' said Soapy, not without sarcasm, but friendly, as one greets good fortune.

The policeman's mind refused to accept Soapy even as a clue. Men who smash windows do not remain to parley with the law's minions. They take to their heels. The policeman saw a man half-way down the block running to catch a car. With drawn club he joined in the pursuit. Soapy, with disgust in his heart, loafed along, twice unsuccessful.

On the opposite side of the street was a restaurant of no great pretensions. It catered to large appetites and modest purses. Its crockery and atmosphere were thick; its soup and napery thin.

Into this place Soapy took his accusive shoes and tell-tale trousers without challenge. At a table he sat and consumed beefsteak, flapjacks, doughnuts, and pie. And then to the waiter he betrayed the fact that the minutest coin and himself were strangers.

'Now, get busy and call a cop,' said Soapy. 'And don't keep a gentleman waiting.'

'No cop for youse,' said the waiter, with a voice like butter cakes and an eye like the cherry in a Manhattan cocktail. 'Hey, Con!'

Neatly upon his left ear on the callous pavement two waiters pitched Soapy. He arose, joint by joint, as a carpenter's rule opens, and beat the dust from his clothes. Arrest seemed but a rosy dream. The Island seemed very far away. A policeman who stood before a drug store two doors away laughed and walked down the street.

Five blocks Soapy travelled before his courage permitted him to woo capture again. This time the opportunity presented what he fatuously termed to himself a 'cinch'. A young woman of a modest and pleasing guise was standing before a show window gazing with sprightly interest at its display of shaving-mugs and inkstands, and two yards from the window a large policeman of severe demeanour leaned against a water-plug.

It was Soapy's design to assume the role of the despicable and execrated 'masher'. The refined and elegant appearance of his victim and the contiguity of the conscientious cop encouraged him to believe that he would soon feel the pleasant official clutch upon his arm that would ensure his winter quarters on the right little, tight little isle.

Soapy straightened the lady missionary's readymade tie, dragged his shrinking cuffs into the open, set his hat at a killing cant and sidled toward the young woman. He made eyes at her, was taken with sudden coughs and 'hems', smiled, smirked, and went brazenly through the impudent and contemptible litany of the 'masher'. With half an eye Soapy saw that the policeman was watching him fixedly. The young woman moved away a few steps, and again bestowed her absorbed attention upon the shaving-mugs. Soapy followed, boldly stepping to her side, raised his hat and said:

'Ah there, Bedelia! Don't you want to come and play in my yard?'

The policeman was still looking. The persecuted young woman had but to beckon a finger and Soapy would be practically *en route* for his insular haven. Already he imagined he could feel the cosy warmth of the station-house. The young woman faced him and, stretching out a hand, caught Soapy's coat-sleeve.

'Sure, Mike,' she said joyfully, 'if you'll blow me to a pail of suds. I'd have spoke to you sooner, but the cop was watching.'

With the young woman playing the clinging ivy to his oak Soapy walked past the policeman overcome with gloom. He seemed doomed to liberty.

At the next corner he shook off his companion and ran. He halted in the district where by night are found the lightest streets, hearts, vows, and librettos. Women in furs and men in greatcoats moved gaily in the wintry air. A sudden fear seized Soapy that some dreadful enchantment had rendered him immune to arrest. The thought brought a little of panic upon it, and when he came upon another policeman lounging grandly in front of a transplendent theatre he caught at the immediate straw of 'disorderly conduct'.

On the sidewalk Soapy began to yell drunken gibberish at the top of his harsh voice. He danced, howled, raved, and otherwise disturbed the welkin.

The policeman twirled his club, turned his back to Soapy, and remarked to a citizen:

' 'Tis one of them Yale lads celebratin' the goose egg they give to the Hartford College. Noisy; but no harm. We've instructions to lave them be.'

Disconsolate, Soapy ceased his unavailing racket. Would never a policeman lay hands on him? In his fancy the Island seemed an unattainable Arcadia. He buttoned his thin coat against the chilling wind.

In a cigar store he saw a well-dressed man lighting a cigar at a swinging light. His silk umbrella he had set by the door on entering. Soapy stepped inside, secured the umbrella and sauntered off with it slowly. The man at the cigar light followed hastily.

'My umbrella,' he said sternly.

'Oh, is it?' sneered Soapy, adding insult to petit larceny. 'Well, why don't you call a policeman? I took it. Your umbrella! Why don't you call a cop? There stands one on the corner.'

The umbrella owner slowed his steps. Soapy did likewise, with a presentiment that luck would again run against him. The policeman looked at the two curiously.

'Of course,' said the umbrella man – 'that is – well, you know how these mistakes occur – I – if it's your umbrella I hope you'll excuse me – I picked it up this morning in a restaurant. – If you recognize it as yours, why – I hope you'll –'

'Of course it's mine,' said Soapy, viciously.

The ex-umbrella man retreated. The policeman hurried to assist a tall blonde in an opera cloak across the street in front of a street car that was approaching two blocks away.

Soapy walked eastward through a street damaged by improvements. He hurled the umbrella wrathfully into an excavation. He muttered against the men who wear helmets and carry clubs. Because he wanted to fall into their clutches, they seemed to regard him as a king who could do no wrong.

At length Soapy reached one of the avenues to the east where the glitter and turmoil was but faint. He set his face down this towards Madison Square, for the homing instinct survives even when the home is a park bench.

But on an unusually quiet corner Soapy came to a standstill. Here was an old church, quaint and rambling and gabled. Through one violet-stained window a soft light glowed, where, no doubt, the organist loitered over the keys, making sure of his mastery of the coming Sabbath anthem. For there drifted out to

Soapy's ears sweet music that caught and held him transfixed against the convolutions of the iron fence.

The moon was above, lustrous and serene; vehicles and pedestrians were few; sparrows twittered sleepily in the eaves – for a little while the scene might have been a country churchyard. And the anthem that the organist played cemented Soapy to the iron fence, for he had known it well in the days when his life contained such things as mothers and roses and ambitions and friends and immaculate thoughts and collars.

The conjunction of Soapy's receptive state of mind and the influences about the old church wrought a sudden and wonderful change in his soul. He viewed with swift horror the pit into which he had tumbled, the degraded days, unworthy desires, dead hopes, wrecked faculties, and base motives that made up his existence.

And also in a moment his heart responded thrillingly to this novel mood. An instantaneous and strong impulse moved him to battle with his desperate fate. He would pull himself out of the mire; he would make a man of himself again; he would conquer the evil that had taken possession of him. There was time; he was comparatively young yet; he would resurrect his old eager ambitions and pursue them without faltering. Those solemn but sweet organ notes had set up a revolution in him. To-morrow he would go into the roaring down-town district and find work. A fur importer had once offered him a place as driver. He would find him to-morrow and ask for the position. He would be somebody in the world. He would –

Soapy felt a hand laid on his arm. He looked quickly around into the broad face of a policeman.

'What are you doin' here?' asked the officer.

'Nothin',' said Soapy.

'Then come along,' said the policeman.

'Three months on the Island,' said the Magistrate in the Police Court the next morning.

The Strength of God

Sherwood Anderson

The Reverend Curtis Hartman was pastor of the Presbyterian Church of Winesburg, and had been in that position ten years. He was forty years old, and by his nature very silent and reticent. To preach, standing in the pulpit before the people, was always a hardship for him and from Wednesday morning until Saturday evening he thought of nothing but the two sermons that must be preached on Sunday. Early on Sunday morning he went into a little room called a study in the bell tower of the church and prayed. In his prayers there was one note that always predominated. 'Give me strength and courage for Thy work, O Lord!' he pleaded, kneeling on the bare floor and bowing his head in the presence of the task that lay before him.

The Reverend Hartman was a tall man with a brown beard. His wife, a stout, nervous woman, was the daughter of a manufacturer of underwear at Cleveland, Ohio. The minister himself was rather a favorite in the town. The elders of the church liked him because he was quiet and unpretentious and Mrs White, the banker's wife, thought him scholarly and refined.

The Presbyterian Church held itself somewhat aloof from the other churches of Winesburg. It was larger and more imposing and its minister was better paid. He even had a carriage of his own and on summer evenings sometimes drove about town with his wife. Through Main Street and up and down Buckeye Street he went, bowing gravely to the people, while his wife, afire with secret pride, looked at him out of the corners of her eyes and worried lest the horse become frightened and run away.

For a good many years after he came to Winesburg things went well with Curtis Hartman. He was not one to arouse keen enthusiasm among the worshippers in his church but on the other hand he made no enemies. In reality he was much in earnest and sometimes suffered prolonged periods of remorse because he could not go crying the word of God in the highways and byways of the town. He wondered if the flame of the spirit really burned in him and dreamed of a day when a strong sweet new current of power would come like a great wind into his voice and his soul and the people would tremble before the spirit of God made manifest in him. 'I am a poor stick and that will never really happen to me,' he mused dejectedly and then a patient smile lit up his features. 'Oh well, I suppose I'm doing well enough,' he added philosophically.

The room in the bell tower of the church, where on Sunday mornings the minister prayed for an increase in him of the power of God, had but one window. It was long and narrow and swung outward on a hinge like a door. On the window, made of little leaded panes, was a design showing the Christ laying his hand upon the head of a child. One Sunday morning in the summer as he sat by his desk in the room with a large Bible opened before him, and the sheets of his sermon scattered about, the minister was shocked to see, in the upper room of the house next door, a woman lying in her bed and smoking a cigarette while she read a book. Curtis Hartman went on tiptoe to the window and closed it softly. He was horror stricken at the thought of a woman smoking and trembled also to think that his eyes, just raised from the pages of the book of God, had looked upon the bare shoulders and white throat of a woman. With his brain in a whirl he went down into the pulpit and preached a long sermon without once thinking of his gestures or his voice. The sermon attracted unusual attention because of its power and clearness. 'I wonder if she is listening, if my voice is carrying a message into her soul,' he thought and began to hope that on future Sunday mornings he might be able to say words that would touch and awaken the woman apparently far gone in secret sin.

The house next door to the Presbyterian Church, through the windows of which the minister had seen the sight that had so upset him, was occupied by two women. Aunt Elizabeth Swift, a grey competent-looking widow with money in the Winesburg National Bank, lived there with her daughter Kate Swift, a school teacher. The school teacher was thirty years old and had a neat trim-looking figure. She had few friends and bore a reputation of having a sharp tongue. When he began to think about her, Curtis Hartman remembered that she had been to Europe and had lived for two years in New York City. 'Perhaps after all her smoking means nothing,' he thought. He began to remember that when he was a student in college and occasionally read novels, good, although somewhat worldly women, had smoked through the pages of a book that had once fallen into his hands. With a rush of new determination he worked on his sermons all through the week and forgot, in his zeal to reach the ears and the soul of this new listener, both his embarrassment in the pulpit and the necessity of prayer in the study on Sunday mornings.

Reverend Hartman's experience with women had been somewhat limited. He was the son of a wagon maker from Muncie, Indiana, and had worked his way through college. The daughter of the underwear manufacturer had boarded in a house where he lived during his school days and he had married her after a formal and prolonged courtship, carried on for the most part by the girl herself. On his marriage day the underwear manufacturer had given his daughter five thousand dollars and he promised to leave her at least twice that amount in his will. The minister had thought himself fortunate in marriage and had never permitted himself to think of other women. He did not want to think of other women. What he wanted was to do the work of God quietly and earnestly.

In the soul of the minister a struggle awoke. From wanting to reach the ears of Kate Swift, and through his sermons to delve into her soul, he began to want also to look again at the figure lying white and quiet in the bed. On a Sunday morning when he could not sleep because of his thoughts he arose and went to walk in the streets. When he had gone along Main Street almost to the old Richmond place he stopped and picking up a stone rushed off to the room in the bell tower. With the stone he broke out a corner of the window and then locked the door and sat down at the desk before the open Bible to wait. When the shade of the window to Kate Swift's room was raised he could see, through the hole, directly into her bed, but she was not there. She also had arisen and had gone for a walk and the hand that raised the shade was the hand of Aunt Elizabeth Swift.

The minister almost wept with joy at this deliverance from the carnal desire to 'peep' and went back to his own house praising God. In an ill moment he forgot, however, to stop the hole in the window. The piece of glass broken out at the corner of the window just nipped off the bare heel of the boy standing motionless and looking with rapt eyes into the face of the Christ.

Curtis Hartman forgot his sermon on that Sunday morning. He talked to his congregation and in his talk said that it was a mistake for people to think of their minister as a man set aside and intended by nature to lead a blameless life. 'Out of my own experience I know that we, who are the ministers of God's word, are beset by the same temptations that assail you,' he declared. 'I have been tempted and have surrendered to temptation. It is only the hand of God, placed beneath my head, that has raised me up. As he has raised me so also will he raise you. Do not despair. In your hour of sin raise your eyes to the skies and you will be again and again saved.'

Resolutely the minister put the thoughts of the woman in the bed out of his mind and began to be something like a lover in the presence of his wife. One evening when they drove out together he turned the horse out of Buckeye Street and in the darkness on Gospel Hill, above Waterworks Pond, put his arm about Sarah Hartman's waist. When he had eaten breakfast in the morning and was ready to retire to his study at the back of his house he went around the table and kissed his wife on the cheek. When thoughts of Kate Swift came into his head, he smiled and raised his eyes to the skies. 'Intercede for me, Master,' he muttered, 'keep me in the narrow path intent on Thy work.'

And now began the real struggle in the soul of the brown-bearded minister. By chance he discovered that Kate Swift was in the habit of lying in her bed in the evenings and reading a book. A lamp stood on a table by the side of the bed and the light streamed down upon her white shoulders and bare throat. On the evening when he made the discovery the minister sat at the desk in the study from nine until after eleven and when her light was put out stumbled out of the church to spend two more hours walking and praying in the streets. He did not want to kiss the shoulders and the throat of Kate Swift and had not allowed his mind to dwell on such thoughts. He did not know what he wanted. 'I am God's child and he must save me from myself,' he cried, in the darkness under the trees as he wandered in the streets. By a tree he stood and looked at the sky that was covered with hurrying clouds. He began to talk to God intimately and closely. 'Please, Father, do not forget me. Give me power to go to-morrow and repair the hole in the window. Lift my eyes again to the skies. Stay with me, Thy servant, in his hour of need.'

Up and down through the silent streets walked the minister and for days and weeks his soul was troubled. He could not understand the temptation that had come to him nor could he fathom the reason for its coming. In a way he began to blame God, saying to himself that he had tried to keep his feet in the true path and had not run about seeking sin. 'Through my days as a young man and all through my life here I have gone quietly about my work,' he declared. 'Why now should I be tempted? What have I done that this burden should be laid on me?'

Three times during the early fall and winter of that year Curtis Hartman crept out of his house to the room in the bell tower to sit in the darkness looking at the figure of Kate Swift lying in her bed and later went to walk and pray in the streets. He could not understand himself. For weeks he would go along scarcely thinking of the school teacher and telling himself that he had conquered the carnal desire to look at her body. And then something would happen. As he sat in the study of his own house, hard at work on a sermon, he would become nervous and begin to walk up and down the room. 'I will go out into the streets,' he told himself and even as he let himself in at the church door he persistently denied to himself the cause of his being there. 'I will not repair the hole in the window and I will train myself to come here at night and sit in the presence of this woman without raising my eyes. I will not be defeated in this thing. The Lord has devised this temptation as a test of my soul and I will grope my way out of darkness into the light of righteousness.'

One night in January when it was bitter cold and snow lay deep on the streets of Winesburg Curtis Hartman paid his last visit to the room in the bell tower of the church. It was past nine o'clock when he left his own house and he set out so hurriedly that he forgot to put on his overshoes. In Main Street no one was abroad but Hop Higgins the night watchman and in the whole town no one was awake but the watchman and young George Willard, who sat in the office of the *Winesburg Eagle* trying to write a story. Along the street to the church went the minister, plowing through the drifts and thinking that this time he would utterly give way to sin. 'I want to look at the woman and to think of kissing her shoulders and I am going to let myself think what I choose,' he declared bitterly and tears came into his eyes. He began to think that he would get out of the ministry and try some other way of life. 'I shall go to some city and get into business,' he declared. 'If my nature is such that I cannot resist sin, I shall give myself over to sin. At least I shall not be a hypocrite, preaching the word of God with my mind thinking of the shoulders and neck of a woman who does not belong to me.'

It was cold in the room of the bell tower of the church on that January night and almost as soon as he came into the room Curtis

Hartman knew that if he stayed he would be ill. His feet were wet from tramping in the snow and there was no fire. In the room in the house next door Kate Swift had not yet appeared. With grim determination the man sat down to wait. Sitting in the chair and gripping the edge of the desk on which lay the Bible he stared into the darkness thinking the blackest thoughts of his life. He thought of his wife and for the moment almost hated her. 'She has always been ashamed of passion and has cheated me,' he thought. 'Man has a right to expect living passion and beauty in a woman. He has no right to forget that he is an animal and in me there is something that is Greek. I will throw off the woman of my bosom and seek other women. I will besiege this school teacher. I will fly in the face of all men and if I am a creature of carnal lusts I will live then for my lusts.'

The distracted man trembled from head to foot, partly from cold, partly from the struggle in which he was engaged. Hours passed and a fever assailed his body. His throat began to hurt and his teeth chattered. His feet on the study floor felt like two cakes of ice. Still he would not give up. 'I will see this woman and will think the thoughts I have never dared to think,' he told himself, gripping the edge of the desk and waiting.

Curtis Hartman came near dying from the effects of that night of waiting in the church, and also he found in the thing that happened what he took to be the way of life for him. On other evenings when he had waited he had not been able to see, through the little hole in the glass, any part of the school teacher's room except that occupied by her bed. In the darkness he had waited until the woman suddenly appeared sitting in the bed in her white night-robe. When the light was turned up she propped herself up among the pillows and read a book. Sometimes she smoked one of the cigarettes. Only her bare shoulders and throat were visible.

On the January night, after he had come near dying with cold and after his mind had two or three times actually slipped away into an odd land of fantasy so that he had by an exercise of will power to force himself back into consciousness, Kate Swift appeared. In the room next door a lamp was lighted and the waiting man stared into an empty bed. Then upon the bed before his eyes a naked woman threw herself. Lying face downward she wept and beat with her fists upon the pillow. With a final outburst of weeping she half arose, and in the presence of the man who had waited to look and to think thoughts the woman of sin began to pray. In the lamplight her figure, slim and strong, looked like the figure of the boy in the presence of the Christ on the leaded window.

Curtis Hartman never remembered how he got out of the church. With a cry he arose, dragging the heavy desk along the floor. The Bible fell, making a great clatter in the silence. When the light in the house next door went out he stumbled down the stairway and into the street. Along the street he went and ran in at the door of the *Winesburg Eagle*. To George Willard, who was tramping up and down in the office undergoing a struggle of his own, he began to talk half incoherently. 'The ways of God are beyond human understanding,' he cried, running in quickly and closing the door. He began to advance upon the young man, his eyes glowing and his voice ringing with fervor. 'I have found the light,' he cried. 'After ten years in this town, God has manifested himself to me in the body of a woman.' His voice dropped and he began to whisper. 'I did not understand,' he said. 'What I took to be a trial of my soul was only a preparation for a new and more beautiful fervor of the spirit. God has appeared to me in the person of Kate Swift, the school teacher, kneeling naked on a bed. Do you know Kate Swift? Although she may not be aware of it, she is an instrument of God, bearing the message of truth.'

Reverend Curtis Hartman turned and ran out of the office. At the door he stopped, and after looking up and down the deserted street, turned again to George Willard. 'I am delivered. Have no fear.' He held up a bleeding fist for the young man to see. 'I smashed the glass of the window,' he cried. 'Now it will have to be wholly replaced: The strength of God was in me and I broke it with my fist.'

The Hunted Beast

T. F. Powys

Mr Walter Gidden, the vicar of East Dodder, climbed the stile slowly. He rested upon it as if he had a long hour in which to do nothing before he went home. Then he looked back. Something had happened, something horrible. Something that he could not bring his mind to think of . . .

Nature sometimes looks with a curious pity at a man upon whom has fallen, from who knows where, an awful event. But the pity of nature is dumb: it is also unthinking. It pities the victim and the torturer. It pities the dead by the look it gives them – and the living it pities by their fears.

Mr Gidden climbed softly over the stile, he leant against it and tried to think.

He was in the lane that led to the village and to his house. Upon either side of the lane the hedges were covered with honeysuckle. The sweet and odorous scent of new-mown hay filled the air. Everywhere there were flowers, and a little way down the lane a tiny rabbit sat and busily scratched itself. Suddenly, coming from nowhere, rich colour went by – a peacock butterfly . . .

Unthinking nature can deceive as well as pity. All seemed the same as it ever had been in this quiet country lane. Evidently nature wished to blot out, for a moment at least, in Mr Gidden's mind, what had happened, but only that the horrid wave should gather force to break.

A great many times had Mr Gidden, happy with the

contentment that belongs to a good man, strayed to that very spot to loiter.

An evil dream might have overtaken him. Perhaps he had lain down beside the stile – he might never have gone into the field. Then nothing had happened – the lane was the same. He knew the blackbird that sang from the ash tree – he knew him by one white feather. Mr Gidden looked down at his boots . . .

Mr Gidden had lived at East Dodder for twenty-five years. He had been married for thirty years. During all that time he had loved his wife and she had loved him. The two living children – there had been a girl, Mary, who had died – were both dutiful and good. The family were united lovingly and their thoughts were for one another . . .

There was no one in sight. Away towards the village a herd of cows was feeding peacefully. No one interrupted them: they might have been feeding there for ever. No crash came, the heavens did not fall, no earthquake happened, the sky was just the same.

But Mr Gidden trembled. Had he the ague? His teeth chattered. Suddenly he seized his own throat: he held tight for a moment, gasped, and let go. Why did not the green summer fields gape and pour out hell-fire? How could all the sweetness of summer be there still – with him standing there?

He now walked along the lane uneasily. He thought he staggered, but he was wrong, for he walked with his usual stride as if nothing had happened.

Before he knew where he was he opened his own gate, and he was careful to close it after him. His wife was sitting upon a garden-seat, sewing. Mr Gidden wondered what she was sewing.

He had returned a little earlier than usual from his afternoon walk; there was nothing untoward in that. It was kind of him, that was all, for he was often late. Mrs Gidden spoke to him and went on with her sewing – she was darning a table-cloth. He might have felt the sun in the lane a little too warm. Or the downs a little fatiguing? She had seen him there, and a little before he reached the summit, she had also noticed the children.

When she saw the children she found a new rent in the table-cloth. Village washerwomen are very careless!

Mrs Gidden had watched before she began to repair the rent she had found. She wished well to those children, employing her kindest thoughts about them. She knew them at that distance away – the two Budden boys and Nellie Webber. Her husband was upon the down and those children in the fields below.

As she had watched him there, there rose in her heart a wonderful feeling of gratitude to God for giving her such a happy life. She hoped to do more good yet, to help others more. She ought to say something to Nellie Webber, who was a trifle too merry with her young limbs, but young girls soon grow . . .

Mr Gidden had gone quietly into the house. She heard the study door shut; he would be still there when tea was ready . . .

Mr Gidden sat at his study table, the round inkpot was in front of him and his favourite pen. He took up the sermon that he had been writing before he went out. He had begun and ended his sermon with the word 'God' – that was curious.

He rose from his chair and took the clock – a heavy one – from the mantelpiece, and placed it upon the table in front of him.

He carefully calculated the movement of time.

Those two Budden boys, when they ran off and left Nellie alone, could not have run far. They must have watched what he had done to Nellie, from some hiding-place near.

As soon as he was out of sight they would have gone to her again. He had probably reached home when they had found her all bloody in the ditch.

Mr Gidden knew a little about boys. Boys like to look at anything strange: they stand and stare for five minutes and then they run away. They would wait and see if she moved. Then they would run home to tell Mrs Webber – ten minutes!

Mrs Webber, a stout talkative woman, who bore an ill character in the village, wouldn't hurry to the policeman's cottage; she would talk to people on her way. No one ever hurried in Dodder. It would be fully half an hour, from the time Mrs Webber set off to tell the policeman, to the moment when Constable Burr would call at the Rectory.

Mr Gidden looked at the clock. What had he done? He must try to think; he must remember what it was.

But his thoughts wandered. It was hard to hold them to the point. Something seemed to be pulling at his coat-tails. That was his past life. His past life pleaded with him and tried to pull him back.

There had been many joys in it – harmless, peaceful joys. 'That may be continued,' said the past, 'for many more years.'

But what had he decided to do? – to die. And for what? He must remember what it was that he had to die for.

He had been walking along the top of the downs when the rabbit screamed. He knew the sound at once and he knew what it was – a rabbit caught in a snare but not killed. He had come upon a rabbit before, caught in a gin, and had killed the poor beast at once with a blow of his stick. He would put this one out of its pain in the same manner. Perhaps if it were only wired he would release it and let it go.

But, this time, Mr Gidden wasn't the first to find the rabbit. No, nor yet the first to hear its scream, for the children had heard it. Mr Gidden watched the children going to the rabbit, and he followed them.

For some reason or other he felt nervous. It occurred to him that the children might think if they saw him that he had come not to save the rabbit but to steal it.

Mr Gidden was not ignorant of the behaviour of village minds. A country child thinks that the wrong he does is only the wrong that another would do if he had the same chance. When once, by mistake, Mr Gidden had surprised two persons lying together in a lane, whom he supposed to be fighting, he had heard a voice say over the hedge, ' 'E do wish old Peter were 'e.'

The children, in their eagerness to get to the rabbit, had not seen the clergyman coming after them, and Mr Gidden was able to conceal himself behind a bush only a little way from the snared rabbit. He watched what went on.

The boys had taken the rabbit out of the snare and had given it to Nellie to hold. Nellie was fourteen years old, a plump, coarse, sturdy girl.

She held the rabbit firmly while the boys examined every part of it. They all laughed to see how the fleas from the rabbit hopped about.

Presently Jack Budden took out from his pocket a blunt knife, and Nellie said jokingly, ' 'Tis they eyes stoats do first bite at.' To the horror of Mr Gidden, Jack, in imitation of the stoats' behaviour, gouged out the rabbit's eyes with the blunt knife.

For a moment while he watched, Mr Gidden could not move. The children placed the rabbit upon the grass to see what it did.

Then a terrible rage overcame Mr Gidden. He rushed out of his hiding-place and beat the blind rabbit to death with his stick. He turned upon the children, meaning to beat them too.

The boys escaped his hands and ran off. But the girl wasn't so fortunate; she did not run so quickly as the boys; perhaps she wanted to know what the clergyman would do to her.

Mr Gidden threw himself upon her. He tore at her clothes. She struggled and fell into the ditch. He struck her, lay upon her in his fury, and held to her throat. His stick was broken; he took up a great bone that lay near and struck her with that. There was blood upon the bone, and Nellie now lay very still.

During the struggle Mr Gidden had wished to do the very worst a man could do. He had wished to violate her – to give her cruelty for cruelty, pain for pain. But her clothes conquered him. He did not know what to do, he did not understand young girls. He looked down at her – she did not move. He was satisfied, he had avenged the rabbit. Though the world delivered no justice, he had delivered it. He had toppled over the world . . .

The Reverend Walter Gidden looked at the clock, he calculated the minutes that must elapse before the policeman would come for him.

Mr Gidden hadn't lived in the country for twenty-five years for nothing, he knew the people a little, he had read the local paper, he had listened to the village news. He might not have quite killed Nellie, but he knew what they would say he had done to her. He also remembered that his wife had said sadly – though a moment after she had remarked more gaily that young girls soon grow – that a cripple had been a little too kind to Nellie a few days before . . .

Mr Gidden rose hurriedly. Some one had opened and shut the front gate, cautiously, sedately, gently.

Mr Gidden looked out of the side window. It was, as he expected, the constable – Mr William Burr. Mr Gidden crossed the room to the larger window that led into the back garden. He leaped out of it.

He climbed some railings, he was in a little field beyond the garden. Two calves were in the field; these galloped away. Mr Gidden lay down in a small pit.

They would not search for him at once. Mr Burr would only enquire after him. Mr Burr would not wish to shock the lady, he would ask about him as if he were merely enquiring about his health. If Mr Gidden was out, Burr would go to the inspector at Stonebridge to ask what he ought to do.

Mr Burr would say, 'Is Mr Gidden at home?' and Mrs Gidden would reply, 'He was sitting in the study a moment ago, but perhaps he has gone out for another little walk.'

But Mr Gidden couldn't stay where he was; even though the hounds were not actually after him he knew himself to be a hunted beast. He left the pit and crept on with his back bent, hiding and running. He came to a hedge that he could not remember ever having noticed before. Everything looked different. The earth and sky were not the same now; the green grass mocked at him.

He clambered through the hedge and found himself in a field

of corn. He crept into the corn, treading carefully. He began to crawl, he crawled on and on, and then he lay down.

He had now time to think. He lay upon his back and looked up at the corn. A little mouse, moving amongst the corn, came to have a look at him. How high the corn was! It touched the sky. Every reed of corn appeared to have a distinct life. Each stalk was wonderful. They grew up high to heaven and to God. Could he but become a stalk of corn or a little mouse!

Mr Gidden endeavoured to calm his mind and to look philosophically at the event that had befallen him and at what must come of it. That morning he had received a letter from his son John, who was a curate in Bloomsbury. His daughter, too, had written from Bedford College. He had read their letters happily, in his study before breakfast. He had felt comfortable and contented; the warm weather, the letters, had pleased him.

He remembered his age – fifty-four. He was in good health except for a little chest weakness, and that always made him take the greater care of himself. He might have lived, in all comfort and happiness, until he was very old. But the bolt had fallen, and he was not going to be taken alive.

That thought twisted and bent him, and yet he held firmly to it. It struggled in him, changing into different forms, trying to escape. He held it firm; he would not let it go. He would never live to make sport for the mob. Let the evil ones toss him to and fro – when he was dead – what would he care?

When his name was cried round the streets of Weyminster by the newsboys he wouldn't know of it. It was his wish now – to die.

Shouts came from the village. He was being called for. Every one, he was sure, must know by this time what he had done. He must go farther, he must fly. He said the last words aloud, and so they reminded him of the prayer for the sick – 'We fly to Thee for succour in behalf of this Thy servant.'

Mr Gidden crept on all fours out of the corn. He came to another hedge; a gap in it was guarded by a broken hurdle, round which nettles grew. Mr Gidden crawled through the nettles. He ran, taking an uncertain course, running by this hedge and by that, crushing the pretty flowers with his feet, breaking through the tall weeds. Sometimes he would creep so that he might more conveniently hide himself.

Once he stopped, peered through some bushes, and looked at the village. The village appeared to be quiet, he even thought he saw Nellie walking over the green with something white round her head – a bandage. But he couldn't believe his own eyes when he remembered what he had done to her. He did not know how hardy children are.

At last, after crossing the road that led to Shelton, he crept into a little spinney where there were pools of water and thick tufts and tussocks of grass. Mr Gidden threw himself down amongst them. His hands and his face burned and tingled; he had both stung and scratched himself. His clothes, that had that morning been so sleek and black, were now all spotted and torn. He leaned over a pool of clear water and saw his face reflected. He was become horrible; the face he saw was distorted with anguish; he looked pale and ghastly. He had never seen even a dying man look as he did. The dying, for the most part, were carefully tended in Dodder. And though they might gasp and their breath rattle – yet they lay upon soft pillows. He was far more awful to look at than the worst of them.

From the place in which Mr Gidden had concealed himself, he could see the downs and the field, too, where the children had been. He saw two men there, and now and again one of them would kneel down as though to examine the ground.

'Of course,' thought Mr Gidden, 'they must have carried her away,' but they were still looking for anything that he might have left to prove his guilt. Perhaps he had left his hat. He fancied now that it had fallen into the ditch. He couldn't remember having his hat upon his head when he reached home. Was he wearing it now? – no – then he must have left it behind him somewhere.

As he lay in the marsh his past life crept up to him, as a little dog might come who feared a whipping.

Mr Gidden had entered the world upon a Christmas Day – the longed-for and prayed-for child of gentle and pious parents. He was born in a comfortable parsonage home in Wiltshire. There was a brook in front of the house, where there used to be kingfishers. Upon the south wall of the house there grew a wonderful magnolia. He had adored, with a vast adoration, the great white flowers. His mother had told him that they were beautiful because they had committed no sin. His mother used to lift him up to touch them. He remembered his own little hands, his clean shirt cuffs, and the stainless flowers. Nothing harmed him then.

There was the great Bible – and the first words that he learned to read – 'And the Lord called Samuel again the third time.'

He read easily.

He had been delicate, and he could never bear to witness the least cruelty. Once he found another little boy cutting off the whiskers of a cat – a common practice in the country. Walter had rushed upon him, brandishing a wooden sword in his hand. The boy fled.

After those magic days of childhood were over, Mr Gidden's life had passed on evenly, nothing surprising ever happened. There was, he had ever believed, a loving God who, when it was for their eternal good, healed the sick and gave to those He healed a new chance to do better and to ask for pardon for their sins.

Those gentle thoughts were now all gone – a brutal thief had stolen them away; they were with him no more. Why was he a man? Had he been but one of those tussocks of grass, all might have been well. Strange hummocks they were, whose roots, after many years of growth, had built up a pedestal for the living grass above – a yard or two above the ground some of them were! Here was Nature's mournful plan, the living built up upon the dead. Only the summit of all the bones was green.

Mr Gidden shut his eyes. Perhaps when he opened them he

would be in his study. Or else, was it a dream? Had he laid him down to sleep near to a bunch of thyme upon the down? Then he had dreamed a rather strange dream. Did he use to walk about in his dreams – perhaps to kill? A girl had been found dead upon the heath a year before. Some one must have killed her, too. Perhaps it was he – Walter Gidden. Thus moves the devil's cruelty in the earth. The worlds shudder, the skies weep. The deed is done.

Mr Gidden raised his head: he heard voices. Two men were walking towards him from the direction of the Shelton road. They were two rabbit-catchers, the very two who had been under the hill, setting their snares. They were accompanied by a little black dog. Mr Gidden did not recognise them.

Mr Gidden crept to the farther side of the copse. His hands were torn by thorns, his knees sank into the mud, but he was going away from the men.

He crept into a ditch and under a low railing. He was in the meadow. He raised himself and ran, hoping to reach the hedge across the meadow before he was seen. But he had not run far before he knew that he could not escape. The men must see him before he reached safety. What was he to do?

The field he was crossing was a water meadow, in which there were ditches. He cast himself into a ditch in which was half a foot of water. The water ran into a tunnel that burrowed under a grassy roadway where the haycarts rumbled in summer and the cows plodded in winter.

Mr Gidden peeped out of the ditch through the meadow-sweet and mint. The two men were coming directly to the place where he lay. He crept into the tunnel to hide. He could not crawl in, the place was too low for that. He moved along like a snake or a worm.

He lay still in the middle of the tunnel. The water trickled over his clothes and soaked him through. He heard voices: the men had evidently come to that very place and were resting beside the little ditch, talking and laughing. They were speaking of some one who had disgraced himself. Mr Gidden supposed they were speaking about him. Presently something dashed into the opening, and a dog barked.

Mr Gidden was filled with horror. They would have him yet, he thought.

The dog spluttered and splashed. Mr Gidden was wary. The little dog came on inquisitively, barking with short, sharp barks. It came near; Mr Gidden clutched at it and held it by the throat. He strangled the dog slowly. When one hand grew tired, he used the other. At length he moved so that he could clasp the dog's throat with both his hands.

After he had strangled the dog, he held its head under the water.

The men did not seem to be aware that the dog had crept into the tunnel; they had moved away and were now calling their dog out of the spinney. They supposed it had run in there. Mr Gidden let the dead dog go.

He buried his own face in the water. He gasped and spluttered like the dog. But he could not drown there, he must take stronger means than that.

He had avenged the cruelty to the rabbit, and now he had killed this dog. Who could prevent the cruelty of the world? No one. But he could end himself, and that would be something done.

For some hours he lay there, and then crept out of the tunnel.

The evening was very still. A few dim stars were in the sky, looking faint, weary, and sad.

Mr Gidden lay on the grass, his limbs were cramped, he could hardly stir. Below him in the ditch was the dead body of the little dog.

Mr Gidden tried to get up; he succeeded at the third attempt. His limbs were heavy, as though Death had already touched him with his clammy hands. He limped out of the field, and cautiously crossed the road, taking nearly the same way that he had come. He went along in the same cornfield that he had hid himself in.

He was near his home, and he heard the supper-bell ring. The sound called him. He listened. He thought he heard his wife calling him by name. His legs, without his command, moved towards his home. In a few moments he would be there.

He stopped suddenly. Some one in the village laughed – a horrible laugh. It was the hunchback. The cripple didn't trouble about Nellie now. He could laugh as he chose.

Mr Gidden turned to go to the sea. He was very careful of himself. He did not wish to faint by the way.

Mr Gidden had always been careful not to take cold. But he had done queer things that day. He had lain in a swamp – in a ditch. He had always been careful about other things too. He was very cleanly, he shaved every morning. If he had the smallest pimple upon his face he would look at it askance and shave the more carefully. The remainder of his body was always as smooth and white as a child's. How would he look after a few days in the sea? – God's Judgment.

Mr Gidden climbed down the cliff slowly: he did not wish to fall. He looked to his steps.

At the bottom of the cliff he picked up a child's boat. He walked, with the boat in his hand, into the sea.

He knew he could not swim. His clothes hung heavy, but still he swam out and the tide helped him. He let himself sink, but rose in a moment gasping, and hitting the water with his hands, letting the little boat go.

The little boat floated away. Mr Gidden began to fight horribly for his life.

He heard the hunchback laugh. The water closed over his head. He thought he was on the top of it, in the child's boat, but he sank deeper.

118

The Master of Mystery

Jack London

There was complaint in the village. The women chattered together with shrill, high-pitched voices. The men were glum and
doubtful of aspect, and the very dogs wandered dubiously about,
alarmed in vague ways by the unrest of the camp and ready to
take to the woods on the first outbreak of trouble. The air was
filled with suspicion. No man was sure of his neighbor, and
each was conscious that he stood in like unsureness with his
fellows. Even the children were oppressed and solemn, and little
Di Ya, the cause of it all, had been soundly thrashed, first by
Hooniah, his mother, and then by his father, Bawn, and was now
whimpering and looking pessimistically out upon the world from
the shelter of the big overturned canoe on the beach.

And to make the matter worse Scundoo, the shaman, was in
disgrace and his known magic could not be called upon to seek
out the evildoer. Forsooth, a month gone, he had promised a fair
south wind so that the tribe might journey to the *potlatch* at
Tonkin, where Taku Jim was giving away the savings of twenty
years; and when the day came, lo, a grievous north wind blew,
and of the first three canoes to venture forth, one was swamped
in the big seas, and two were pounded to pieces on the rocks,
and a child was drowned. He had pulled the string of the wrong
bag, he explained – a mistake. But the people refused to listen;
the offerings of meat and fish and fur ceased to come to his
door; and he sulked within – so they thought – fasting in bitter
penance; in reality, eating generously from his well-stored cache

119

and meditating upon the fickleness of the mob.

The blankets of Hooniah were missing. They were good blankets, of most marvelous thickness and warmth, and her pride in them was greatened in that they had been come by so cheaply. Ty-Kwan, of the next village but one, was a fool to have so easily parted with them. But then, she did not know they were the blankets of the murdered Englishman, because of whose take-off the United States cutter nosed along the coast for a time, while its launches puffed and snorted among the secret inlets. And not knowing that Ty-Kwan had disposed of them in haste so that his own people might not have to render account to the Government, Hooniah's pride was unshaken. And because the women envied her, her pride was without end and boundless, till it filled the village and spilled over along the Alaskan shore from Dutch Harbor to St Mary's. Her totem had become justly celebrated, and her name known on the lips of men wherever men fished and feasted, what of the blankets and their marvelous thickness and warmth. It was a most mysterious happening, the manner of their going.

'I but stretched them up in the sun by the sidewall of the house,' Hooniah disclaimed for the thousandth time to her Thlinket sisters. 'I but stretched them up and turned my back; for Di Ya, dough-thief and eater of raw flour that he is, with head into the big iron pot, overturned and stuck there, his legs waving like the branches of a forest tree in the wind. And I did but drag him out and twice knock his head against the door for riper understanding, and behold, the blankets were not!'

'The blankets were not!' the women repeated in awed whispers.

'A great loss,' one added. A second, 'Never were there such blankets.' And a third, 'We be sorry, Hooniah, for thy loss.' Yet each woman was glad in her heart that the odious, dissension-breeding blankets were gone.

'I but stretched them up in the sun,' Hooniah began again.

'Yea, yea,' Bawn spoke up, wearied. 'But there were no gossips in the village from other places. Wherefore it be plain that some of

120

our own tribespeople have laid unlawful hand upon the blankets.'

'How can that be, O Bawn?' the women chorused indignantly. 'Who should there be?'

'Then has there been witchcraft,' Bawn continued stolidly enough, though he stole a sly glance at their faces.

'*Witchcraft!*' And at the dread word their voices hushed and they looked fearfully at each other.

'Ay,' Hooniah affirmed, the latent malignancy of her nature flashing into a moment's exultation. 'And word has been sent to Klok-No-Ton, and strong paddles. Truly shall he be here with the afternoon tide.'

The little groups broke up and fear descended upon the village. Of all misfortune, witchcraft was the most appalling. With the intangible and unseen things only the shamans could cope, and neither man, woman, nor child could know until the moment of ordeal whether devils possessed their souls or not. And of all shamans Klok-No-Ton, who dwelt in the next village, was the most terrible. None found more evil spirits than he, none visited his victims with more frightful tortures. Even had he found, once, a devil residing within the body of a three-months babe – a most obstinate devil which could only be driven out when the babe had lain for a week on thorns and briers. The body was thrown into the sea after that, but the waves tossed it back again and again as a curse upon the village, nor did it finally go away till two strong men were staked out at low tide and drowned.

And Hooniah had sent for this Klok-No-Ton. Better had it been if Scundoo, their own shaman, were undisgraced. For he had ever a gentler way, and he had been known to drive forth two devils from a man who afterward begat seven healthy children. But Klok-No-Ton! They shuddered with dire foreboding at thought of him, and each one felt himself the center of accusing eyes, and looked accusingly upon his fellows – each one and all, save Sime, and Sime was a scoffer whose evil end was destined with a certitude his success could not shake.

'Hoh! Hoh!' he laughed. 'Devils and Klok-No-Ton! – than

121

whom no greater devil can be found in Thlinket Land.'

'Thou fool! Even now he cometh with witcheries and sorceries; so beware thy tongue, lest evil befall thee and thy days be short in the land!'

So spoke La-lah, otherwise the Cheater, and Sime laughed scornfully.

'I am Sime, unused to fear, unafraid of the dark. I am a strong man, as my father before me, and my head is clear. Nor you nor I have seen with our eyes the unseen evil things –'

'But Scundoo hath,' La-lah made answer. 'And likewise Klok-No-Ton. This we know.'

'How dost thou know, son of a fool?' Sime thundered, the choleric blood darkening his thick bull neck.

'By the word of their mouths – even so.'

Sime snorted. 'A shaman is only a man. May not his words be crooked, even as thine and mine? Bah! Bah! And once more, bah! And this for thy shamans and thy shamans' devils! and this! and this!'

And Sime snapped his fingers to right and left.

When Klok-No-Ton arrived on the afternoon tide, Sime's defiant laugh was unabated; nor did he forebear to make a joke when the shaman tripped on the sand in the landing. Klok-No-Ton looked at him sourly, and without greeting stalked straight through their midst to the house of Scundoo.

Of the meeting with Scundoo none of the tribespeople might know, for they clustered reverently in the distance and spoke in whispers while the masters of mystery were together.

'Greeting, O Scundoo!' Klok-No-Ton rumbled, wavering perceptibly from doubt of his reception.

He was a giant in stature and towered massively above little Scundoo, whose thin voice floated upward like the faint far rasping of a cricket.

'Greeting, Klok-No-Ton,' Scundoo returned. 'The day is fair with thy coming.'

'Yet it would seem . . .' Klok-No-Ton hesitated.

'Yea, yea,' the little shaman put in impatiently, 'that I have fallen on ill days, else would I not stand in gratitude to you in that you do my work.'

'It grieves me, friend Scundoo . . .'

'Nay, I am made glad, Klok-No-Ton.'

'But will I give thee half of that which be given me.'

'Not so, good Klok-No-Ton,' murmured Scundoo, with a deprecatory wave of the hand. 'It is I who am thy slave, and my days shall be filled with desire to befriend thee.'

'As I —'

'As thou now befriendest me.'

'That being so, it is then a bad business, these blankets of the woman Hooniah?'

The big shaman blundered tentatively in his quest, and Scundoo smiled a wan, gray smile, for he was used to reading men, and all men seemed very small to him.

'Ever hast thou dealt in strong medicine,' he said. 'Doubtless the evildoer will be briefly known to thee.'

'Ay, briefly known when I set eyes upon him.' Again Klok-No-Ton hesitated. 'Have there been gossips from other places?' he asked.

Scundoo shook his head. 'Behold! Is this not a most excellent mucluc?'

He held up the foot-covering of sealskin and walrus hide, and his visitor examined it with interest.

'It did come to me by a close-driven bargain.'

Klok-No-Ton nodded attentively.

'I got it from the man La-lah. He is a remarkable man, and often have I thought . . .'

'So?' Klok-No-Ton ventured impatiently.

'Often have I thought,' Scundoo concluded, his voice falling as he came to a full pause. 'It is a fair day, and thy medicine be strong, Klok-No-Ton.'

Klok-No-Ton's face brightened. 'Thou art a great man,

Scundoo, a shaman of shamans. I go now. I shall remember thee always. And the man La-lah, as you say, is remarkable.'

Scundoo smiled yet more wan and gray, closed the door on the heels of his departing visitor, and barred and double-barred it.

Sime was mending his canoe when Klok-No-Ton came down the beach, and he broke off from his work only long enough to load his rifle ostentatiously and place it near him.

The shaman noted the action and called out: 'Let all the people come together on this spot! It is the word of Klok-No-Ton, devilseeker and driver of devils!'

He had been minded to assemble them at Hooniah's house, but it was necessary that all should be present, and he was doubtful of Sime's obedience and did not wish trouble. Sime was a good man to let alone, his judgement ran, and a bad one for the health of any shaman.

'Let the woman Hooniah be brought,' Klok-No-Ton commanded, glaring ferociously about the circle and sending chills up and down the spines of those he looked upon.

Hooniah waddled forward, head bent and gaze averted.

'Where be thy blankets?'

'I but stretched them up in the sun, and behold, they were not!' she whined.

'So?'

'It was because of Di Ya.'

'So?'

'Him have I beaten sore, and he shall yet be beaten, for that he brought trouble upon us who be poor people.'

'The blankets!' Klok-No-Ton bellowed hoarsely, foreseeing her desire to lower the price to be paid. 'The blankets, woman! Thy wealth is known.'

'I but stretched them up in the sun,' she sniffled, 'and we be poor people and have nothing.'

He stiffened suddenly, with a hideous distortion of the face, and Hooniah shrank back. But so swiftly did he spring forward, with inturned eye-balls and loosened jaw, that she stumbled and fell groveling at his feet. He waved his arms about, wildly flagellating the air, his body writhing and twisting in torment. An epilepsy seemed to come upon him. A white froth flecked his lips, and his body was convulsed with shiverings and tremblings.

The women broke into a wailing chant, swaying backward and forward in abandonment, while one by one the men succumbed to the excitement. Only Sime remained. He, perched upon his canoe, looked on in mockery; yet the ancestors whose seed he bore pressed heavily upon him, and he swore his strongest oaths that his courage might be cheered. Klok-No-Ton was horrible to behold. He had cast off his blanket and torn his clothes from him, so that he was quite naked, save for a girdle of eagle-claws about his thighs. Shrieking and yelling, his long black hair flying like a blot of night, he leaped frantically about the circle. A certain rude rhythm characterized his frenzy, and when all were under its sway, swinging their bodies in accord with his and venting their cries in unison, he sat bolt upright, with arm outstretched and long, talon-like finger extended. A low moaning, as of the dead, greeted this, and the people cowered with shaking knees as the dread finger passed them slowly by. For death went with it, and life remained with those who watched it go; and being rejected, they watched with eager intentness.

Finally, with a tremendous cry, the fateful finger rested upon La-lah. He shook like an aspen, seeing himself already dead, his household goods divided, and his widow married to his brother. He strove to speak, to deny, but his tongue clove to his mouth and his throat was sanded with an intolerable thirst. Klok-No-Ton seemed half to swoon away, now that his work was done; but he waited with closed eyes, listening for the great blood-cry to go up – the great blood-cry, familiar to his ear from a thousand conjurations, when the tribespeople flung themselves like wolves upon the trembling victim. But there was only silence, then a low tittering from nowhere in particular which spread and spread until a vast laughter welled up to the sky.

'Wherefore?' he cried.

'Na! Na!' the people laughed. 'Thy medicine be ill, O Klok-No-Ton!'

'It be known to all,' La-lah stuttered. 'For eight weary months have I been gone afar with the Siwash sealers, and but this day am I come back to find the blankets of Hooniah gone ere I came!'

'It be true!' they cried with one accord. 'The blankets of Hooniah were gone ere he came!'

'And thou shalt be paid nothing for thy medicine which is of no avail,' announced Hooniah, on her feet once more and smarting from a sense of ridiculousness.

But Klok-No-Ton saw only the face of Scundoo and its wan, gray smile, heard only the faint far cricket's rasping. 'I got it from the man La-lah, and often have I thought,' and, 'It is a fair day and thy medicine be strong.'

He brushed by Hooniah, and the circle instinctively gave way for him to pass. Sime flung a jeer from the top of the canoe, the women snickered in his face, cries of derision rose in his wake, but he took no notice, pressing onward to the house of Scundoo. He hammered on the door, beat it with his fists, and howled vile imprecations. Yet there was no response, save that in the lulls Scundoo's voice rose eerily in incantation. Klok-No-Ton raged about like a madman, but when he attempted to break in the door with a huge stone, murmurs arose from the men and women. And he, Klok-No-Ton, knew that he stood shorn of his strength and authority before an alien people. He saw a man stoop for a stone, and a second, and a bodily fear ran through him.

'Harm not Scundoo, who is a master!' a woman cried out.

'Better you return to your own village,' a man advised menacingly.

Klok-No-Ton turned on his heel and went down among them to the beach, a bitter rage at his heart, and in his head a just apprehension for his defenseless back. But no stones were cast. The children swarmed mockingly about his feet, and the air was wild with laughter and derision, but that was all. Yet he did not breathe freely until his canoe was well out upon the water, when he rose up and laid a futile curse upon the village and its people, not forgetting to specify Scundoo who had made a mock of him.

Ashore there was a clamor for Scundoo and the whole population crowded his door, entreating and imploring in confused babel till he came forth and raised his hand.

'In that ye are my children I pardon freely,' he said. 'But never again. For the last time thy foolishness goes unpunished. That which ye wish shall be granted, and it be already known to me. This night, when the moon has gone behind the world to look upon the mighty dead, let all the people gather in the blackness before the house of Hooniah. Then shall the evildoer stand forth and take his merited reward. I have spoken.'

'It shall be death!' Bawn vociferated, 'for that it hath brought worry upon us, and shame.'

'So be it,' Scundoo replied, and shut his door.

'Now shall all be made clear and plain, and content rest upon us once again,' La-lah declaimed oracularly.

'Because of Scundoo, the little man,' Sime sneered.

'Because of the medicine of Scundoo, the little man,' La-lah corrected.

'Children of foolishness, these Thlinket people!' Sime smote his thigh a resounding blow. 'It passeth understanding that grown women and strong men should get down in the dirt to dream-things and wonder tales.'

'I am a traveled man,' La-lah answered. 'I have journeyed on the deep seas and seen signs and wonders, and I know that these things be so. I am La-lah –'

'The Cheater –'

'So called, but the Far-Journeyer right-named.'

'I am not so great a traveler –' Sime began.

'Then hold thy tongue,' Bawn cut in, and they separated in anger.

When the last silver moonlight had vanished beyond the world, Scundoo came among the people huddled about the house of

Hooniah. He walked with a quick, alert step, and those who saw him in the light of Hooniah's slush-lamp noticed that he came empty-handed, without rattles, masks, or shaman's paraphernalia, save for a great sleepy raven carried under one arm.

'Is there wood gathered for a fire, so that all may see when the work be done?' he demanded.

'Yea,' Bawn answered. 'There be wood in plenty.'

'Then let all listen, for my words be few. With me have I brought Jelchs, the Raven, diviner of mystery and seer of things. Him, in his blackness, shall I place under the big black pot of Hooniah, in the blackest corner of her house. The slush-lamp shall cease to burn, and all remain in outer darkness. It is very simple. One by one shall ye go into the house, lay hand upon the pot for the space of one long intake of the breath, and withdraw again. Doubtless Jelchs will make outcry when the hand of the evildoer is nigh him. Or who knows but otherwise he may manifest his wisdom. Are ye ready?'

'We be ready,' came the multivoiced response.

'Then will I call the name aloud, each in his turn and hers, till all are called.'

La-lah was first chosen, and he passed in at once. Every ear strained, and through the silence they could hear his footsteps creaking across the rickety floor. But that was all. Jelchs made no outcry, gave no sign. Bawn was next chosen, for it well might be that a man should steal his own blankets with intent to cast shame upon his neighbors. Hooniah followed, and other women and children, but without result.

'Sime!' Scundoo called out.

'Sime!' he repeated.

But Sime did not stir.

'Art thou afraid of the dark?' La-lah, his own integrity being proved, demanded fiercely.

Sime chuckled. 'I laugh at it all, for it is a great foolishness. Yet will I go in, not in belief in wonders, but in token that I am unafraid.'

128

And he passed in boldly, and came out still mocking.

'Some day shalt thou die with great suddenness,' La-lah whispered, righteously indignant.

'I doubt not,' the scoffer answered airily. 'Few men of us die in our beds, what with the shamans and the deep sea.'

When half the villagers had safely undergone the ordeal, the excitement, because of its repression, became painfully intense. When two-thirds had gone through, a young woman, close on her first child-bed, broke down, and in nervous shrieks and laughter gave form to her terror.

Finally the turn came for the last of all to go in – and nothing had yet happened. And Di Ya was the last of all. It must surely be he. Hooniah let out a lament to the stars, while the rest drew back from the luckless lad. He was half dead from fright, and his legs gave under him so that he staggered on the threshold and nearly fell. Scundoo shoved him inside and closed the door. A long time went by, during which could be heard only the boy's weeping. Then, very slowly, came the creak of his steps to the far corner, a pause, and the creaking of his return. The door opened and he came forth. Nothing had happened and he was the last.

'Let the fire be lighted,' Scundoo commanded.

'Surely the thing has failed,' Hooniah whispered hoarsely.

'Yea,' Bawn answered complacently. 'Scundoo groweth old, and we stand in need of a new shaman.'

Sime threw his chest out arrogantly and strutted up to the little shaman. 'Hoh! Hoh! As I said, nothing has come of it!'

'So it would seem, so it would seem,' Scundoo answered meekly. 'And it would seem strange to those unskilled in the affairs of mystery.'

'As thou?' Sime queried.

'Mayhap even as I.' Scundoo spoke quite softly, his eyelids drooping, slowly drooping, down, down, till his eyes were all but hidden. 'So I am minded of another test. *Let every man, woman, and child, now and at once, hold their hands up above their heads!*'

So unexpected was the order, and so imperatively was it given, that it was obeyed without question. Every hand was in the air.

'Let each look on the other's hands, and let all look,' Scundoo commanded, 'so that –'

But a noise of laughter, which was more of wrath, drowned his voice. All eyes had come to rest upon Sime. Every hand but his was black with soot, and his was guiltless of the smirch of Hooniah's pot.

A stone hurtled through the air and struck him on the cheek.

'It is a lie!' he yelled. 'A lie! I know naught of Hooniah's blankets!'

A second stone gashed his brow, a third whistled past his head, the great blood-cry went up, and everywhere were people groping for missiles.

'Where hast thou hidden them?' Scundoo's shrill, sharp voice cut through the tumult like a knife.

'In the large skin-bale in my house, the one slung by the ridgepole,' came the answer. 'But it was a joke –'

Scundoo nodded his head, and the air went thick with flying stones. Sime's wife was crying, but his little boy, with shrieks and laughter, was flinging stones with the rest.

Hooniah came waddling back with the precious blankets. Scundoo stopped her.

'We be poor people and have little,' she whimpered. 'So be not hard upon us, O Scundoo.'

The people ceased from the quivering stone pile they had builded, and looked on.

'Nay, it was never my way, good Hooniah,' Scundoo made answer, reaching for the blankets. 'In token that I am not hard, these only shall I take. Am I not wise, my children?'

'Thou art indeed wise, O Scundoo!' they cried in one voice.

And Scundoo, the Master of Mystery, went away into the darkness, the blankets around him and Jelchs nodding sleepily under his arm.

The Angel of the Lord

Melville Davisson Post

I always thought my father took a long chance, but somebody
had to take it and certainly I was the one least likely to be
suspected. It was a wild country. There were no banks. We had
to pay for the cattle, and somebody had to carry the money. My
father and my uncle were always being watched. My father was
right, I think.

'Abner,' he said, 'I'm going to send Martin. No one will ever
suppose that we would trust this money to a child.'

My uncle drummed on the table and rapped his heels on the
floor. He was a bachelor, stern and silent. But he could talk . . .
and when he did, he began at the beginning and you heard him
through; and what he said – well, he stood behind it.

'To stop Martin,' my father went on, 'would be only to lose
the money; but to stop you would be to get somebody killed.'

I knew what my father meant. He meant that no one would
undertake to rob Abner until after he had shot him to death.

I ought to say a word about my Uncle Abner. He was one of
those austere, deeply religious men who were the product of the
Reformation. He always carried a Bible in his pocket and he
read it where he pleased. Once the crowd at Roy's Tavern tried to
make sport of him when he got his book out by the fire; but they
never tried it again. When the fight was over Abner paid Roy
eighteen silver dollars for the broken chairs and the table – and
he was the only man in the tavern who could ride a horse. Abner
belonged to the church militant, and his God was a war lord.

131

So that is how they came to send me. The money was in greenbacks in packages. They wrapped it up in newspaper and put it into a pair of saddle-bags, and I set out. I was about nine years old. No, it was not as bad as you think. I could ride a horse all day when I was nine years old – most any kind of a horse. I was tough as whit'-leather, and I knew the country I was going into. You must not picture a little boy rolling a hoop in the park.

It was an afternoon in early autumn. The clay roads froze in the night; they thawed out in the day and they were a bit sticky. I was to stop at Roy's Tavern, south of the river, and go on in the morning. Now and then I passed some cattle driver, but no one overtook me on the road until almost sundown; then I heard a horse behind me and a man came up. I knew him. He was a cattleman named Dix. He had once been a shipper, but he had come in for a good deal of bad luck. His partner, Alkire, had absconded with a big sum of money due the grazers. This had ruined Dix; he had given up his land, which wasn't very much, to the grazers. After that he had gone over the mountain to his people, got together a pretty big sum of money and bought a large tract of grazing land. Foreign claimants had sued him in the courts on some old title and he had lost the whole tract and the money that he had paid for it. He had married a remote cousin of ours and he had always lived on her lands, adjoining those of my Uncle Abner.

Dix seemed surprised to see me on the road.

'So it's you, Martin,' he said; 'I thought Abner would be going into the upcountry.'

One gets to be a pretty cunning youngster, even at this age, and I told no one what I was about.

'Father wants the cattle over the river to run a month,' I returned easily, 'and I'm going up there to give his orders to the grazers.'

He looked me over, then he rapped the saddlebags with his knuckles. 'You carry a good deal of baggage, my lad.'

I laughed. 'Horse feed,' I said. 'You know my father! A horse must be fed at dinner time, but a man can go till he gets it.'

One was always glad of any company on the road, and we fell into an idle talk. Dix said he was going out into the Ten Mile country; and I have always thought that was, in fact, his intention. The road turned south about a mile our side of the tavern. I never liked Dix; he was of an apologetic manner, with a cunning, irresolute face.

A little later a man passed us at a gallop. He was a drover named Marks, who lived beyond my Uncle Abner, and he was riding hard to get in before night. He hailed us, but he did not stop; we got a shower of mud and Dix cursed him. I have never seen a more evil face. I suppose it was because Dix usually had a grin about his mouth, and when that sort of face gets twisted there's nothing like it.

After that he was silent. He rode with his head down and his fingers plucking at his jaw, like a man in some perplexity. At the crossroads he stopped and sat for some time in the saddle, looking before him. I left him there, but at the bridge he overtook me. He said he had concluded to get some supper and go on after that.

Roy's Tavern consisted of a single big room, with a loft above it for sleeping quarters. A narrow covered way connected this room with the house in which Roy and his family lived. We used to hang our saddles on wooden pegs in this covered way. I have seen that wall so hung with saddles that you could not find a place for another stirrup. But tonight Dix and I were alone in the tavern. He looked cunningly at me when I took the saddle-bags with me into the big room and when I went with them up the ladder into the loft. But he said nothing – in fact, he had scarcely spoken. It was cold; the road had begun to freeze when we got in. Roy had lighted a big fire. I left Dix before it. I did not take off my clothes, because Roy's beds were mattresses of wheat straw covered with heifer skins – good enough for summer but pretty cold on such a night, even with the heavy, hand-woven coverlet in big white and black checks.

I put the saddle-bags under my head and lay down. I went at once to sleep, but I suddenly awaked. I thought there was a candle in the loft, but it was a gleam of light from the fire below, shining through a crack in the floor. I lay and watched it, the coverlet pulled up to my chin. Then I began to wonder why the fire burned so brightly. Dix ought to be on his way some time and it was a custom for the last man to rake out the fire. There was not a sound. The light streamed steadily through the crack.

Presently it occurred to me that Dix had forgotten the fire and that I ought to go down and rake it out. Roy always warned us about the fire when he went to bed. I got up, wrapped the great coverlet around me, went over to the gleam of light and looked down through the crack in the floor. I had to lie out at full length to get my eye against the board. The hickory logs had turned to great embers and glowed like a furnace of red coals.

Before this fire stood Dix. He was holding out his hands and turning himself about as though he were cold to the marrow; but with all that chill upon him, when the man's face came into the light I saw it covered with a sprinkling of sweat.

I shall carry the memory of that face. The grin was there at the mouth, but it was pulled about; the eyelids were drawn in; the teeth were clamped together. I have seen a dog poisoned with strychnine look like that.

I lay there and watched the thing. It was as though something potent and evil dwelling within the man were in travail to re-form his face upon its image. You cannot realize how that devilish labor held me – the face worked as though it were some plastic stuff, and the sweat oozed through. And all the time the man was cold; and he was crowding into the fire and turning himself about and putting out his hands. And it was as though the heat would no more enter in and warm him than it will enter in and warm the ice.

It seemed to scorch him and leave him cold – and he was fearfully and desperately cold! I could smell the singe of the fire on him, but it had no power against this diabolic chill. I began myself to shiver, although I had the heavy coverlet wrapped around me.

The thing was a fascinating horror; I seemed to be looking down into the chamber of some abominable maternity. The room was filled with the steady red light of the fire. Not a shadow moved in it. And there was silence. The man had taken off his boots and he twisted before the fire without a sound. It was like the shuddering tales of possession or transformation by a drug. I thought the man would burn himself to death. His clothes smoked. How could he be so cold?

Then, finally, the thing was over! I did not see it for his face was in the fire. But suddenly he grew composed and stepped back into the room. I tell you I was afraid to look! I do not know what thing I expected to see there, but I did not think it would be Dix.

Well, it was Dix; but not the Dix that any of us knew. There was a certain apology, a certain indecision, a certain servility in that other Dix, and these things showed about his face. But there was none of these weaknesses in this man.

His face had been pulled into planes of firmness and decision; the slack in his features had been taken up; the furtive moving of the eye was gone. He stood now squarely on his feet and he was full of courage. But I was afraid of him as I have never been afraid of any human creature in this world! Something that had been servile in him, that had skulked behind disguises, that had worn the habiliments of subterfuge, had now come forth; and it had molded the features of the man to its abominable courage.

Presently he began to move swiftly about the room. He looked out at the window and he listened at the door; then he went softly into the covered way. I thought he was going on his journey; but then he could not be going with his boots there beside the fire. In a moment he returned with a saddle blanket in his hand and came softly across the room to the ladder.

Then I understood the thing that he intended, and I was motionless with fear. I tried to get up, but I could not. I could only lie there with my eye strained to the crack in the floor. His foot was on the ladder, and I could already feel his hand on my throat and that blanket on my face, and the suffocation of death in me, when far away on the hard road I heard a horse!

He heard it, too, for he stopped on the ladder and turned his evil face about toward the door. The horse was on the long hill beyond the bridge, and he was coming as though the devil rode in his saddle. It was a hard, dark night. The frozen road was like flint; I could hear the iron of the shoes ring. Whoever rode that horse rode for his life or for something more than his life, or he was mad. I heard the horse strike the bridge and thunder across it. And all the while Dix hung there on the ladder by his hands and listened. Now he sprang softly down, pulled on his boots and stood up before the fire, his face – this new face – gleaming with its evil courage. The next moment the horse stopped.

I could hear him plunge under the bit, his iron shoes ripping the frozen road; then the door leaped back and my Uncle Abner was in the room. I was so glad that my heart almost choked me and for a moment I could hardly see – everything was in a sort of mist.

Abner swept the room in a glance, then he stopped.

'Thank God!' he said; 'I'm in time.' And he drew his hand down over his face with the fingers hard and close as though he pulled something away.

'In time for what?' said Dix.

Abner looked him over. And I could see the muscles of his big shoulders stiffen as he looked. And again he looked him over. Then he spoke and his voice was strange.

'Dix,' he said, 'is it you?'

'Who would it be but me?' said Dix.

'It might be the devil,' said Abner. 'Do you know what your face looks like?'

'No matter what it looks like!' said Dix.

'And so,' said Abner, 'we have got courage with this new face.'

Dix threw up his head.

'Now, look here, Abner,' he said, 'I've had about enough of your big manner. You ride a horse to death and you come plunging in here; what the devil's wrong with you?'

'There's nothing wrong with me,' replied Abner, and his voice was low. 'But there's something damnably wrong with you, Dix.'

'The devil take you,' said Dix, and I saw him measure Abner with his eye. It was not fear that held him back; fear was gone out of the creature; I think it was a kind of prudence.

Abner's eyes kindled, but his voice remained low and steady. 'Those are big words,' he said.

'Well,' cried Dix, 'get out of the door then and let me pass!'

'Not just yet,' said Abner; 'I have something to say to you.'

'Say it then,' cried Dix, 'and get out of the door.'

'Why hurry?' said Abner. 'It's a long time until daylight, and I have a good deal to say.'

'You'll not say it to me,' said Dix. 'I've got a trip to make tonight; get out of the door.'

Abner did not move. 'You've got a longer trip to make tonight than you think, Dix,' he said; 'but you're going to hear what I have to say before you set out on it.'

I saw Dix rise on his toes and I knew what he wished for. He wished for a weapon; and he wished for the bulk of bone and muscle that would have a chance against Abner. But he had neither the one nor the other. And he stood there on his toes and began to curse – low, vicious, withering oaths, that were like the swish of a knife.

Abner was looking at the man with a curious interest.

'It is strange,' he said, as though speaking to himself, 'but it explains the thing. While one is the servant of neither, one has the courage of neither; but when he finally makes his choice he gets what his master has to give him.'

Then he spoke to Dix.

'Sit down!' he said; and it was in that deep, level voice that Abner used when he was standing close behind his words. Every man in the hills knew that voice; one had only a moment to decide after he heard it. Dix knew that, and yet for one instant he hung there on his toes, his eyes shimmering like a weasel's, his mouth twisting. He was not afraid! If he had had the ghost of a chance against Abner he would have taken it. But he knew he had not, and with an oath he threw the saddle blanket into a corner and sat down by the fire.

Abner came away from the door then. He took off his great coat. He put a log on the fire and he sat down across the hearth from Dix. The new hickory sprang crackling into flames. For a good while there was silence; the two men sat at either end of the hearth without a word. Abner seemed to have fallen into a study of the man before him. Finally he spoke:

'Dix,' he said, 'do you believe in the providence of God?'

Dix flung up his head.

'Abner,' he cried, 'if you are going to talk nonsense I promise you upon my oath that I will not stay to listen.'

Abner did not at once reply. He seemed to begin now at another point.

'Dix,' he said, 'you've had a good deal of bad luck . . . Perhaps you wish it put that way.'

'Now, Abner,' he cried, 'you speak the truth; I have had hell's luck.'

'Hell's luck you have had,' replied Abner. 'It is a good word. I accept it. Your partner disappeared with all the money of the grazers on the other side of the river; you lost the land in your lawsuit; and you are to-night without a dollar. That was a big tract of land to lose. Where did you get so great a sum of money?'

'I have told you a hundred times,' replied Dix. 'I got it from my people over the mountains. You know where I got it.'

'Yes,' said Abner. 'I know where you got it, Dix. And I know another thing. But first I want to show you this,' and he took a little penknife out of his pocket. 'And I want to tell you that I believe in the providence of God, Dix.'

'I don't care a fiddler's damn what you believe in,' said Dix.

'But you do care what I know,' replied Abner.

'What do you know?' said Dix.

'I know where your partner is,' replied Abner.

I was uncertain about what Dix was going to do, but finally he answered with a sneer.

'Then you know something that nobody else knows.'

'Yes,' replied Abner, 'there is another man who knows.'

'Who?' said Dix.

'You,' said Abner.

Dix leaned over in his chair and looked at Abner closely.

'Abner,' he cried, 'you are talking nonsense. Nobody knows where Alkire is. If I knew I'd go after him.'

'Dix,' Abner answered, and it was again in that deep, level voice, 'if I had got here five minutes later you would have gone after him. I can promise you that, Dix.

'Now, listen! I was in the upcountry when I got your word about the partnership; and I was on my way back when at Big Run I broke a stirrup-leather. I had no knife and I went into the store and bought this one; then the storekeeper told me that Alkire had gone to see you. I didn't want to interfere with him and I turned back . . . So I did not become your partner. And so I did not disappear . . . What was it that prevented? The broken stirrup-leather? The knife? In old times, Dix, men were so blind that God had to open their eyes before they could see His angel in the way before them . . . They are still blind, but they ought not to be that blind . . . Well, on the night that Alkire disappeared I met him on his way to your house. It was out there at the bridge. He had broken a stirrup-leather and he was trying to fasten it with a nail. He asked me if I had a knife, and I gave him this one. It was beginning to rain and I went on, leaving him there in the road with the knife in his hand.'

Abner paused; the muscles of his great iron jaw contracted.

'God forgive me,' he said; 'it was His angel again! I never saw Alkire after that.'

'Nobody ever saw him after that,' said Dix. 'He got out of the hills that night.'

'No,' replied Abner, 'it was not in the night when Alkire started on his journey; it was in the day.'

'Abner,' said Dix, 'you talk like a fool. If Alkire had traveled the road in the day somebody would have seen him.'

'Nobody could see him on the road he traveled,' replied Abner.

'What road?' said Dix.

'Dix,' replied Abner, 'you will learn that soon enough.'

Abner looked hard at the man.

'You saw Alkire when he started on his journey,' he continued; 'but did you see who it was that went with him?'

'Nobody went with him,' replied Dix; 'Alkire rode alone.'

'Not alone,' said Abner; 'there was another.'

'I didn't see him,' said Dix.

'And yet,' continued Abner, 'you made Alkire go with him.'

I saw cunning enter Dix's face. He was puzzled, but he thought Abner off the scent.

'And I made Alkire go with somebody, did I? Well, who was it? Did you see him?'

'Nobody ever saw him.'

'He must be a stranger.'

'No,' replied Abner, 'he rode the hills before we came into them.'

'Indeed!' said Dix. 'And what kind of a horse did he ride?'

'White!' said Abner.

Dix got some inkling of what Abner meant now, and his face grew livid.

'What are you driving at?' he cried. 'You sit here beating around the bush. If you know anything, say it out; let's hear it. What is it?'

Abner put out his big sinewy hand as though to thrust Dix back into his chair.

'Listen!' he said. 'Two days after that I wanted to get out into the Ten Mile country and I went through your lands; I rode a path through the narrow valley west of your house. At a point on the path where there is an apple tree something caught my eye

140

and I stopped. Five minutes later I knew exactly what had happened under that apple tree . . . Someone had ridden there; he had stopped under that tree; then something happened and the horse had run away – I knew that by the tracks of a horse on this path. I knew that the horse had a rider and that it had stopped under this tree, because there was a limb cut from the tree at a certain height. I knew the horse had remained there, because the small twigs of the apple limb had been pared off, and they lay in a heap on the path. I knew that something had frightened the horse and that it had run away, because the sod was torn up where it had jumped . . . Ten minutes later I knew that the rider had not been in the saddle when the horse jumped; I knew what it was that had frightened the horse; and I knew that the thing had occurred the day before. Now, how did I know that?

'Listen! I put my horse into the tracks of that other horse under the tree and studied the ground. Immediately I saw where the weeds beside the path had been crushed, as though some animal had been lying down there, and in the very center of that bed I saw a little heap of fresh earth. That was strange, Dix, that fresh earth where the animal had been lying down! It had come there after the animal had got up, or else it would have been pressed flat. But where had it come from?

'I got off and walked around the apple tree, moving out from it in an ever-widening circle. Finally I found an ant heap, the top of which had been scraped away as though one had taken up the loose earth in his hands. Then I went back and plucked up some of the earth. The under clods of it were colored as with red paint . . . No, it wasn't paint.

'There was a brush fence some fifty yards away. I went over to it and followed it down.

'Opposite the apple tree the weeds were again crushed as though some animal had lain there. I sat down in that place and drew a line with my eye across a log of the fence to a limb of the apple tree. Then I got on my horse and again put him in the tracks of that other horse under the tree; the imaginary line passed through the pit of my stomach! . . . I am four inches taller than Alkire.'

It was then that Dix began to curse. I had seen his face work while Abner was speaking and that spray of sweat had reappeared. But he kept the courage he had got.

'Lord Almighty, man!' he cried. 'How prettily you sum it up! We shall presently have Lawyer Abner with his brief. Because my renters have killed a calf; because one of their horses frightened at the blood has bolted, and because they cover the blood with earth so the other horses traveling the path may not do the like; straightway I have shot Alkire out of his saddle . . . Man! What a mare's nest! And now, Lawyer Abner, with your neat little conclusions, what did I do with Alkire after I had killed him? Did I cause him to vanish into the air with a smell of sulphur or did I cause the earth to yawn and Alkire to descend into its bowels?'

'Dix,' replied Abner, 'your words move somewhat near the truth.'

'Upon my soul,' cried Dix, 'you compliment me. If I had that trick of magic, believe me, you would be already some distance down.'

Abner remained a moment silent.

'Dix,' he said, 'what does it mean when one finds a plot of earth resodded?'

'Is that a riddle?' cried Dix. 'Well, confound me, if I don't answer it! You charge me with murder and then you fling in this neat conundrum. Now, what could be the answer to that riddle, Abner? If one had done a murder this sod would overlie a grave and Alkire would be in it in his bloody shirt. Do I give the answer?'

'You do not,' replied Abner.

'No!' cried Dix. 'Your sodded plot no grave, and Alkire not within it waiting for the trump of Gabriel! Why, man, where are your little damned conclusions?'

'Dix,' said Abner, 'you do not deceive me in the least; Alkire is not sleeping in a grave.'

'Then in the air,' sneered Dix, 'with the smell of sulphur?'

'Nor in the air,' said Abner.

'Then consumed with fire, like the priests of Baal?'

'Nor with fire,' said Abner.

Dix had got back the quiet of his face; this banter had put him where he was when Abner entered. 'This is all fools' talk,' he said; 'if I had killed Alkire, what could I have done with the body? And the horse! What could I have done with the horse? Remember, no man has ever seen Alkire's horse any more than he has seen Alkire – and for the reason that Alkire rode him out of the hills that night. Now, look here, Abner, you have asked me a good many questions. I will ask you one. Among your little conclusions do you find that I did this thing alone or with the aid of others?'

'Dix,' replied Abner, 'I will answer that upon my own belief you had no accomplice.'

'Then,' said Dix, 'how could I have carried off the horse? Alkire I might carry; but his horse weighed thirteen hundred pounds!'

'Dix,' said Abner, 'no man helped you do this thing; but there were men who helped you to conceal it.'

'And now,' cried Dix, 'the man is going mad! Who could I trust with such work, I ask you? Have I a renter that would not tell it when he moved on to another's land, or when he got a quart of cider in him? Where are the men who helped me?'

'Dix,' said Abner, 'they have been dead these fifty years.'

I heard Dix laugh then, and his evil face lighted as though a candle were behind it. And, in truth, I thought he had got Abner silenced.

'In the name of Heaven!' he cried. 'With such proofs it is a wonder that you did not have me hanged.'

'And hanged you should have been,' said Abner.

'Well,' cried Dix, 'go and tell the sheriff, and mind you lay before him those little, neat conclusions: How from a horse track and the place where a calf was butchered you have reasoned on

143

Alkire's murder, and to conceal the body and the horse you have reasoned on the aid of men who were rotting in their graves when I was born; and see how he will receive you!'

Abner gave no attention to the man's flippant speech. He got his great silver watch out of his pocket, pressed the stem and looked. Then he spoke in his deep, even voice.

'Dix,' he said, 'it is nearly midnight; in an hour you must be on your journey, and I have something more to say. Listen! I knew this thing had been done the previous day because it had rained on the night that I met Alkire, and the earth of this ant heap had been disturbed after that. Moreover, this earth had been frozen, and that showed a night had passed since it had been placed there. And I knew the rider of that horse was Alkire because, beside the path near the severed twigs lay my knife, where it had fallen from his hand. This much I learned in some fifteen minutes; the rest took somewhat longer.

'I followed the track of the horse until it stopped in the little valley below. It was easy to follow while the horse ran, because the sod was torn; but when it ceased to run there was no track that I could follow. There was a little stream threading the valley, and I began at the wood and came slowly up to see if I could find where the horse had crossed. Finally I found a horse track and there was also a man's track, which meant that you had caught the horse and were leading it away. But where?

'On the rising ground above there was an old orchard where there had once been a house. The work about that house had been done a hundred years. It was rotted down now. You had opened this orchard into the pasture. I rode all over the face of this hill and finally I entered this orchard. There was a great, flat, moss-covered stone lying a few steps from where the house had stood. As I looked I noticed that the moss growing from it into the earth had been broken along the edges of the stone, and then I noticed that for a few feet about the stone the ground had been resodded. I got down and lifted up some of this new sod. Under it the earth had been soaked with that . . . red paint.

144

'It was clever of you, Dix, to resod the ground; that took only a little time and it effectually concealed the place where you had killed the horse; but it was foolish of you to forget that the broken moss around the edges of the great flat stone could not be mended.'

'Abner!' cried Dix. 'Stop!' And I saw that spray of sweat, and his face working like kneaded bread, and the shiver of that abominable chill on him.

Abner was silent for a moment and then he went on, but from another quarter.

'Twice,' said Abner, 'the Angel of the Lord stood before me and I did not know it; but the third time I knew it. It is not in the cry of the wind, nor in the voice of many waters that His presence is made known to us. That man in Israel had only the sign that the beast under him would not go on. Twice I had as good a sign, and tonight, when Marks broke a stirrup-leather before my house and called me to the door and asked me for a knife to mend it, I saw and I came!'

The log that Abner had thrown on was burned down, and the fire was again a mass of embers; the room was filled with that dull red light. Dix had got on to his feet, and he stood now twisting before the fire, his hands reaching out to it, and that cold creeping in his bones, and the smell of the fire on him.

Abner rose. And when he spoke his voice was like a thing that has dimensions and weight.

'Dix,' he said, 'you robbed the grazers; you shot Alkire out of his saddle; and a child you would have murdered!'

And I saw the sleeve of Abner's coat begin to move, then it stopped. He stood staring at something against the wall. I looked to see what the thing was, but I did not see it. Abner was looking beyond the wall, as though it had been moved away.

And all the time Dix had been shaking with that hellish cold, and twisting on the hearth and crowding into the fire. Then he fell back, and he was the Dix I knew – his face was slack; his eye was furtive; and he was full of terror.

It was his weak whine that awakened Abner. He put up his hand and brought the fingers hard down over his face, and then he looked at this new creature, cringing and beset with fears.

'Dix,' he said, 'Alkire was a just man; he sleeps as peacefully in that abandoned well under his horse as he would sleep in the churchyard. My hand has been held back; you may go. Vengeance is mine, I will repay, saith the Lord.'

'But where shall I go, Abner?' the creature wailed; 'I have no money and I am cold.'

Abner took out his leather wallet and flung it toward the door.

'There is money,' he said – 'a hundred dollars – and there is my coat. Go! But if I find you in the hills to-morrow, or if I ever find you, I warn you in the name of the living God that I will stamp you out of life!'

I saw the loathsome thing writhe into Abner's coat and seize the wallet and slip out through the door; and a moment later I heard a horse. And I crept back on to Roy's heifer skin.

When I came down at daylight my Uncle Abner was reading by the fire.

The Sisterhood

Catherine Louisa Pirkis

I

'They want you at Redhill, now,' said Mr Dyer, taking a packet of papers from one of his pigeon-holes. 'The idea seems gaining ground in many quarters that in cases of mere suspicion, women detectives are more satisfactory than men, for they are less likely to attract attention. And this Redhill affair, so far as I can make out, is one of suspicion only.'

It was a dreary November morning; every gas jet in the Lynch Court office was alight, and a yellow curtain of outside fog draped its narrow windows.

'Nevertheless, I suppose one can't afford to leave it uninvestigated at this season of the year, with country-house robberies beginning in so many quarters,' said Miss Brooke.

'No; and the circumstances in this case certainly seem to point in the direction of the country-house burglar. Two days ago a somewhat curious application was made privately, by a man giving the name of John Murray, to Inspector Gunning, of the Reigate police – Redhill, I must tell you, is in the Reigate police district. Murray stated that he had been a greengrocer in South London, had sold his business there, and had, with the proceeds of the sale, bought two small houses in Redhill, intending to let the one and live in the other. These houses are situated in a blind alley, known as Paved Court, a narrow turning leading off the London and Brighton coach road. Paved Court has been known

147

to the sanitary authorities for the past ten years as a regular fever nest, and as the houses which Murray bought – numbers 7 and 8 – stand at the very end of the blind alley, with no chance of thorough ventilation, I dare say the man got them for next to nothing. He told the Inspector that he had had great difficulty in procuring a tenant for the house he wished to let, number 8, and that consequently when, about three weeks back, a lady, dressed as a nun, made him an offer for it, he immediately closed with her. The lady gave her name simply as "Sister Monica", and stated that she was a member of an undenominational Sisterhood that had recently been founded by a wealthy lady, who wished her name kept a secret. Sister Monica gave no references, but, instead, paid a quarter's rent in advance, saying that she wished to take possession of the house immediately, and open it as a home for crippled orphans.'

'Gave no references – home for cripples,' murmured Loveday, scribbling hard and fast in her note-book.

'Murray made no objection to this,' continued Mr Dyer, 'and, accordingly, the next day, Sister Monica, accompanied by three other Sisters and some sickly children, took possession of the house, which they furnished with the barest possible necessaries from cheap shops in the neighbourhood. For a time, Murray said, he thought he had secured most desirable tenants, but during the last ten days suspicions as to their real character have entered his mind, and these suspicions he thought it his duty to communicate to the police. Among their possessions, it seems, these Sisters number an old donkey and a tiny cart, and this they start daily on a sort of begging tour through the adjoining villages, bringing back every evening a perfect hoard of broken victuals and bundles of old garments. Now comes the extraordinary fact on which Murray bases his suspicions. He says, and Gunning verifies his statement, that in whatever direction those Sisters turn the wheels of their donkey-cart, burglaries, or attempts at burglaries, are sure to follow. A week ago they went along towards Horely, where, at an outlying house, they received much kindness from a wealthy gentleman. That very night an attempt was made to break into that gentleman's house – an attempt, however, that was happily frustrated by the barking of the house-dog. And so on in other instances that I need not go into. Murray suggests that it might be as well to have the daily movements of these Sisters closely watched, and that extra vigilance should be exercised by the police in the districts that have had the honour of a morning call from them. Gunning coincides with this idea, and so has sent to me to secure your services.'

Loveday closed her note-book. 'I suppose Gunning will meet me somewhere and tell me where I'm to take up my quarters?' she said.

'Yes; he will get into your carriage at Merstham – the station before Redhill – if you will put your hand out of the window, with the morning paper in it. By the way, he takes it for granted that you will take the 11.05 train from Victoria. Murray, it seems, has been good enough to place his little house at the disposal of the police, but Gunning does not think espionage could be so well carried on there as from other quarters. The presence of a stranger in an alley of that sort is bound to attract attention. So he has hired a room for you in a draper's shop that immediately faces the head of the court. There is a private door to this shop of which you will have the key, and can let yourself in and out as you please. You are supposed to be a nursery governess on the lookout for a situation, and Gunning will keep you supplied with letters to give colour to the idea. He suggests that you need only occupy the room during the day, at night you will find far more comfortable quarters at Laker's Hotel, just outside the town.'

This was about the sum total of the instructions that Mr Dyer had to give.

The 11.05 train from Victoria, that carried Loveday to her work among the Surrey Hills, did not get clear of the London fog till well away on the other side of Purley. When the train halted at Merstham, in response to her signal, a tall, soldier-like individual made for her carriage, and, jumping in, took the seat facing her. He introduced himself to her as Inspector Gunning, recalled to her memory a former occasion on which they had met, and then, naturally enough, turned the talk upon the present suspicious circumstances they were bent upon investigating.

'It won't do for you and me to be seen together,' he said; 'of course I am known for miles round, and any one seen in my company will be at once set down as my coadjutor, and spied upon accordingly. I walked from Redhill to Merstham on purpose to avoid recognition on the platform at Redhill, and half-way here, to my great annoyance, found that I was being followed by a man in a workman's dress and carrying a basket of tools. I doubled, however, and gave him the slip, taking a short cut down a lane which, if he had been living in the place, he would have known as well as I did. By Jove!' this was added with a sudden start, 'there is the fellow, I declare; he has weathered me after all, and has no doubt taken good stock of us both, with the train going at this snail's pace. It was unfortunate that your face should have been turned towards that window, Miss Brooke.'

'My veil is something of a disguise, and I will put on another cloak before he has a chance of seeing me again,' said Loveday.

All she had seen in the brief glimpse that the train had allowed, was a tall, powerfully-built man walking along the siding of the line. His cap was drawn low over his eyes, and in his hand he carried a workman's basket.

Gunning seemed much annoyed at the circumstance. 'Instead of landing at Redhill,' he said, 'we'll go on to Three Bridges, and wait there for a Brighton train to bring us back, that will enable you to get to your room somewhere between the lights; I don't want to have you spotted before you've so much as started your work.'

Then they went back to their discussion of the Redhill Sisterhood.

'They call themselves "undenominational", whatever that means,' said Gunning, 'they say they are connected with no religious sect whatever, they attend sometimes one place of worship, sometimes another, sometimes none at all. They refuse to give up the name of the founder of their order, and really no one has any right to demand it of them, for, as no doubt you see, up to the present moment the case is one of mere suspicion, and it may be a pure coincidence that attempts at burglary have followed their footsteps in this neighbourhood. By the way, I have heard of a man's face being enough to hang him, but until I saw Sister Monica's, I never saw a woman's face that could perform the same kind of office for her. Of all the lowest criminal types of faces I have ever seen, I think hers is about the lowest and most repulsive.'

After the Sisters, they passed in review the chief families resident in the neighbourhood.

'This,' said Gunning, unfolding a paper, 'is a map I have specially drawn up for you – it takes in the district for ten miles round Redhill, and every country house of any importance is marked on it in red ink. Here, in addition, is an index of those houses, with special notes of my own to every house.'

Loveday studied the map for a minute or so, then turned her attention to the index.

'Those four houses you've marked, I see, are those that have been already attempted. I don't think I'll run them through, but I'll mark them "doubtful"; you see the gang – for, of course, it is a gang – might follow our reasoning on the matter, and look upon those houses as our weak point. Here's one I'll run through, "house empty during winter months", – that means plate and jewellery sent to the bankers. Oh! and this one may as well be crossed off, "father and four sons all athletes and sportsmen", that means firearms always handy – I don't think burglars will be likely to trouble them. Ah! now we come to something! Here's a house to be marked "tempting" in a burglar's list. "Wootton Hall, lately changed hands and rebuilt, with complicated passages and corridors. Splendid family plate in daily use and left entirely in the care of the butler." I wonder does the master of that house trust to his "complicated passages" to preserve his plate for him? A dismissed dishonest servant would supply a dozen maps of the place for half a sovereign. What do these initials, "E.L." against the next house in the list, North Cape, stand for?'

'Electric lighted. I think you might almost cross that house off also. I consider electric lighting one of the greatest safeguards against burglars that a man can give his house.'

'Yes, if he doesn't rely exclusively upon it; it might be a nasty trap under certain circumstances. I see this gentleman also has magnificent presentation and other plate.'

'Yes ... Mr Jameson is a wealthy man and very popular in the neighbourhood; his cups and epergnes are worth looking at.'

'Is it the only house in the district that is lighted with electricity?'

'Yes; and, begging your pardon, Miss Brooke, I only wish it were not so. If electric lighting were generally in vogue it would save the police a lot of trouble on these dark winter nights.'

'The burglars would find some way of meeting such a condition of things, depend upon it; they have reached a very high development in these days. They no longer stalk about as they did fifty years ago with blunderbuss and bludgeon; they plot, plan, contrive, and bring imagination and artistic resource to their aid. By the way, it often occurs to me that the popular detective stories, for which there seems so large a demand at the present day, must be, at times, uncommonly useful to the criminal classes.'

At Three Bridges they had to wait so long for a return train that it was nearly dark when Loveday got back to Redhill. Mr Gunning did not accompany her thither, having alighted at a previous station. Loveday had directed her portmanteau to be sent direct to Laker's Hotel, where she had engaged a room by telegram from Victoria Station. So, unburthened by luggage, she slipped quietly out of the Redhill Station and made her way straight for the draper's shop in the London Road. She had no difficulty in finding it, thanks to the minute directions given her by the Inspector.

Street lamps were being lighted in the sleepy little town as she went along, and as she turned into the London Road, shop-keepers were lighting up their windows on both sides of the way. A few yards down this road, a dark patch between the lighted shops showed her where Paved Court led off from the thorough-fare. A side door of one of the shops that stood at the corner of the court seemed to offer a post of observation whence she could see without being seen, and here Loveday, shrinking into the shadows, ensconced herself in order to take stock of the little alley and its inhabitants. She found it much as it had been described to her – a collection of four-roomed houses of which more than half were unlet. Numbers 7 and 8 at the head of the court presented a slightly less neglected appearance than the other tenements. Number 7 stood in total darkness, but in the upper window of number 8 there showed what seemed to be a night-light burning, so Loveday conjectured that this possibly was the room set apart as a dormitory for the little cripples.

While she stood thus surveying the home of the suspected Sisterhood, the Sisters themselves – two, at least, of them – came into view, with their donkey-cart and their cripples, in the main road. It was an odd little cortège. One Sister habited in a nun's dress of dark blue serge, led the donkey by the bridle; another Sister, similarly attired, walked alongside the low cart, in which were seated two sickly-looking children. They were evidently returning from one of their long country circuits, and, unless they had lost their way and been belated, it certainly seemed a late hour for the sickly little cripples to be abroad.

As they passed under the gas lamp at the corner of the court, Loveday caught a glimpse of the faces of the Sisters. It was easy, with Inspector Gunning's description before her mind, to identify the older and taller woman as Sister Monica, and a more coarse-featured and generally repellent face Loveday admitted to herself she had never before seen. In striking contrast to this forbidding countenance was that of the younger Sister. Loveday could only catch a brief passing view of it, but that one brief view was enough to impress it on her memory as of unusual sadness and beauty. As the donkey stopped at the corner of the court, Loveday heard this sad-looking young woman addressed as 'Sister Anna' by one of the cripples, who asked plaintively when they were going to have something to eat.

'Now, at once,' said Sister Anna, lifting the little one, as it seemed to Loveday, tenderly out of the cart, and carrying him on her shoulder down the court to the door of number 8, which opened to them at their approach. The other Sister did the same with the other child; then both Sisters returned, unloaded the cart of sundry bundles and baskets, and, this done, led off the old donkey and trap down the road, possibly to a neighbouring costermonger's stables.

A man, coming along on a bicycle, exchanged a word of greeting with the Sisters as they passed, then swung himself off his machine at the corner of the court, and walked it along the paved way to the door of number 7. This he opened with a key, and then, pushing the machine before him, entered the house.

Loveday took it for granted that this man must be the John Murray of whom she had heard. She had closely scrutinized him as he had passed her, and had seen that he was a dark, well-featured man of about fifty years of age.

She congratulated herself on her good fortune in having seen so much in such a brief space of time, and, coming forth from her sheltered corner, turned her steps in the direction of the draper's shop on the other side of the road.

It was easy to find. 'Golightly' was the singular name that figured above the shop-front, in which were displayed a variety of goods calculated to meet the wants of servants and the poorer classes generally. A tall, powerfully-built man appeared to be looking in at the window. Loveday's foot was on the doorstep of the draper's private entrance, her hand on the door-knocker, when this individual, suddenly turning, convinced her of his identity with the journey-man workman who had so disturbed Mr Gunning's equanimity. It was true he wore a bowler instead of a journeyman's cap, and he no longer carried a basket of tools, but there was no possibility for any one, with so good an eye for an outline as Loveday possessed, not to recognize the carriage of the head and shoulders as that of the man she had seen walking along the railway siding. He gave her no time to make minute observation of his appearance, but turned quickly away, and disappeared down a by-street.

Loveday's work seemed to bristle with difficulties now. Here was she, as it were, unearthed in her own ambush; for there could be but little doubt that during the whole time she had stood watching those Sisters, that man, from a safe vantage-point, had been watching her.

She found Mrs Golightly a civil and obliging person. She showed Loveday to her room above the shop, brought her the letters which Inspector Gunning had been careful to have posted to her during the day. Then she supplied her with pen and ink and, in response to Loveday's request, with some strong coffee that she said, with a little attempt at a joke, would 'keep a dormouse awake all through the winter without winking'.

While the obliging landlady busied herself about the room, Loveday had a few questions to ask about the Sisterhood who lived down the court opposite. On this head, however, Mrs Golightly could tell her no more than she already knew, beyond the fact that they started every morning on their rounds at eleven o'clock punctually, and that before that hour they were never to be seen outside their door.

Loveday's watch that night was to be a fruitless one. Although she sat, with her lamp turned out and safely screened from observation, until close upon midnight, with eyes fixed upon numbers 7 and 8, Paved Court, not so much as a door opening or shutting at either house rewarded her vigil. The lights flitted from the lower to the upper floors in both houses, and then disappeared, somewhere between nine and ten in the evening; and after that, not a sign of life did either tenement show.

And all through the long hours of that watch, again and again there seemed to flit before her mind's eye, as if in some sort it were fixed upon its retina, the sweet, sad face of Sister Anna.

Why it was this face should so haunt her, she found it hard to say.

'It has a mournful past and a mournful future written upon it as a hopeless whole,' she said to herself. 'It is the face of an Andromeda! "Here am I", it seems to say, "tied to my stake, helpless and hopeless".'

The church clocks were sounding the midnight hour as Loveday made her way through the dark streets to her hotel outside the town. As she passed under the railway arch that ended in the open country road, the echo of not very distant footsteps caught her ear. When she stopped they stopped, when she went on they went on, and she knew that once more she was being followed and watched, although the darkness of the arch prevented her seeing even the shadow of the man who was thus dogging her steps.

The next morning broke keen and frosty. Loveday studied her map and her country-house index over a seven o'clock breakfast, and then set off for a brisk walk along the country road. No doubt in London the streets were walled in and roofed with yellow fog; here, however, bright sunshine playing in and out of the bare tree-boughs and leafless hedges on to a thousand frost spangles, turned the prosaic macadamized road into a gangway fit for Queen Titania herself and her fairy train.

Loveday turned her back on the town and set herself to follow the road as it wound away over the hill in the direction of a village called Northfield. Early as she was, she was not to have that road to herself. A team of strong horses trudged by on their way to their work in the fuller's-earth pits. A young fellow on a bicycle flashed past at a tremendous pace, considering the upward slant of the road. He looked hard at her as he passed, then slackened speed, dismounted, and awaited her coming on the brow of the hill.

'Good-morning, Miss Brooke,' he said, lifting his cap as she came alongside of him. 'May I have five minutes' talk with you?'

The young man who thus accosted her had not the appearance of a gentleman. He was a handsome, bright-faced young fellow of about two-and-twenty, and was dressed in ordinary cyclist's dress; his cap was pushed back from his brow over thick, curly, fair hair, and Loveday, as she looked at him, could not repress the thought how well he would look at the head of a troop of cavalry, giving the order to charge the enemy.

He led his machine to the side of the footpath.

'You have the advantage of me,' said Loveday; 'I haven't the remotest notion who you are.'

'No,' he said; 'although I know you, you cannot possibly know me. I am a north-country man, and I was present, about a month ago, at the trial of old Mr Craven, of Troyte's Hill – in fact, I acted as reporter for one of the local papers. I watched your face so closely as you gave your evidence that I should know it anywhere, among a thousand.'

'And your name is . . . ?'

'George White, of Grenfell. My father is part proprietor of one of the Newcastle papers. I am a bit of a literary man myself, and sometimes figure as a reporter, sometimes as leader-writer, to that paper.' Here he gave a glance towards his side pocket, from which protruded a small volume of Tennyson's poems.

The facts he had stated did not seem to invite comment, and Loveday ejaculated merely:

'Indeed!'

The young man went back to the subject that was evidently filling his thoughts. 'I have special reasons for being glad to have met you this morning, Miss Brooke,' he went on, making his footsteps keep pace with hers. 'I am in great trouble, and I believe you are the only person in the whole world who can help me out of that trouble.'

'I am rather doubtful as to my power of helping any one out of trouble,' said Loveday; 'so far as my experience goes, our troubles are as much a part of ourselves as our skins are of our bodies.'

'Ah, but not such trouble as mine,' said White eagerly. He broke off for a moment, then, with a sudden rush of words, told her what that trouble was. For the past year he had been engaged to be married to a young girl, who, until quite recently, had been fulfilling the duties of a nursery governess in a large house in the neighbourhood of Redhill.

'Will you kindly give me the name of that house?' interrupted Loveday.

'Certainly; Wootton Hall, the place is called, and Annie Lee is my sweetheart's name. I don't care who knows it!' He threw his head back as he said this, as if he would be delighted to announce the fact to the whole world. 'Annie's mother,' he went on, 'died when she was a baby, and we both thought her father was dead also, when suddenly, about a fortnight ago, it came to her knowledge that, instead of being dead, he was serving his time at Portland for some offence committed years ago.'

'Do you know how this came to Annie's knowledge?'

'Not the least in the world; I only know that I suddenly got a letter from her announcing the fact, and, at the same time, breaking off her engagement with me. I tore the letter into a thousand pieces, and wrote back saying I would not allow the engagement to be broken off, but would marry her if she would have me. To this letter she did not reply; there came instead a few lines from Mrs Copeland, the lady at Wootton Hall, saying that Annie had thrown up her engagement, and joined some Sisterhood, and that she, Mrs Copeland, had pledged her word to Annie to reveal to no one the name and whereabouts of that Sisterhood.'

'And I suppose you imagine I am able to do what Mrs Copeland is pledged not to do?'

'That's just it, Miss Brooke!' cried the young man enthusiastically. 'You do such wonderful things; everyone knows you do. It seems as if, when anything is wanting to be found out, you just walk into a place, look round you, and, in a moment, everything becomes clear as noonday.'

'I can't quite lay claim to such wonderful powers as that. As it happens, however, in the present instance, no particular skill is needed to find out what you wish to know, for I fancy I have already come upon the traces of Miss Annie Lee.'

'Miss Brooke!'

'Of course, I cannot say for certain, but it is a matter you can easily settle for yourself – settle, too, in a way that will confer a great obligation on me.'

'I shall be only too delighted to be of any, the slightest, service to you!' cried White, enthusiastically as before.

'Thank you. I will explain. I came down here specially to watch the movements of a certain Sisterhood who have somehow aroused the suspicions of the police. Well, I find that instead of being able to do this, I am myself so closely watched – possibly by confederates of these Sisters – that unless I can do my work by deputy I may as well go back to town at once.'

'Ah! I see – you want me to be that deputy.'

'Precisely. I want you to go to the room in Redhill that I have hired, take your place at the window – screened, of course, from observation – at which I ought to be seated – watch as closely as possible the movements of these Sisters, and report them to me at the hotel, where I shall remain shut in from morning till night – it is the only way in which I can throw my persistent spies off the scent. Now, in doing this for me, you will be doing yourself a good turn, for I have little doubt but what under the blue serge hood of one of the Sisters you will discover the pretty face of Miss Annie Lee.'

As they talked they had walked, and now stood on the top of the hill at the head of the one little street that constituted the whole of the village of Northfield.

On their left hand stood the village school and the master's house; nearly facing these, on the opposite side of the road, beneath a clump of elms, stood the village pound. Beyond this pound, on either side of the way, were two rows of small cottages with tiny squares of garden in front, and in the midst of these small cottages a swinging sign beneath a lamp announced a 'Postal and Telegraph Office'.

'Now that we have come into the land of habitations again,' said Loveday, 'it will be best for us to part. It will not do for you and me to be seen together, or my spies will be transferring their attentions from me to you, and I shall have to find another deputy. You had better start on your bicycle for Redhill at once, and I will walk back at leisurely speed. Come to me at my hotel without fail at one o'clock and report proceedings. I do not say anything definite about remuneration, but I assure you, if you carry out my instructions to the letter, your services will be amply rewarded by me and by my employers.'

There were yet a few more details to arrange. White had been, he said, only a day and night in the neighbourhood, and special directions as to the locality had to be given to him. Loveday advised him not to attract attention by going to the draper's private door, but to enter the shop as if he were a customer, and then explain matters to Mrs Golightly, who, no doubt, would be in her place behind the counter; tell her he was the brother of the Miss Smith who had hired her room, and ask permission to go through the shop to that room, as he had been commissioned by his sister to read and answer any letters that might have arrived there for her.

'Show her the key of the side door – here it is,' said Loveday; 'it will be your credentials, and tell her you did not like to make use of it without acquainting her with the fact.'

The young man took the key, endeavouring to put it in his waistcoat pocket, found the space there occupied, and so transferred it to the keeping of a side pocket in his tunic.

All this time Loveday stood watching him.

'You have a capital machine there,' she said, as the young man mounted his bicycle once more, 'and I hope you will turn it to account in following the movements of these Sisters about the neighbourhood. I feel confident you will have something definite to tell me when you bring me your first report at one o'clock.'

White once more broke into a profusion of thanks, and then, lifting his cap to the lady, started his machine at a fairly good pace.

Loveday watched him out of sight down the slope of the hill, then, instead of following him as she had said she would 'at a leisurely pace', she turned her steps in the opposite direction along the village street.

It was an altogether ideal country village. Neatly-dressed, chubby-faced children, now on their way to the school, dropped quaint little curtseys, or tugged at curly locks as Loveday passed; every cottage looked the picture of cleanliness and trimness, and, although so late in the year, the gardens were full of late flowering chrysanthemums and early flowering Christmas roses.

At the end of the village, Loveday came suddenly into view of a large, handsome, red-brick mansion. It presented a wide frontage to the road, from which it lay back amid extensive pleasure grounds. On the right hand, and a little in the rear of the house, stood what seemed to be large and commodious stables, and immediately adjoining these stables was a low-built, red-brick shed, that had evidently been recently erected.

That low-built, red-brick shed excited Loveday's curiosity.

'Is this house called North Cape?' she asked of a man, who chanced at that moment to be passing with a pickaxe and shovel.

The man answered in the affirmative, and Loveday then asked another question: Could he tell her what was that small shed so close to the house – it looked like a glorified cowhouse – now what could be its use?

The man's face lighted up as if it were a subject on which he liked to be questioned. He explained that that small shed was the engine-house where the electricity that lighted North Cape was made and stored. Then he dwelt with pride upon the fact, as if he held a personal interest in it, that North Cape was the only house, far or near, that was thus lighted.

161

'I suppose the wires are carried underground to the house,' said Loveday, looking in vain for signs of them anywhere.

The man was delighted to go into details on the matter. He had helped to lay those wires, he said: they were two in number, one for supply and one for return, and were laid three feet below ground, in boxes filled with pitch. They were switched on to jars in the engine-house, where the electricity was stored, and, after passing underground, entered the family mansion under the flooring at its western end.

Loveday listened attentively to these details, and then took a minute and leisurely survey of the house and its surroundings. This done, she retraced her steps through the village, pausing, however, at the 'Postal and Telegraph Office' to despatch a telegram to Inspector Gunning.

It was one to send the Inspector to his cipher-book. It ran as follows:

Rely solely on chemist and coal-merchant throughout the day. L.B.

After this, she quickened her pace, and in something over three-quarters of an hour was back again at her hotel.

There she found more of life stirring than when she had quitted it in the early morning. There was to be a meeting of the 'Surrey Stags' about a couple of miles off, and a good many hunting men were hanging about the entrance of the house, discussing the chances of sport after last night's frost. Loveday made her way through the throng in leisurely fashion, and not a man but what had keen scrutiny from her sharp eyes. No, there was no cause for suspicion there; they were evidently one and all just what they seemed to be – loud-voiced, hard-riding men, bent on a day's sport; but – and here Loveday's eyes travelled beyond the hotel courtyard to the other side of the road – who was that man with a bill-hook hacking at the hedge there – a thin-featured, round-shouldered old fellow, with a bent-about hat? It might be

162

as well not to take it too rashly for granted that her spies had withdrawn, and had left her free to do her work in her own fashion.

She went upstairs to her room. It was situated on the first floor in the front of the house, and consequently commanded a good view of the high road. She stood well back from the window, and at an angle whence she could see and not be seen, took a long, steady survey of the hedger. And the longer she looked the more convinced she was that the man's real work was something other than the bill-hook seemed to imply. He worked, so to speak, with his head over his shoulder, and when Loveday supplemented her eyesight with a strong field-glass, she could see more than one stealthy glance shot from beneath his bent-about hat in the direction of her window.

There could be little doubt about it: her movements were to be as closely watched today as they had been yesterday. Now it was of first importance that she should communicate with Inspector Gunning in the course of the afternoon: the question to solve was how it was to be done?

To all appearance Loveday answered the question in extra-ordinary fashion. She pulled up her blind, she drew back her curtain, and seated herself, in full view, at a small table in the window recess. Then she took a pocket ink-stand from her pocket, a packet of correspondence cards from her letter-case, and with rapid pen set to work on them.

About an hour and a half afterwards, White, coming in, according to his promise, to report proceedings, found her still seated at the window, not, however, with writing materials before her, but with needle and thread in her hand, with which she was mending her gloves.

'I return to town by the first train tomorrow morning,' she said as he entered, 'and I find these wretched things want no end of stitches. Now for your report.'

White appeared to be in an elated frame of mind. 'I've seen her!' he cried, 'my Annie – they've got her, those confounded

Sisters; but they sha'n't keep her – no, not if I have to pull the house down about their ears to get her out!'

'Well, now you know where she is, you can take your time about getting her out,' said Loveday. 'I hope, however, you haven't broken faith with me, and betrayed yourself by trying to speak with her, because, if so, I shall have to look for another deputy.'

'Honour, Miss Brooke!' answered White indignantly. 'I stuck to my duty, though it cost me something to see her hanging over those kids and tucking them into the cart, and never say a word to her, never so much as wave my hand.'

'Did she go out with the donkey-cart today?'

'No, she only tucked the kids into the cart with a blanket, and then went back to the house. Two old Sisters, ugly as sin, went out with them. I watched them from the window, jolt, jolt, jolt, round the corner, out of sight, and then I whipped down the stairs, and on to my machine, and was after them in a trice, and managed to keep them well in sight for over an hour and a half.'

'And their destination today was?'

'Wootton Hall.'

'Ah, just as I expected.'

'Just as you expected?' echoed White.

'I forgot. You do not know the nature of the suspicions that are attached to this Sisterhood, and the reasons I have for thinking that Wootton Hall, at this season of the year, might have an especial attraction for them.'

White continued staring at her. 'Miss Brooke,' he said presently, in an altered tone, 'whatever suspicions may attach to the Sisterhood, I'll stake my life on it, my Annie has had no share in any wickedness of any sort.'

'Oh, quite so; it is most likely that your Annie has, in some way, been inveigled into joining these Sisters – has been taken possession of by them, in fact, just as they have taken possession of the little cripples.'

'That's it! that's it!' he cried excitedly; 'that was the idea that occurred to me when you spoke to me on the hill about them, otherwise you may be sure . . .'

'Did they get relief of any sort at the Hall?' interrupted Loveday.

'Yes; one of the two ugly old women stopped outside the lodge gates with the donkey-cart, and the other beauty went up to the house alone. She stayed there, I should think, about a quarter of an hour, and when she came back was followed by a servant, carrying a bundle and a basket.'

'Ah! I've no doubt they brought away with them something else beside old garments and broken victuals.'

White stood in front of her, fixing a hard, steady gaze upon her.

'Miss Brooke,' he said presently, in a voice that matched the look on his face, 'what do you suppose was the real object of these women in going to Wootton Hall this morning?'

'Mr White, if I wished to help a gang of thieves break into Wootton Hall tonight, don't you think I should be greatly interested in procuring for them the information that the master of the house was away from home; that two of the menservants, who slept in the house, had recently been dismissed and their places had not yet been filled; also that the dogs were never unchained at night, and that their kennels were at the side of the house at which the butler's pantry is not situated? These are particulars I have gathered in this house without stirring from my chair, and I am satisfied that they are likely to be true. At the same time, if I were a professional burglar, I should not be content with information that was likely to be true, but would be careful to procure such that was certain to be true, and so would set accomplices to work at the fountain head. Now do you understand?'

White folded his arms and looked down on her.

'What are you going to do?' he asked, in short, brusque tones.

Loveday looked him full in the face. 'Communicate with the police immediately,' she answered; 'and I should feel greatly obliged if you would at once take a note from me to Inspector Gunning at Reigate.'

'And what becomes of Annie?'

'I don't think you need have any anxiety on that head. I have no doubt that when the circumstances of her admission to the Sisterhood are investigated, it will be proved that she has been as much deceived and imposed upon as the man, John Murray, who so foolishly let his house to these women. Remember, Annie has Mrs Copeland's good word to support her integrity.'

White stood silent for awhile.

'What sort of a note do you wish me to take to the Inspector?' he presently asked.

'You shall read it as I write it, if you like,' answered Loveday. She took a correspondence card from her letter-case, and, with an indelible pencil, wrote as follows:

Wootton Hall is threatened tonight – concentrate attention there. L.B.

White read the words as she wrote them with a curious expression passing over his handsome features.

'Yes,' he said, curtly as before; 'I'll deliver that, I give you my word, but I'll bring back no answer to you. I'll do no more spying for you – it's a trade that doesn't suit me. There's a straightforward way of doing straightforward work, and I'll take that way – no other – to get my Annie out of that den.'

He took the note, which she sealed and handed to him, and strode out of the room.

Loveday, from the window, watched him mount his bicycle. Was it her fancy, or did there pass a swift, furtive glance of recognition between him and the hedger on the other side of the way as he rode out of the courtyard?

She seemed determined to make that hedger's work easy for him. The short winter's day was closing in now, and her room must consequently have been growing dim to outside observation. She lighted the gas chandelier which hung from the ceiling, and, still with blinds and curtains undrawn, took her old place at the window, spread writing materials before her, and commenced a long and elaborate report to her chief at Lynch Court.

About half an hour afterwards, she threw a casual glance across the road, and saw that the hedger had disappeared, but that two ill-looking tramps sat munching bread and cheese under the hedge to which his bill-hook had done so little service. Evidently the intention was, one way or another, not to lose sight of her so long as she remained in Redhill.

Meantime, White had delivered Loveday's note to the Inspector at Reigate, and had disappeared on his bicycle once more.

Gunning read it without a change of expression. Then he crossed the room to the fireplace and held the card as close to the bars as he could without scorching it.

'I had a telegram from her this morning,' he explained to his confidential man, 'telling me to rely upon chemicals and coals throughout the day, and that, of course, meant that she would write to me in invisible ink. No doubt this message about Wootton Hall means nothing . . .'

He broke off abruptly, exclaiming: 'Eh! what's this!' as, having withdrawn the card from the fire, Loveday's real message stood out in bold, clear characters between the lines of the false one.

Thus it ran:

North Cape will be attacked tonight – a desperate gang – be prepared for a struggle. Above all, guard the electrical engine-house. On no account attempt to communicate with me; I am so closely watched that any endeavour to do so may frustrate your chance of trapping the scoundrels. L.B.

That night when the moon went down behind Reigate Hill an exciting scene was enacted at North Cape. The *Surrey Gazette*, in its issue the following day, gave the sub-joined account of it under the heading, 'Desperate Encounter with Burglars'.

'Last night, "North Cape", the residence of Mr Jameson, was the scene of an affray between the police and a desperate gang of burglars. "North Cape" is lighted throughout by electricity, and the burglars, four in number, divided in half – two being told off to enter and rob the house, and two to remain at the engine-shed, where the electricity is stored, so that, at a given signal, should need arise, the wires might be unswitched, the inmates of the house thrown into sudden darkness and confusion, and the escape of the marauders thereby facilitated. Mr Jameson, however, had received timely warning from the police of the intended attack, and he, with his two sons, all well-armed, sat in darkness in the inner hall awaiting the coming of the thieves. The police were stationed, some in the stables, some in out-buildings nearer to the house, and others in more distant parts of the grounds. The burglars effected their entrance by means of a ladder placed to a window of the servants' staircase, which leads straight down to the butler's pantry and to the safe where the silver is kept. The fellows, however, had no sooner got into the house than two policemen, issuing from their hiding-place outside, mounted the ladder after them and thus cut off their retreat. Mr Jameson and his two sons, at the same moment, attacked them in front, and thus overwhelmed by numbers the scoundrels were easily secured. It was at the engine-house outside that the sharpest struggle took place. The thieves had forced open the door of this engine-shed with their jemmies immediately on their arrival, under the very eyes of the police, who lay in ambush in the stables, and when one of the men, captured in the house, contrived to sound an alarm on his whistle, these outside watchers made a rush for the electrical jars, in order to unswitch the wires. Upon this the police closed upon them, and a hand-to-hand struggle followed, and if it had not been for the timely assistance of Mr Jameson and his sons, who had fortunately conjectured that their presence here might be useful, it is more than likely that one of the burglars, a powerfully-built man, would have escaped.

'The names of the captured men are John Murray, Arthur and George Lee (father and son), and a man with so many *aliases* that it is difficult to know which is his real name. The whole thing had been most cunningly and carefully planned. The elder Lee, lately released from penal servitude for a similar offence, appears to have been prime mover in the affair. This man had, it seems, a son and a daughter, who, through the kindness of friends, had been fairly well placed in life; the son at an electrical engineer's in London, the daughter as nursery governess at Wootton Hall. Directly this man was released from Portland, he seems to have found out his children and done his best to ruin them both. He was constantly at Wootton Hall endeavouring to induce his daughter to act as an accomplice to a robbery of the house. This so worried the girl that she threw up her situation and joined a Sisterhood that had recently been established in the neighbourhood. Upon this, Lee's thoughts turned in another direction. He induced his son, who had saved a little money, to throw up his work in London, and join him in his disreputable career. The boy is a handsome young fellow, but appears to have in him the makings of a first-class criminal. In his work as an electrical engineer he had made the acquaintance of the man John Murray, who, it is said, has been rapidly going downhill of late. Murray was the owner of the house rented by the Sisterhood that Miss Lee had joined, and the idea evidently struck the brains of these three scoundrels that this Sisterhood, whose antecedents were not generally known, might be utilized to draw off the attention of the police from themselves and from the especial house in the neighbourhood that they had planned to attack. With this end in view, Murray made an application to the police to have the Sisters watched, and still further to give colour to the suspicions he had endeavoured to set afloat concerning them, he and his confederates made feeble attempts at burglary upon the houses at which the Sisters had called, begging for scraps. It is a matter for congratulation that the plot, from beginning to end, has been thus successfully unearthed, and it is felt on all sides that great credit is due to Inspector Gunning and his skilled coadjutors for the vigilance and promptitude they have displayed throughout the affair.'

Loveday read aloud this report, with her feet on the fender of the Lynch Court office.

'Accurate, so far as it goes,' she said, as she laid down the paper.

'But we want to know a little more,' said Mr Dyer. 'In the first place, I would like to know what it was that diverted your suspicions from the unfortunate Sisters?'

'The way in which they handled the children,' answered Loveday promptly. 'I have seen female criminals of all kinds handling children, and I have noticed that although they may occasionally – even this is rare – treat them with a certain rough sort of kindness, of tenderness they are utterly incapable. Now Sister Monica, I must admit, is not pleasant to look at; at the same time, there was something absolutely beautiful in the way in which she lifted the little cripple out of the cart, put his tiny thin hand round her neck, and carried him into the house. By the way, I would like to ask some rabid physiognomist how he would account for Sister Monica's repulsiveness of features as contrasted with young Lee's undoubted good looks – heredity, in this case, throws no light on the matter.'

'Another question,' said Mr Dyer, not paying heed to Loveday's digression; 'how was it you transferred your suspicions to John Murray?'

'I did not do so immediately, although at the very first it had struck me as odd that he should be so anxious to do the work of the police for them. The chief thing I noticed concerning Murray, on the first and only occasion on which I saw him, was that he had had an accident with his bicycle, for in the right-hand corner of his lamp-glass there was a tiny star, and the lamp itself had a dent on the same side, had also lost its hook, and was fastened to the machine by a bit of electric fuse. The next morning, as I was walking up the hill towards Northfield, I was accosted by a young man mounted on that selfsame bicycle – not a doubt of it – star in glass, dent, fuse, all there.'

'Ah, that sounded an important key-note, and led you to connect Murray and the younger Lee immediately.'

'It did, and, of course, also at once gave the lie to his statement that he was a stranger in the place, and confirmed my opinion that there was nothing of the north-countryman in his accent. Other details in his manner and appearance gave rise to other suspicions. For instance, he called himself a press reporter by profession, and his hands were coarse and grimy, as only a mechanic's could be. He said he was a bit of a literary man, but the Tennyson that showed so obtrusively from his pocket was new, and in parts uncut, and totally unlike the well-thumbed volume of the literary student. Finally, when he tried and failed to put my latch-key into his waistcoat pocket, I saw the reason lay in the fact that the pocket was already occupied by a soft coil of electric fuse, the end of which protruded. Now, an electric fuse is what an electrical engineer might almost unconsciously carry about with him, it is so essential a part of his working tools, but it is a thing that a literary man or a press reporter could have no possible use for.'

'Exactly, exactly. And it was, no doubt, that bit of electric fuse that turned your thoughts to the one house in the neighbourhood lighted by electricity, and suggested to your mind the possibility of electrical engineers turning their talents to account in that direction. Now, will you tell me what, at that stage of your day's work, induced you to wire to Gunning that you would bring your invisible ink bottle into use?'

'That was simply a matter of precaution; it did not compel me to the use of invisible ink, if I saw other safe methods of communication. I felt myself being hemmed in on all sides with spies, and I could not tell what emergency might arise. I don't think I have ever had a more difficult game to play. As I walked and talked with the young fellow up the hill, it became clear to me that if I wished to do my work I must lull the suspicions of the gang, and seem to walk into their trap. I saw by the persistent way in which Wootton Hall was forced on my notice that it was wished to fix my suspicions there. I accordingly, to all appearance, did so, and allowed the fellows to think they were making a fool of me.'

'Ha! ha! Capital, that – the biter bit, with a vengeance! Splendid idea to make that young rascal himself deliver the letter that was to land him and his pals in jail. And he all the time laughing in his sleeve and thinking what a fool he was making of you! Ha, ha, ha!' And Mr Dyer made the office ring again with his merriment.

'The only person one is at all sorry for in this affair is poor little Sister Anna,' said Loveday pityingly; 'and yet, perhaps, all things considered, after her sorry experience of life, she may not be so badly placed in a Sisterhood where practical Christianity – not religious hysterics – is the one and only rule of the order.'

The Gylston Slander

Herbert Jenkins

It was through Roger Freynes, the eminent K.C., that Malcolm Sage first became interested in the series of anonymous letters that had created considerable scandal in the little village of Gylston.

Tucked away in the north-west corner of Hampshire, Gylston was a village of some eight hundred inhabitants. The vicar, the Rev. John Crayne, had held the living for some twenty years. Aided by his wife and daughter, Muriel, a pretty and high-spirited girl of nineteen, he devoted himself to the parish, and in return enjoyed great popularity.

Life at the vicarage was an ideal of domestic happiness. Mr and Mrs Crayne were devoted to each other and to their daughter, and she to them. Muriel Crayne had grown up among the villagers, devoting herself to parish work as soon as she was old enough to do so. She seemed to find her life sufficient for her needs, and many were the comparisons drawn by other parents in Gylston between the vicar's daughter and their own restless offspring.

A year previously a new curate had arrived in the person of the Rev. Charles Blade. His frank, straightforward personality, coupled with his good looks and masculine bearing, had caused him to be greatly liked, not only by the vicar and his family, but by all the parishioners.

Suddenly and without warning the peace of the vicarage was destroyed. One morning Mr Crayne received by post an anonymous letter, in which the names of his daughter and the curate were linked together in a way that caused him both pain and anxiety.

A man with a strong sense of humour himself, he cordially despised the anonymous letter-writer, and his first instinct had been to ignore that which he had just received. On second thoughts, however, he reasoned that the writer would be unlikely to rest content with a single letter; but would, in all probability, make the same calumnious statements to others.

After consulting with his wife, he had reluctantly questioned his daughter. At first she was inclined to treat the matter lightly; but on the grave nature of the accusations being pointed out to her, she had become greatly embarrassed and assured him that the curate had never been more than ordinarily attentive to her.

The vicar decided to allow the matter to rest there, and accordingly he made no mention of the letter to Blade.

A week later his daughter brought him a letter she had found lying in the vicarage grounds. It contained a passionate declaration of love, and ended with a threat of what might happen if the writer's passion were not reciprocated.

Although the letter was unsigned, the vicar could not disguise from himself the fact that there was a marked similarity between the handwriting of the two anonymous letters and that of his curate. He decided, therefore, to ask Blade if he could throw any light on the matter.

At first the young man had appeared bewildered; then he had pledged his word of honour, not only that he had not written the letters, but that there was no truth in the statements they contained.

With that the vicar had to rest content; but worse was to follow.

Two evenings later, one of the churchwardens called at the vicarage and, after behaving in what to the vicar seemed a very strange manner, he produced from his pocket a letter he had received that morning, in which were repeated the scandalous statements contained in the first epistle.

From then on the district was deluged with anonymous letters, all referring to the alleged passion of the curate for the vicar's daughter, and the intrigue they were carrying on together. Some of the letters were frankly indelicate in their expression and, as the whole parish seethed with the scandal, the vicar appealed to the police for aid.

One peculiarity of the letters was that all were written upon the same paper, known as 'Olympic Script.' This was supplied locally to a number of people in the neighbourhood, among others, the vicar, the curate, and the schoolmaster.

Soon the story began to find its way into the newspapers, and Blade's position became one full of difficulty and embarrassment. He had consulted Robert Freynes, who had been at Oxford with his father, and the K.C., convinced of the young man's innocence, had sought Malcolm Sage's aid.

'You see, Sage,' Freynes had remarked, 'I'm sure the boy is straight and incapable of such conduct; but it's impossible to talk to that ass Murdy. He has no more imagination than a tin-linnet.'

Freynes's reference was to Chief Inspector Murdy, of Scotland Yard, who had been entrusted with the inquiry, the local police having proved unequal to the problem.

Although Malcolm Sage had promised Robert Freynes that he would undertake the inquiry into the Gylston scandal, it was not until nearly a week later that he found himself at liberty to motor down into Hampshire.

One afternoon the vicar of Gylston, on entering his church, found a stranger on his knees in the chancel. Note-book in hand, he was transcribing the inscription of a monumental brass.

As the vicar approached, he observed that the stranger was vigorously shaking a fountain-pen, from which the ink had evidently been exhausted.

At the sound of Mr Crayne's footsteps the stranger looked up, turning towards him a pair of gold-rimmed spectacles, above which a bald conical head seemed to contradict the keenness of the eyes and the youthful lines of the face beneath.

'You are interested in monumental brasses?' inquired the vicar, as he entered the chancel, and the stranger rose to his feet. 'I am the vicar,' he explained. There was a look of eager interest in the pale grey eyes that looked out from a placid, scholarly face.

'I was taking the liberty of copying the inscription on this,' replied Malcolm Sage, indicating the time-worn brass at his feet, 'only unfortunately my fountain-pen has given out.'

'There is pen and ink in the vestry,' said the vicar, impressed by the fact that the stranger had chosen the finest brass in the church, one that had been saved from Cromwell's Puritans by the ingenuity of the then incumbent, who had caused it to be covered with cement. Then as an afterthought the vicar added, 'I can get your pen filled at the vicarage. My daughter has some ink; she always uses a fountain-pen.'

Malcolm Sage thanked him, and for the next half-hour the vicar forgot the worries of the past few weeks in listening to a man who seemed to have the whole subject of monumental brasses and Norman architecture at his finger-ends.

Subsequently Malcolm Sage was invited to the vicarage, where another half-hour was occupied in Mr Crayne showing him his collection of books on brasses.

As Malcolm Sage made a movement to depart, the vicar suddenly remembered the matter of the ink, apologised for his remissness, and left the room, returning a few minutes later with a bottle of fountain-pen ink. Malcolm Sage drew from his pocket his pen, and proceeded to replenish the ink from the bottle. Finally he completed the transcription of the lettering of the brass from a rubbing produced by the vicar.

Reluctant to allow so interesting a visitor to depart, Mr Crayne pressed him to take tea; but Malcolm Sage pleaded an engagement.

As they crossed the hall, a fair girl suddenly rushed out from a door on the right. She was crying hysterically. Her hair was disordered, her deep violet eyes rimmed with red, and her moist lips seemed to stand out strangely red against the alabaster paleness of her skin.

'Muriel!'

Malcolm Sage glanced swiftly at the vicar. The look of scholarly calm had vanished from his features, giving place to a set sternness that reflected the tone in which he had uttered his daughter's name.

At the sight of a stranger the girl had paused, then, as if realising her tear-stained face and disordered hair, she turned and disappeared through the door from which she had rushed.

'My daughter,' murmured the vicar, a little sadly, Malcolm Sage thought. 'She has always been very highly strung and emotional,' he added, as if considering some explanation necessary. 'We have to be very stern with her on such occasions. It is the only way to repress it.'

'You find it answer?' remarked Malcolm Sage.

'She has been much better lately, although she has been sorely tried. Perhaps you have heard.'

Malcolm Sage nodded absently, as he gazed intently at the thumb-nail of his right hand. A minute later he was walking down the drive, his thoughts occupied with the pretty daughter of the vicar of Gylston.

At the curate's lodgings he was told that Mr Blade was away, and would not return until late that night.

As he turned from the gate, Malcolm Sage encountered a pale-faced, narrow-shouldered man with a dark moustache and a hard, peevish mouth.

To Malcolm Sage's question as to which was the way to the inn, he nodded in the direction from which he had come and continued on his way.

'A man who has failed in what he set out to accomplish,' was Malcolm Sage's mental diagnosis of John Gray, the Gylston schoolmaster.

It was not long before Malcolm Sage realised that the village of Gylston was intensely proud of itself. It had seen in the London papers accounts of the mysterious scandal of which it was the centre. A Scotland Yard officer had been down, and had subjected many of the inhabitants to a careful cross-examination. In consequence Gylston realised that it was a village to be reckoned with.

The Tired Traveller was the centre of all rumour and gossip. Here each night in the public-bar, or in the private-parlour, according to their social status, the inhabitants would forgather and discuss the problem of the mysterious letters. Every sort of theory was advanced, and every sort of explanation offered. Whilst popular opinion tended to the view that the curate was the guilty party, there were some who darkly shook their heads and muttered, 'We shall see.'

It was remembered and discussed with relish that John Gray, the schoolmaster, had for some time past shown a marked admiration for the vicar's daughter. She, however, had made it clear that the cadaverous, saturnine pedagogue possessed for her no attractions.

During the half-hour that Malcolm Sage spent at the Tired Traveller, eating a hurried meal, he heard all there was to be heard about local opinion.

The landlord, a rubicund old fellow whose baldness extended to his eyelids, was bursting with information. By nature capable of making a mystery out of a sunbeam, he revelled in the scandal that hummed around him.

After a quarter of an hour's conversation, the landlord's conversation, Malcolm Sage found himself possessed of a bewildering amount of new material.

'A young gal don't have them highsterics for nothin',' mine host remarked darkly. 'Has fits of 'em every now and then ever since she was a flapper, sobbin' and cryin' fit to break 'er heart, and the vicar that cross with her.'

'That is considered the best way to treat hysterical people,' remarked Malcolm Sage.

'Maybe,' was the reply, 'but she's only a gal, and a pretty one too,' he added inconsequently.

'Then there's the schoolmaster,' he continued, ' 'ates the curate like poison, he does. Shouldn't be surprised if it was him that done it. 'E's always been a bit sweet in that quarter himself, has Mr Gray. Got talked about a good deal one time, 'angin' about arter Miss Muriel,' added the loquacious publican.

By the time Malcolm Sage had finished his meal, the landlord was well in his stride of scandalous reminiscence. It was with obvious reluctance that he allowed so admirable a listener to depart, and it was with manifest regret that he watched Malcolm Sage's car disappear round the curve in the road.

A little way beyond the vicarage, an admonitory triangle caused Tims to slow up. Just by the bend Malcolm Sage observed a youth and a girl standing in the recess of a gate giving access to a meadow. Although they were in the shadow cast by the hedge, Malcolm Sage's quick eyes recognised in the girl the vicar's daughter. The youth looked as if he might be one of the lads of the village.

In the short space of two or three seconds Malcolm Sage noticed the change in the girl. Although he could not see her face very clearly, the vivacity of her bearing and the ready laugh were suggestive of a gaiety contrasting strangely with the tragic figure he had seen in the afternoon.

Muriel Crayne was obviously of a very mercurial temperament, he decided, as the car swung round the bend.

The next morning, in response to a telephone message, Inspector Murdy called on Malcolm Sage.

'Well, Mr Sage,' he cried, as he shook hands, 'going to have another try to teach us our job?' And his blue eyes twinkled good-humouredly.

The inspector had already made up his mind. He was a man with many successes to his record, achieved as a result of undoubted astuteness in connection with the grosser crimes, such as train-murders, post-office hold-ups and burglaries. He was incapable, however, of realising that there existed a subtler form of law-breaking, arising from something more intimately associated with the psychic than the material plane.

'Did you see Mr Blade?' inquired Malcolm Sage.

'Saw the whole blessed lot,' was the cheery reply. 'It's all as clear as milk.' And he laughed.

'What did Mr Blade say?' inquired Malcolm Sage, looking keenly across at the inspector.

'Just that he had nothing to say.'

'His exact words. Can you remember them?' queried Malcolm Sage.

'Oh, yes!' replied the inspector. 'He said, "Inspector Murdy, I have nothing to say," and then he shut up like a real Whitstable.'

'He was away yesterday,' remarked Malcolm Sage, who then told the inspector of his visit. 'How about John Gray, the schoolmaster?' he queried.

'He practically told me to go to the devil,' was the genial reply. Inspector Murdy was accustomed to rudeness; his profession invited it, and to his rough-and-ready form of reasoning, rudeness meant innocence; politeness, guilt.

He handed to Malcolm Sage a copy of a list of people who purchased 'Olympic Script' from Mr Grainger, the local Whiteley, volunteering the information that the curate was the biggest consumer, as if that settled the question of his guilt.

'And yet the vicar would not hear of the arrest of Blade,' murmured Malcolm Sage, turning the copper ash-tray round with his restless fingers.

The inspector shrugged his massive shoulders.

'Sheer good nature and kindliness, Mr Sage,' he said. 'He's as gentle as a woman.'

'I once knew a man,' remarked Malcolm Sage, 'who said that in the annals of crime lay the master-key to the world's mysteries, past, present and to come.'

'A dreamer, Mr Sage,' smiled the inspector. 'We haven't time for dreaming at the Yard,' he added good-temperedly, as he rose and shook himself like a Newfoundland dog.

'I suppose it never struck you to look elsewhere than at the curate's lodgings for the writer of the letters?' inquired Malcolm Sage quietly.

'It never strikes me to look about for some one when I'm sitting on his chest,' laughed Inspector Murdy.

'True,' said Malcolm Sage. 'By the way,' he continued, without looking up, 'in future can you let me see every letter as it is received? You might also keep careful record of how they are delivered.'

'Certainly, Mr Sage. Anything that will make you happy.'

'Later I may get you to ask the vicar to seal up any subsequent anonymous letters that reach him without allowing any one to see the contents. Do you think he would do that?'

'Without doubt if I ask him,' said the inspector, surprise in his eyes as he looked down upon the cone of baldness beneath him, realising what a handicap it is to talk to a man who keeps his eyes averted.

'He must then put the letters in a place where no one can possibly obtain access to them. One thing more,' continued Malcolm Sage, 'will you ask Miss Crayne to write out the full story of the letters as far as she personally is acquainted with it?'

'Very well, Mr Sage,' said the inspector, with the air of one humouring a child. 'Now I'll be going.' He walked towards the door, then suddenly stopped and turned.

'I suppose you think I'm wrong about the curate?'

'I'll tell you later,' was the reply.

'When you find the master-key?' laughed the inspector, as he opened the door.

'Yes, when I find the master-key,' said Malcolm Sage quietly and, as the door closed behind Inspector Murdy, he continued to finger the copper ash-tray as if that were the master-key.

II

Malcolm Sage was seated at a small green-covered table playing solitaire. A velvet smoking-jacket and a pair of wine-coloured morocco slippers suggested that the day's work was done.

Patience, chess, and the cinema were his unfailing sources of inspiration when engaged upon a more than usually difficult case. He had once told Sir James Walton that they clarified his brain and co-ordinated his thoughts, the cinema in particular. The fact that in the surrounding darkness were hundreds of other brains, vital and active, appeared to stimulate his own imagination.

Puffing steadily at a gigantic meerschaum, he moved the cards with a deliberation which suggested that his attention rather than his thoughts was absorbed in the game.

Nearly a month had elapsed since he had agreed to take up the inquiry into the authorship of the series of anonymous letters with which Gylston and the neighbourhood had been flooded; yet still the matter remained a mystery.

A celebrated writer of detective stories had interested himself in the affair, with the result that the Press throughout the country had 'stunted' Gylston as if it had been a heavy-weight championship, or a train murder.

For a fortnight Malcolm Sage had been on the Continent in connection with the theft of the Adair Diamonds. Two days previously, after having restored the famous jewels to Lady Adair, he had returned to London, to find that the Gylston affair had developed a new and dramatic phase. The curate had been arrested for an attempted assault upon Miss Crayne and, pleading 'not guilty,' had been committed for trial.

The incident that led up to this had taken place on the day that Malcolm Sage left London. Late that afternoon Miss Crayne had arrived at the vicarage in a state bordering on collapse. On becoming more collected, she stated that on returning from paying a call, and when half-way through a copse, known locally as 'Gypsies Wood,' Blade had sprung out upon her and violently protested his passion. He had gripped hold of her wrists, the mark of his fingers was to be seen on the delicate skin, and threatened to kill her and himself. She had been terrified, thinking he meant to kill her. The approach of a farm labourer had saved her, and the curate had disappeared through the copse.

This story was borne out by Joseph Higgins, the farm labourer in question. He had arrived to find Miss Crayne in a state of great alarm and agitation, and he had walked with her as far as the vicarage gate. He did not, however, actually see the curate.

On the strength of this statement the police had applied for a warrant, and had subsequently arrested the curate. Later he appeared before the magistrates, had been remanded, and finally committed for trial, bail being allowed.

Blade protested his innocence alike of the assault and the writing of the letters; but two handwriting experts had testified to the similarity of the handwriting of the anonymous letters with that of the curate. Furthermore, they were all written upon 'Olympic Script,' the paper that Blade used for his sermons.

Malcolm Sage had just started a new deal when the door opened and Rogers showed in Robert Freynes. With a nod, Malcolm Sage indicated the chair opposite. His visitor dropped into it and, taking a pipe from his pocket, proceeded to fill and light it.

Placing his meerschaum on the mantelpiece, Malcolm Sage produced a well-worn briar from his pocket, which, having got into commission, he proceeded once more with the game.

'It's looking pretty ugly for Blade,' remarked Freynes, recognising by the substitution of the briar for the meerschaum that Malcolm Sage was ready for conversation.

'Tell me.'

'It's those damned handwriting experts,' growled Freynes. 'They're the greatest anomaly of our legal system. The judge always warns the jury of the danger of accepting their evidence; yet each side continues to produce them. It's an insult to intelligence and justice.'

'To hang a man because his "s" resembles that of an implicating document,' remarked Malcolm Sage, as he placed a red queen on a black knave, 'is about as sensible as to imprison him because he has the same accent as a footpad.'

'Then there's Blade's astonishing apathy,' continued Freynes. 'He seems quite indifferent to the gravity of his position. Refuses to say a word. Any one might think he knew the real culprit and was trying to shield him,' and he sucked moodily at his pipe.

'The handwriting expert,' continued Malcolm Sage imperturbably, 'is too concerned with the crossing of a "t," the dotting of an "i," or the tail of a "g," to give time and thought to the way in which the writer uses, for instance, the compound tenses of verbs. Blade was no more capable of writing those letters than our friend Murdy is of transliterating the Rosetta Stone.'

'Yes; but can we prove it?' asked Freynes gloomily, as with the blade of a penknife he loosened the tobacco in the bowl of his pipe. 'Can we prove it?' he repeated and, snapping the knife to, he replaced it in his pocket.

'Blade's sermons,' Malcolm Sage continued, 'and such letters of his as you have been able to collect, show that he adopted a very definite and precise system of punctuation. He frequently uses the colon and the semicolon, and always in the right place. In a parenthetical clause preceded by the conjunction "and," he uses a comma *after* the "and," not before it as most people do. Before such words as "yet" and "but," he without exception uses a semicolon. The word "only," he always puts in its correct place. In short, he is so academic as to savour somewhat of the pomposity of the eighteenth century.'

'Go on,' said Freynes, as Malcolm Sage paused, as if to give the other a chance of questioning his reasoning.

'Turning to the anonymous letters,' continued Malcolm Sage, 'it must be admitted that the handwriting is very similar; but there all likeness to Blade's sermons and correspondence ends. Murdy has shown me nearly all the anonymous letters, and in the whole series there is not one instance of the colon or the semicolon being used. The punctuation is of the vaguest, consisting largely of the dash, which after all is a literary evasion.

'In these letters the word "but" frequently appears without any punctuation mark before it. At other times it has a comma, a dash, or a full stop.'

He paused and for the next two minutes devoted himself to the game before him. Then he continued:

'Such phrases as "If only you knew," "I should have loved to have been," "different than," which appear in these letters, would have been absolutely impossible to a man of Blade's meticulous literary temperament.'

As Malcolm Sage spoke, Robert Freynes's brain had been working rapidly. Presently he brought his hand down with a smack upon his knee.

'By heavens, Sage!' he cried, 'this is a new pill for the handwriting expert. I'll put you in the box. We've got a fighting chance after all.'

'The most curious factor in the whole case,' continued Malcolm Sage, 'is the way in which the letters were delivered. One was thrown into a fly on to Miss Crayne's lap, she tells us, when she and her father were driving home after dining at the Hall. Another was discovered in the vicarage garden. A third was thrown through Miss Crayne's bedroom window. A few of the earlier group were posted in the neighbouring town of Whitchurch, some on days that Blade was certainly not there.'

'That was going to be one of my strongest points,' remarked Freynes.

'The letters always imply that there is some obstacle existing between the writer and the girl he desires. What possible object could Blade have in writing letters to various people suggesting an intrigue between his vicar's daughter and himself; yet these letters were clearly written by the same hand that addressed those to the girl, her father and her mother.'

Freynes nodded his head comprehendingly.

'If Blade were in love with the girl,' continued Malcolm Sage, 'what was there to prevent him from pressing his suit along legitimate and accepted lines. Murdy frankly acknowledges that there has been nothing in Blade's outward demeanour to suggest that Miss Crayne was to him anything more than the daughter of his vicar.'

'What do you make of the story of the assault?'

'As evidence it is worthless,' replied Malcolm Sage, 'being without corroboration. The farm-hand did not actually see Blade.'

Freynes nodded his agreement.

'Having convinced myself that Blade had nothing to do with the writing of the letters, I next tried to discover if there were anything throwing suspicion on others in the neighbourhood, who were known to use "Olympic Script" as notepaper.

'The schoolmaster, John Gray, was one. He is an admirer of Miss Crayne, according to local gossip; but it was obvious from the first that he had nothing to do with the affair. One by one I eliminated all the others, until I came back once more to Blade.

'It was clear that the letters were written with a fountain-pen, and Blade always uses one. That, however, is not evidence, as millions of people use fountain-pens. By the way, what is your line of defence?' he inquired.

'Smashing the handwriting experts,' was the reply. 'I was calling four myself, on the principle that God is on the side of the big battalions; but now I shall depend entirely on your evidence.'

'The assault?' queried Malcolm Sage.

'There I'm done,' said Freynes, 'for although Miss Crayne's evidence is not proof, it will be sufficient for a jury. Besides, she's a very pretty and charming girl. I suppose,' he added, 'Blade must have made some sort of declaration, which she, in the light of the anonymous letters, entirely misunderstood.'

'What does he say?'

'Denies it absolutely, although he admits being in the neighbourhood of the "Gypsies Wood," and actually catching sight of

Miss Crayne in the distance; but he says he did not speak to her.'

'Is he going into the witness-box?'

'Certainly,' then after a pause he added, 'Kelton is prosecuting, and he's as moral as a swan. He'll appeal to the jury as fathers of daughters, and brothers of sisters.'

Malcolm Sage made no comment; but continued smoking mechanically, his attention apparently absorbed in the cards before him.

'If you can smash the handwriting experts,' continued the K.C., 'I may be able to manage the girl's testimony.'

'It will not be necessary,' said Malcolm Sage, carefully placing a nine of clubs upon an eight of diamonds.

'Not necessary?'

'I have asked Murdy to come round,' continued Malcolm Sage, still intent upon his game. 'I think that was his ring.'

A minute later the door opened to admit the burly inspector, more blue-eyed and genial than ever, and obviously in the best of spirits.

'Good-evening, Mr Sage,' he cried cheerfully. 'Congratulations on the Adair business. Good-evening, sir,' he added, as he shook hands with Freynes.

He dropped heavily into a seat, and taking a cigar from the box on the table, which Malcolm Sage had indicated with a nod, he proceeded to light it. No man enjoyed a good cigar more than Inspector Murdy.

'Well, what do you think of it?' he inquired, looking from Malcolm Sage to Freynes. 'It's a clear case now, I think.' He slightly stressed the word 'now.'

'You mean it's Blade?' inquired Malcolm Sage, as he proceeded to gather up the cards.

'Who else?' inquired the inspector, through a cloud of smoke.

'That is the question which involves your being here now, Murdy,' said Malcolm Sage dryly.

'We've got three handwriting experts behind us,' said the inspector complacently.

'That is precisely where they should be,' retorted Malcolm Sage quietly. 'In the biblical sense,' he added.

Freynes laughed, whilst Inspector Murdy looked from one to the other. He did not quite catch the allusion.

'You have done as I suggested?' inquired Malcolm Sage, when he had placed the cards in their box and removed the card-table.

'Here are all the letters received up to a fortnight ago,' said the inspector, holding out a bulky packet. 'Those received since have each been sealed up separately by the vicar, who is keeping half of them, whilst I have the other half; but really, Mr Sage, I don't understand –'

'Thank you, Murdy,' said Malcolm Sage, as he took the packet. 'It is always a pleasure to work with Scotland Yard. It is so thorough.'

The inspector beamed; for he knew the compliment was sincere.

Without a word Malcolm Sage left the room, taking the packet with him.

'A bit quaint at times, ain't he, sir?' remarked Inspector Murdy to Freynes; 'but one of the best. I'd trust him with anything.'

Freynes nodded encouragingly.

'There are some of them down at the Yard that don't like him,' he continued. 'They call him "Sage and Onions;" but most of us who have worked with him swear by Mr Sage. He's never out for the limelight himself, and he's always willing to give another fellow a leg up. After all, it's our living,' he added, a little inconsequently.

Freynes appreciated the inspector's delicacy in refraining from any mention of the Gylston case during Malcolm Sage's absence. After all, they represented respectively the prosecution and the defence. For nearly half an hour the two talked together upon unprofessional subjects. When Malcolm Sage returned, he found them discussing the prospects of Dempsey against Carpentier.

Handing back the packet of letters to Inspector Murdy, Malcolm Sage resumed his seat, and proceeded to relight his pipe.

'Spotted the culprit, Mr Sage?' inquired the inspector, with something that was very much like a wink in the direction of Freynes.

'I think so,' was the quiet reply. 'You might meet me at Gylston Vicarage to-morrow at three. I'll telegraph to Blade to be there too. You had better bring the schoolmaster also.'

'You mean –' began the inspector, rising.

'Exactly,' said Malcolm Sage. 'It's past eleven, and we all require sleep.'

III

The next afternoon the study of the vicar of Gylston presented a strange appearance.

Seated at Mr Crayne's writing-table was Malcolm Sage, a small attaché-case at his side, whilst before him were several piles of sealed packets. Grouped about the room were Inspector Murdy, Robert Freynes, Mr Gray, and the vicar.

All had their eyes fixed upon Malcolm Sage; but with varying expressions. Those of the schoolmaster were frankly cynical. The inspector and Freynes looked as if they expected to see produced from the attaché-case a guinea-pig or a white rabbit, pink-eyed and kicking; whilst the vicar had obviously not yet recovered from his surprise at discovering that the stranger, who had shown such a remarkable knowledge of monumental brasses and Norman architecture, was none other than the famous investigator about whom he had read so much in the newspapers.

With quiet deliberation Malcolm Sage opened the attaché-case and produced a spirit lamp, which he lighted. He then placed a metal plate upon a rest above the flame. On this he imposed a thicker plate of a similar metal that looked like steel; but it had a handle across the middle, rather resembling that of a tool used by plasterers.

He then glanced up, apparently unconscious of the almost

feverish interest with which his every movement was being watched.

'I should like Miss Crayne to be present,' he said.

As he spoke the door opened and the curate entered, his dark, handsome face lined and careworn. It was obvious that he had suffered. He bowed, and then looked about him, without any suggestion of embarrassment.

Malcolm Sage rose and held out his hand, Freynes followed suit.

'Ask Miss Muriel to come here,' said the vicar to the maid as she was closing the door.

The curate took the seat that Malcolm Sage indicated beside him. Silently the six men waited.

A few minutes later Miss Crayne entered, pale but self-possessed. She closed the door behind her. Suddenly she caught sight of the curate. Her eyes widened, and her paleness seemed to become accentuated. A moment later it was followed by a crimson flush. She hesitated, her hands clenched at her side, then with a manifest effort she appeared to control herself and, with a slight smile and inclination of her head, took the chair the schoolmaster moved towards her. Instinctively she turned her eyes toward Malcolm Sage.

'Inspector Murdy,' he said, without raising his eyes, 'will you please open two of those packets.' He indicated the pile upon his left. 'I should explain,' he continued, 'that each of these contains one of the most recent of the series of letters with which we are concerned. Each was sealed up by Mr Crayne immediately it reached him, in accordance with Inspector Murdy's request. Therefore, only the writer, the recipient and the vicar have had access to these letters.'

Malcolm Sage turned his eyes interrogatingly upon Mr Crayne, who bowed.

Meanwhile the inspector had cut open the two top envelopes, unfolded the sheets of paper they contained, and handed them to Malcolm Sage.

190

All eyes were fixed upon his long, shapely fingers as he smoothed out one of the sheets of paper upon the vicar's blotting-pad. Then, lifting the steel plate by the handle, he placed it upon the upturned sheet of paper.

The tension was almost unendurable. The heavy breathing of Inspector Murdy seemed like the blowing of a grampus. Mr Gray glanced across at him irritably. The vicar coughed slightly, then looked startled that he had made so much noise.

Every one bent forward, eagerly expecting something; yet without quite knowing what. Malcolm Sage lifted the metal plate from the letter. There in the centre of the page, in bluish-coloured letters, which had not been there when the paper was smoothed out upon the blotting-pad, appeared the words:

Malcolm Sage,
August 12th, 1919.
No. 138.

For some moments they all gazed at the paper as if the mysterious blue letters exercised upon them some hypnotic influence.

'Secret ink!'

It was Robert Freynes who spoke. Accustomed as he was to dramatic moments, he was conscious of a strange dryness at the back of his throat, and a consequent huskiness of voice.

His remark seemed to break the spell. Instinctively every one turned to him. The significance of the bluish-coloured characters was slowly dawning upon the inspector; but the others still seemed puzzled to account for their presence.

Immediately he had lifted the plate from the letter, Malcolm Sage had drawn a sheet of plain sermon paper from the rack before him. This he subjected to the same treatment as the letter. When a few seconds later he exposed it, there in the centre appeared the same words:

Malcolm Sage,
August 12th, 1919.

but on this sheet the number was 203.

Then the true significance of the two sheets of paper seemed to dawn upon the onlookers.

Suddenly there was a scream, and Muriel Crayne fell forward on to the floor.

'Oh! father, father, forgive me!' she cried, and the next moment she was beating the floor with her hands in violent hysterics.

IV

'From the first I suspected the truth,' remarked Malcolm Sage, as he, Robert Freynes and Inspector Murdy sat smoking in the car that Tims was taking back to London at its best pace. 'Eighty-five years ago a somewhat similar case occurred in France, that of Marie de Morel, when an innocent man was sentenced to ten years' imprisonment, and actually served eight before the truth was discovered.'

The inspector whistled under his breath.

'This suspicion was strengthened by the lengthy account of the affair written by Miss Crayne, which Murdy obtained from her. The punctuation, the phrasing, the inaccurate use of auxiliary verbs, were identical with that of the anonymous letters.

'Another point was that the similarity of the handwriting of the anonymous letters to Blade's became more pronounced as the letters themselves multiplied. The writer was becoming more expert as an imitator.'

Freynes nodded his head several times.

'The difficulty, however, was to prove it,' continued Malcolm Sage. 'There was only one way; to substitute secretly marked paper for that in use at the vicarage.

'I accordingly went down to Gylston, and the vicar found me

keenly interested in monumental brasses, his pet subject, and Norman architecture. He invited me to the vicarage. In his absence from his study I substituted a supply of marked Olympic Script in place of that in his letter-rack, and also in the drawer of his writing-table. As a further precaution, I arranged for my fountain-pen to run out of ink. He kindly supplied me with a bottle, obviously belonging to his daughter. I replenished my pen, which was full of a chemical that would enable me, if necessary, to identify any letter in the writing of which it had been used. When I placed my pen, which is a self-filler, in the ink, I forced this liquid into the bottle.'

The inspector merely stared. Words had forsaken him for the moment.

'It was then necessary to wait until the ink in Miss Crayne's pen had become exhausted, and she had to replenish her supply of paper from her father's study. After that discovery was inevitable.'

'But suppose she had denied it?' questioned the inspector.

'There was the ink which she alone used, and which I could identify,' was the reply.

'Why did you ask Gray to be present?' inquired Freynes.

'As his name had been associated with the scandal it seemed only fair,' remarked Malcolm Sage, then turning to Inspector Murdy he said, 'I shall leave it to you, Murdy, to see that a proper confession is obtained. The case has had such publicity that Mr Blade's innocence must be made equally public.'

'You may trust me, Mr Sage,' said the inspector. 'But why did the curate refuse to say anything?'

'Because he is a high-minded and chivalrous gentleman,' was the quiet reply.

'He knew?' cried Freynes.

'Obviously,' said Malcolm Sage. 'It is the only explanation of his silence. I taxed him with it after the girl had been taken away, and he acknowledged that his suspicions amounted almost to certainty.'

'Yet he stayed behind,' murmured the inspector with the air of a man who does not understand. 'I wonder why?'

'To minister to the afflicted, Murdy,' said Malcolm Sage. 'That is the mission of the Church.'

'I suppose you meant that French case when you referred to the "master-key," ' remarked the inspector, as if to change the subject.

Malcolm Sage nodded.

'But how do you account for Miss Crayne writing such letters about herself,' inquired the inspector, with a puzzled expression in his eyes. 'Pretty funny letters some of them for a parson's daughter.'

'I'm not a pathologist, Murdy,' remarked Malcolm Sage dryly, 'but when you try to suppress hysteria in a young girl by sternness, it's about as effectual as putting ointment on a plague-spot.'

'Sex-repression?' queried Freynes.

Malcolm Sage shrugged his shoulders; then after a pause, during which he lighted the pipe he had just refilled, he added:

'When you are next in Great Russell Street, drop in at the British Museum and look at the bust of Faustina. You will see that her chin is similar in modelling to that of Miss Crayne. The girl was apparently very much attracted to Blade, and proceeded to weave what was no doubt to her a romance, later it became an obsession. It all goes to show the necessity for pathological consideration of certain crimes.'

'But who was Faustina?' inquired the inspector, unable to follow the drift of the conversation.

'Faustina,' remarked Malcolm Sage, 'was the domestic fly in the philosophical ointment of an emperor,' and Inspector Murdy laughed; for, knowing nothing of the marriage or the *Meditations* of Marcus Aurelius, it seemed to him the only thing to do.

The Young Man in Holy Orders

Robert Louis Stevenson

The Reverend Mr Simon Rolles had distinguished himself in the Moral Sciences, and was more than usually proficient in the study of Divinity. His essay 'On the Christian Doctrine of the Social Obligations' obtained for him, at the moment of its production, a certain celebrity in the University of Oxford; and it was understood in clerical and learned circles that young Mr Rolles had in contemplation a considerable work – a folio, it was said – on the authority of the Fathers of the Church. These attainments, these ambitious designs, however, were far from helping him to any preferment; and he was still in quest of his first curacy when a chance ramble in that part of London, the peaceful and rich aspect of the garden, a desire for solitude and study, and the cheapness of the lodging, led him to take up his abode with Mr Raeburn, the nurseryman of Stockdove Lane.

It was his habit every afternoon, after he had worked seven or eight hours on St. Ambrose or St. Chrysostom, to walk for a while in meditation among the roses. And this was usually one of the most productive moments of his day. But even a sincere appetite for thought, and the excitement of grave problems awaiting solution, are not always sufficient to preserve the mind of the philosopher against the petty shocks and contacts of the world. And when Mr Rolles found General Vandeleur's secretary, ragged and bleeding, in the company of his landlord; when he saw both change colour and seek to avoid his questions; and, above all, when the former denied his own identity with the most unmoved assurance, he speedily forgot the Saints and Fathers in the vulgar interest of curiosity.

'I cannot be mistaken,' thought he. 'That is Mr Hartley beyond a doubt. How comes he in such a pickle? why does he deny his name? and what can be his business with that black-looking ruffian, my landlord?'

As he was thus reflecting, another peculiar circumstance attracted his attention. The face of Mr Raeburn appeared at a low window next the door; and, as chance directed, his eyes met those of Mr Rolles. The nurseryman seemed disconcerted, and even alarmed; and immediately after the blind of the apartment was pulled sharply down.

'This may all be very well,' reflected Mr Rolles; 'it may all be excellently well; but I confess freely that I do not think so. Suspicious, underhand, untruthful, fearful of observation – I believe upon my soul,' he thought, 'the pair are plotting some disgraceful action.'

The detective that there is in all of us awoke and became clamant in the bosom of Mr Rolles; and with a brisk; eager step, that bore no resemblance to his usual gait, he proceeded to make the circuit of the garden. When he came to the scene of Harry's escalade, his eye was at once arrested by a broken rosebush and marks of trampling on the mould. He looked up, and saw scratches on the brick; and a rag of trouser floating from a broken bottle. This, then, was the mode of entrance chosen by Mr Raeburn's particular friend! It was thus that General Vandeleur's secretary came to admire a flower-garden! The young clergyman whistled softly to himself as he stopped to examine the ground. He could make out where Harry had landed from his perilous leap; he recognised the flat foot of Mr Raeburn where it had sunk deeply in the soil as he pulled up the Secretary by the collar; nay, on a closer inspection, he seemed to distinguish the marks of groping fingers, as though something had been spilt abroad and eagerly collected.

'Upon my word,' he thought, 'the thing grows vastly interesting.'

And just then he caught sight of something almost entirely buried in the earth. In an instant he had disinterred a dainty morocco case, ornamented and clasped in gilt. It had been trodden heavily underfoot, and thus escaped the hurried search of Mr Raeburn. Mr Rolles opened the case, and drew a long breath of almost horrified astonishment; for there lay before him, in a cradle of green velvet, a diamond of prodigious magnitude and of the finest water. It was of the bigness of a duck's egg; beautifully shaped; and without a flaw; and as the sun shone upon it, it gave forth a lustre like that of electricity, and seemed to burn in his hand with a thousand internal fires.

He knew little of precious stones; but the Rajah's Diamond was a wonder that explained itself; a village child, if he found it, would run screaming for the nearest cottage; and a savage would prostrate himself in adoration before so imposing a fetish. The beauty of the stone flattered the young clergyman's eyes; the thought of its incalculable value overpowered his intellect. He knew that what he held in his hand was worth more than many years' purchase of an archiepiscopal see; that it would build cathedrals more stately than Ely or Cologne; that he who possessed it was set free for ever from the primal curse, and might follow his own inclinations without concern or hurry, without let or hindrance. And as he suddenly turned it, the rays leaped forth again with renewed brilliancy, and seemed to pierce his very heart.

Decisive actions are often taken in a moment and without any conscious deliverance from the rational parts of man. So it was now with Mr Rolles. He glanced hurriedly round, beheld, like Mr Raeburn before him, nothing but the sunlit flower-garden, the tall tree-tops, and the house with blinded windows; and in a trice he had shut the case, thrust it into his pocket, and was hastening to his study with the speed of guilt.

The Reverend Simon Rolles had stolen the Rajah's Diamond.

Early in the afternoon the police arrived with Harry Hartley. The nurseryman, who was beside himself with terror, readily discovered his hoard; and the jewels were identified and inventoried in the presence of the Secretary. As for Mr Rolles, he showed himself in a most obliging temper, communicated what he knew with freedom, and professed regret that he could do no more to help the officers in their duty.

'Still,' he added, 'I suppose your business is nearly at an end.'

'By no means,' replied the man from Scotland Yard; and he narrated the second robbery of which Harry had been the immediate victim, and gave the young clergyman a description of the more important jewels that were still not found, dilating particularly on the Rajah's Diamond.

'It must be worth a fortune,' observed Mr Rolles.

'Ten fortunes – twenty fortunes,' cried the officer.

'The more it is worth,' remarked Simon shrewdly, 'the more difficult it must be to sell. Such a thing has a physiognomy not to be disguised, and I should fancy a man might as easily negotiate St Paul's Cathedral.'

'Oh, truly!' said the officer; 'but if the thief be a man of any intelligence, he will cut it into three or four, and there will be still enough to make him rich.'

'Thank you,' said the clergyman. 'You cannot imagine how much your conversation interests me.'

Whereupon the functionary admitted that they knew many strange things in his profession, and immediately after took his leave.

Mr Rolles regained his apartment. It seemed smaller and barer than usual; the materials for his great work had never presented so little interest; and he looked upon his library with the eye of scorn. He took down, volume by volume, several Fathers of the Church, and glanced them through; but they contained nothing to his purpose.

'These old gentlemen,' thought he, 'are no doubt very valuable writers, but they seem to me conspicuously ignorant of life. Here am I, with learning enough to be a Bishop, and I positively do not know how to dispose of a stolen diamond. I glean a hint from a common policeman, and with all my folios, I cannot so much as put it into execution. This inspires me with very low ideas of University training.'

Herewith he kicked over his book-shelf and, putting on his hat, hastened from the house to the club of which he was a member. In such a place of mundane resort he hoped to find some man of good counsel and a shrewd experience in life. In the reading-room he saw many of the country clergy and an Archdeacon; there were three journalists and a writer upon the Higher Metaphysic, playing pool; and at dinner only the raff of ordinary club frequenters showed their commonplace and obliterated countenances. None of these, thought Mr Rolles, would know more on dangerous topics than he knew himself; none of them were fit to give him guidance in his present strait. At length, in the smoking-room, up many weary stairs, he hit upon a gentleman of somewhat portly build and dressed with conspicuous plainness. He was smoking a cigar and reading the *Fortnightly Review*; his face was singularly free from all sign of preoccupation or fatigue; and there was something in his air which seemed to invite confidence and to expect submission. The more the young clergyman scrutinised his features, the more he was convinced that he had fallen on one capable of giving pertinent advice.

'Sir,' said he, 'you will excuse my abruptness; but I judge you from your appearance to be pre-eminently a man of the world.'

'I have indeed considerable claims to that distinction,' replied the stranger, laying aside his magazine with a look of mingled amusement and surprise.

'I, sir,' continued the Curate, 'am a recluse, a student, a creature of ink-bottles and patristic folios. A recent event has brought my folly vividly before my eyes, and I desire to instruct myself in life. By life,' he added, 'I do not mean Thackeray's novels; but the crimes and secret possibilities of our society, and the principles of wise conduct among exceptional events. I am a patient reader; can the thing be learnt in books?'

'You put me in a difficulty,' said the stranger. 'I confess I have no great notion of the use of books, except to amuse a railway journey; although, I believe, there are some very exact treatises on astronomy, the use of the globes, agriculture, and the art of making paper flowers. Upon the less apparent provinces of life I fear you will find nothing truthful. Yet stay,' he added, 'have you read Gaboriau?'

Mr Rolles admitted he had never even heard the name.

'You may gather some notions from Gaboriau,' resumed the stranger. 'He is at least suggestive; and as he is an author much studied by Prince Bismarck, you will, at the worst, lose your time in good society.'

'Sir,' said the curate, 'I am infinitely obliged by your politeness.'

'You have already more than repaid me,' returned the other.

'How?' inquired Simon.

'By the novelty of your request,' replied the gentleman; and with a polite gesture, as though to ask permission, he resumed the study of the *Fortnightly Review*.

On his way home Mr Rolles purchased a work on precious stones and several of Gaboriau's novels. These last he eagerly skimmed until an advanced hour in the morning; but although they introduced him to many new ideas, he could nowhere discover what to do with a stolen diamond. He was annoyed, moreover, to find the information scattered amongst romantic story-telling, instead of soberly set forth after the manner of a manual; and he concluded that, even if the writer had thought much upon these subjects, he was totally lacking in educational method. For the character and attainments of Lecoq, however, he was unable to contain his admiration.

'He was truly a great creature,' ruminated Mr Rolles. 'He knew the world as I know Paley's Evidences. There was nothing that he could not carry to a termination with his own hand, and against the largest odds. Heavens!' he broke out suddenly, 'is not this the lesson? Must I not learn to cut diamonds for myself?'

It seemed to him as if he had sailed at once out of his perplexities; he remembered that he knew a jeweller, one B. Macculloch, in Edinburgh, who would be glad to put him in the way of the necessary training; a few months, perhaps a few years, of sordid toil, and he would be sufficiently expert to divide and sufficiently cunning to dispose with advantage of the Rajah's Diamond. That done, he might return to pursue his researches at leisure, a wealthy and luxurious student, envied and respected by all. Golden visions attended him through his slumber, and he awoke refreshed and light-hearted with the morning sun.

Mr Raeburn's house was on that day to be closed by the police, and this afforded a pretext for his departure. He cheerfully prepared his baggage, transported it to King's Cross, where he left it in the cloak-room, and returned to the club to while away the afternoon and dine.

'If you dine here to-day, Rolles,' observed an acquaintance, 'you may see two of the most remarkable men in England – Prince Florizel of Bohemia, and old Jack Vandeleur.'

'I have heard of the Prince,' replied Mr Rolles; 'and General Vandeleur I have even met in Society.'

'General Vandeleur is an ass!' returned the other. 'This is his brother John, the biggest adventurer, the best judge of precious stones, and one of the most acute diplomatists in Europe. Have you never heard of his duel with the Duc de Val d'Orge? of his exploits and atrocities when he was Dictator of Paraguay? of his dexterity in recovering Sir Samuel Levi's jewellery? nor of his services in the Indian Mutiny – services by which the Government profited, but which the Government dared not recognise? You make me wonder what we mean by fame, or even by infamy; for Jack Vandeleur has prodigious claims to both. Run downstairs,' he continued, 'take a table near them, and keep your ears open. You will hear some strange talk, or I am much misled.'

'But how shall I know them?' inquired the clergyman.

'Know them!' cried his friend; 'why, the Prince is the finest gentleman in Europe, the only living creature who looks like a king; and as for Jack Vandeleur, if you can imagine Ulysses at seventy years of age, and with a sabre-cut across his face, you have the man before you! Know them, indeed! Why, you could pick either of them out of a Derby day!'

Rolles eagerly hurried to the dining-room. It was as his friend had asserted; it was impossible to mistake the pair in question. Old John Vandeleur was of a remarkable force of body, and obviously broken to the most difficult exercises. He had neither the carriage of a swordsman, nor of a sailor, nor yet of one much inured to the saddle; but something made up of all these, and the result and expression of many different habits and dexterities. His features were bold and aquiline; his expression arrogant and predatory; his whole appearance that of a swift, violent, unscrupulous man of action; and his copious white hair and the deep sabre-cut that traversed his nose and temple added a note of savagery to a head already remarkable and menacing in itself.

In his companion, the Prince of Bohemia, Mr Rolles was astonished to recognise the gentleman who had recommended him the study of Gaboriau. Doubtless Prince Florizel, who rarely visited the club, of which, as of most others, he was an honorary member, had been waiting for John Vandeleur when Simon accosted him on the previous evening.

The other diners had modestly retired into the angles of the room, and left the distinguished pair in a certain isolation, but the young clergyman was unrestrained by any sentiment of awe, and, marching boldly up, took his place at the nearest table.

The conversation was, indeed, new to the student's ears. The ex-Dictator of Paraguay stated many extraordinary experiences in different quarters of the world; and the Prince supplied a commentary which, to a man of thought, was even more interesting than the events themselves. Two forms of experience were thus brought together and laid before the young clergyman; and he did not know which to admire the most – the desperate actor or the skilled expert in life; the man who spoke boldly of his own deeds and perils, or the man who seemed, like a god, to know all things and to have suffered nothing. The manner of each aptly fitted with his part in the discourse. The Dictator indulged in brutalities alike of speech and gesture; his hand opened and shut and fell roughly on the table; and his voice was loud and heavy. The Prince, on the other hand, seemed the very type of urbane docility and quiet; the least movement, the least inflection, had with him a weightier significance than all the shouts and pantomime of his companion; and if ever, as must frequently have been the case, he described some experience personal to himself, it was so aptly dissimulated as to pass unnoticed with the rest.

At length the talk wandered on to the late robberies and the Rajah's Diamond.

'That diamond would be better in the sea,' observed Prince Florizel.

'As a Vandeleur,' replied the Dictator, 'your Highness may imagine my dissent.'

'I speak on grounds of public policy,' pursued the Prince. 'Jewels so valuable should be reserved for the collection of a Prince or the treasury of a great nation. To hand them about among the common sort of men is to set a price on Virtue's head; and if the Rajah of Kashgar – a Prince, I understand, of great enlightenment – desired vengeance upon the men of Europe, he could hardly have gone more efficaciously about his purpose than by sending us this apple of discord. There is no honesty too robust for such a trial. I myself, who have many duties and many privileges of my own – I myself, Mr Vandeleur, could scarce handle the intoxicating crystal and be safe. As for you, who are a diamond hunter by taste and profession, I do not believe there is a crime in the calendar you would not perpetrate – I do not believe you have a friend in the world whom you would not eagerly betray – I do not know if you have a family, but if you have I declare you would sacrifice your children – and all this for what? Not to be richer, nor to have more comforts or more respect, but simply to call this diamond yours for a year or two until you die, and now and again to open a safe and look at it as one looks at a picture.'

'It is true,' replied Vandeleur. 'I have hunted most things, from men and women down to mosquitoes; I have dived for coral; I have followed both whales and tigers; and a diamond is the tallest quarry of the lot. It has beauty and worth; it alone can properly reward the ardours of the chase. At this moment, as your Highness may fancy, I am upon the trail; I have a sure knack, a wide experience; I know every stone of price in my brother's collection as a shepherd knows his sheep; and I wish I may die if I do not recover them every one!'

'Sir Thomas Vandeleur will have great cause to thank you,' said the Prince.

'I am not so sure,' returned the Dictator, with a laugh. 'One of the Vandeleurs will. Thomas or John – Peter or Paul – we are all apostles.'

'I did not catch your observation,' said the Prince with some disgust.

And at the same moment the waiter informed Mr Vandeleur that his cab was at the door.

Mr Rolles glanced at the clock, and saw that he also must be moving; and the coincidence struck him sharply and unpleasantly, for he desired to see no more of the diamond hunter.

Much study having somewhat shaken the young man's nerves, he was in the habit of travelling in the most luxurious manner; and for the present journey he had taken a sofa in the sleeping carriage.

'You will be very comfortable,' said the guard; 'there is no one in your compartment, and only one old gentleman in the other end.'

It was close upon the hour, and the tickets were being examined, when Mr Rolles beheld this other fellow-passenger ushered by several porters into his place; certainly, there was not another man in the world whom he would not have preferred –

for it was old John Vandeleur, the ex-Dictator.

The sleeping carriages on the Great Northern line were divided into three compartments – one at each end for travellers, and one in the centre fitted with the conveniences of a lavatory. A door running in grooves separated each of the others from the lavatory; but as there were neither bolts nor locks, the whole suite was practically common ground.

When Mr Rolles had studied his position, he perceived himself without defence. If the Dictator chose to pay him a visit in the course of the night, he could do no less than receive it; he had no means of fortification, and lay open to attack as if he had been lying in the fields. The situation caused him some agony of mind. He recalled with alarm the boastful statements of his fellow-traveller across the dining-table, and the professions of immorality which he had heard him offering to the disgusted Prince. Some persons, he remembered to have read, are endowed with a singular quickness of perception for the neighbourhood of precious metals; through walls and even at considerable distances they are said to divine the presence of gold. Might it not be the same with diamonds? he wondered; and if so, who was more likely to enjoy this transcendental sense than the person who gloried in the appellation of the Diamond Hunter? From such a man he recognised that he had everything to fear, and longed eagerly for the arrival of the day.

In the meantime he neglected no precaution, concealed his diamond in the most internal pocket of a system of greatcoats, and devoutly recommended himself to the care of Providence.

The train pursued its usual even and rapid course; and nearly half the journey had been accomplished before slumber began to triumph over uneasiness in the breast of Mr Rolles. For some time he resisted its influence; but it grew upon him more and more, and a little before York he was fain to stretch himself upon one of the couches and suffer his eyes to close; and almost at the same instant consciousness deserted the young clergyman. His last thought was of his terrifying neighbour.

When he awoke it was still pitch dark, except for the flicker of the veiled lamp; and the continual roaring and oscillation testified to the unrelaxed velocity of the train. He sat upright in a panic, for he had been tormented by the most uneasy dreams; it was some seconds before he recovered his self-command; and even after he had resumed a recumbent attitude sleep continued to flee him, and he lay awake with his brain in a state of violent agitation, and his eyes fixed upon the lavatory door. He pulled his clerical felt hat over his brow still farther to shield him from the light; and he adopted the usual expedients, such as counting a thousand or banishing thought, by which experienced invalids are accustomed to woo the approach of sleep. In the case of Mr Rolles they proved one and all vain; he was harassed by a dozen different anxieties – the old man in the other end of the carriage haunted him in the most alarming shapes; and in whatever attitude he chose to lie the diamond in his pocket occasioned him a sensible physical distress. It burned, it was too large, it bruised his ribs; and there were infinitesimal fractions of a second in which he had half a mind to throw it from the window.

While he was thus lying, a strange incident took place.

The sliding-door into the lavatory stirred a little, and then a little more, and was finally drawn back for the space of about twenty inches. The lamp in the lavatory was unshaded, and in the lighted aperture thus disclosed, Mr Rolles could see the head of Mr Vandeleur in an attitude of deep attention. He was conscious that the gaze of the Dictator rested intently on his own face; and the instinct of self-preservation moved him to hold his breath, to refrain from the least movement, and keeping his eyes lowered, to watch his visitor from underneath the lashes. After about a moment, the head was withdrawn and the door of the lavatory replaced.

The Dictator had not come to attack, but to observe; his action was not that of a man threatening another, but that of a man who was himself threatened; if Mr Rolles was afraid of him, it appeared that he, in his turn, was not quite easy on the score of Mr Rolles. He had come, it would seem, to make sure that his only fellow-traveller was asleep; and, when satisfied on that point, he had at once withdrawn.

The clergyman leaped to his feet. The extreme of terror had given place to a reaction of foolhardy daring. He reflected that the rattle of the flying train concealed all other sounds, and determined, come what might, to return the visit he had just received. Divesting himself of his cloak, which might have interfered with the freedom of his action, he entered the lavatory and paused to listen. As he had expected, there was nothing to be heard above the roar of the train's progress; and laying his hand on the door at the farther side, he proceeded cautiously to draw it back for about six inches. Then he stopped, and could not contain an ejaculation of surprise.

John Vandeleur wore a fur travelling cap with lappets to protect his ears; and this may have combined with the sound of the express to keep him in ignorance of what was going forward. It is certain, at least, that he did not raise his head, but continued without interruption to pursue his strange employment. Between his feet stood an open hat-box; in one hand he held the sleeve of his sealskin great-coat; in the other a formidable knife, with which he had just slit up the lining of the sleeve. Mr Rolles had read of persons carrying money in a belt; and as he had no acquaintance with any but cricket-belts, he had never been able rightly to conceive how this was managed. But here was a stranger thing before his eyes; for John Vandeleur, it appeared, carried diamonds in the lining of his sleeve; and even as the young clergyman gazed, he could see one glittering brilliant drop after another into the hat-box.

He stood riveted to the spot, following this unusual business with his eyes. The diamonds were, for the most part, small, and not easily distinguishable either in shape or fire. Suddenly the Dictator appeared to find a difficulty; he employed both hands and stooped over his task; but it was not until after considerable manoeuvring that he extricated a large tiara of diamonds from the lining, and held it up for some seconds' examination before he placed it with the others in the hat-box. The tiara was a ray of light to Mr Rolles; he immediately recognised it for a part of the treasure stolen from Harry Hartley by the loiterer. There was no room for mistake; it was exactly as the detective had described it; there were the ruby stars, with a great emerald in the centre; there were the interlacing crescents; and there were the pear-shaped pendants, each a single stone, which gave a special value to Lady Vandeleur's tiara.

Mr Rolles was hugely relieved. The Dictator was as deeply in the affair as he was; neither could tell tales upon the other. In the first glow of happiness, the clergyman suffered a deep sigh to escape him; and as his bosom had become choked and his throat dry during his previous suspense, the sigh was followed by a cough.

Mr Vandeleur looked up; his face contracted with the blackest and most deadly passion; his eyes opened widely and his under jaw dropped in an astonishment that was upon the brink of fury. By an instinctive movement he had covered the hat-box with the coat. For half a minute the two men stared upon each other in silence. It was not a long interval, but it sufficed for Mr Rolles; he was one of those who think swiftly on dangerous occasions; he decided on a course of action of a singularly daring nature; and although he felt he was setting his life upon the hazard, he was the first to break silence.

'I beg your pardon,' said he.

The Dictator shivered slightly, and when he spoke his voice was hoarse.

'What do you want here?' he asked.

'I take a particular interest in diamonds,' replied Mr Rolles, with an air of perfect self-possession. 'Two connoisseurs should be acquainted. I have here a trifle of my own which may perhaps serve for an introduction.'

And so saying, he quietly took the case from his pocket,

showed the Rajah's Diamond to the Dictator for an instant, and replaced it in security.

'It was once your brother's,' he added.

John Vandeleur continued to regard him with a look of almost painful amazement; but he neither spoke nor moved.

'I was pleased to observe,' resumed the young man, 'that we have gems from the same collection.'

The Dictator's surprise overpowered him.

'I beg your pardon,' he said; 'I begin to perceive that I am growing old! I am positively not prepared for little incidents like this. But set my mind at rest upon one point: do my eyes deceive me, or are you indeed a parson?'

'I am in holy orders,' answered Mr Rolles.

'Well,' cried the other, 'as long as I live I will never hear another word against the cloth!'

'You flatter me,' said Mr Rolles.

'Pardon me,' replied Vandeleur; 'pardon me, young man. You are no coward, but it still remains to be seen whether you are not the worst of fools. Perhaps,' he continued, leaning back upon his seat, 'perhaps you would oblige me with a few particulars. I must suppose you had some object in the stupefying impudence of your proceedings, and I confess I have a curiosity to know it.'

'It is very simple,' replied the clergyman; 'it proceeds from my great inexperience of life.'

'I shall be glad to be persuaded,' answered Vandeleur.

Whereupon Mr Rolles told him the whole story of his connection with the Rajah's Diamond, from the time he found it in Raeburn's garden to the time when he left London in the Flying Scotchman. He added a brief sketch of his feelings and thoughts during the journey, and concluded in these words:-

'When I recognised the tiara I knew we were in the same attitude toward Society, and this inspired me with a hope, which I trust you will say was not ill-founded, that you might become in some sense my partner in the difficulties and, of course, the profits of my situation. To one of your special knowledge and obviously great experience the negotiation of the diamond would give but little trouble, while to me it was a matter of impossibility. On the other part, I judged that I might lose nearly as much by cutting the diamond, and that not improbably with an unskilful hand, as might enable me to pay you with proper generosity for your assistance. The subject was a delicate one to broach; and perhaps I fell short in delicacy. But I must ask you to remember that for me the situation was a new one, and I was entirely unacquainted with the etiquette in use. I believe without vanity that I could have married or baptized you in a very acceptable manner; but every man has his own aptitudes, and this sort of bargain was not among the list of my accomplishments.'

'I do not wish to flatter you,' replied Vandeleur; 'but upon my word, you have an unusual disposition for a life of crime. You have more accomplishments than you imagine; and though I have encountered a number of rogues in different quarters of the world, I never met with one so unblushing as yourself. Cheer up, Mr Rolles, you are in the right profession at last! As for helping you, you may command me as you will. I have only a day's business in Edinburgh on a little matter for my brother; and once that is concluded, I return to Paris, where I usually reside. If you please, you may accompany me thither. And before the end of a month I believe I shall have brought your little business to a satisfactory conclusion.'

II

Francis Scrymgeour, a clerk in the Bank of Scotland at Edinburgh, had attained the age of twenty-five in a sphere of quiet, creditable, and domestic life. His mother died while he was young; but his father, a man of sense and probity, had given him an excellent education at school, and brought him up at home to orderly and frugal habits. Francis, who was of a docile and affectionate disposition, profited by these advantages with

210

zeal, and devoted himself heart and soul to his employment. A walk upon Saturday afternoon, an occasional dinner with members of his family, and a yearly tour of a fortnight in the Highlands or even on the continent of Europe, were his principal distractions, and he grew rapidly in favour with his superiors, and enjoyed already a salary of nearly two hundred pounds a year, with the prospect of an ultimate advance to almost double that amount. Few young men were more contented, few more willing and laborious than Francis Scrymgeour. Sometimes at night, when he had read the daily paper, he would play upon the flute to amuse his father, for whose qualities he entertained a great respect.

One day he received a note from a well-known firm of Writers to the Signet, requesting the favour of an immediate interview with him. The letter was marked 'Private and Confidential,' and had been addressed to him at the bank, instead of at home – two unusual circumstances which made him obey the summons with the more alacrity. The senior member of the firm, a man of much austerity of manner, made him gravely welcome, requested him to take a seat, and proceeded to explain the matter in hand in the picked expressions of a veteran man of business. A person, who must remain nameless, but of whom the lawyer had every reason to think well – a man, in short, of some station in the country – desired to make Francis an annual allowance of five hundred pounds. The capital was to be placed under the control of the lawyer's firm and two trustees who must also remain anonymous. There were conditions annexed to this liberality, but he was of opinion that his new client would find nothing either excessive or dishonourable in the terms; and he repeated these two words with emphasis, as though he desired to commit himself to nothing more.

Francis asked their nature.

'The conditions,' said the Writer to the Signet, 'are, as I have twice remarked, neither dishonourable nor excessive. At the same time I cannot conceal from you that they are most unusual.

Indeed, the whole case is very much out of our way; and I should certainly have refused it had it not been for the reputation of the gentleman who entrusted it to my care, and, let me add, Mr Scrymgeour, the interest I have been led to take in yourself by many complimentary and, I have no doubt, well-deserved reports.'

Francis entreated him to be more specific.

'You cannot picture my uneasiness as to these conditions,' he said.

'They are two,' replied the lawyer, 'only two; and the sum, as you will remember, is five hundred a year – and unburdened, I forgot to add, unburdened.'

And the lawyer raised his eyebrows at him with solemn gusto.

'The first,' he resumed, 'is of remarkable simplicity. You must be in Paris by the afternoon of Sunday, the 15th; there you will find, at the box-office of the Comédie Française, a ticket for admission taken in your name and waiting you. You are requested to sit out the whole performance in the seat provided, and that is all.'

'I should certainly have preferred a week-day,' replied Francis. 'But, after all, once in a way –'

'And in Paris, my dear sir,' added the lawyer soothingly. 'I believe I am something of a precisian myself, but upon such a consideration, and in Paris, I should not hesitate an instant.'

And the pair laughed pleasantly together.

'The other is of more importance,' continued the Writer to the Signet. 'It regards your marriage. My client, taking a deep interest in your welfare, desires to advise you absolutely in the choice of a wife. Absolutely, you understand,' he repeated.

'Let us be more explicit, if you please,' returned Francis. 'Am I to marry anyone, maid or widow, black or white, whom this invisible person chooses to propose?'

'I was to assure you that suitability of age and position should be a principle with your benefactor,' replied the lawyer. 'As to race, I confess the difficulty had not occurred to me, and I failed to inquire; but if you like I will make a note of it at once, and advise you on the earliest opportunity.'

'Sir,' said Francis, 'it remains to be seen whether this whole affair is not a most unworthy fraud. The circumstances are inexplicable – I had almost said incredible; and until I see a little more daylight, and some plausible motive, I confess I should be very sorry to put a hand to the transaction. I appeal to you in this difficulty for information. I must learn what is at the bottom of it all. If you do not know, cannot guess, or are not at liberty to tell me, I shall take my hat and go back to my bank as I came.'

'I do not know,' answered the lawyer, 'but I have an excellent guess. Your father, and no one else, is at the root of this apparently unnatural business.'

'My father!' cried Francis, in extreme disdain. 'Worthy man, I know every thought of his mind, every penny of his fortune!'

'You misinterpret my words,' said the lawyer. 'I do not refer to Mr Scrymgeour, senior; for he is not your father. When he and his wife came to Edinburgh, you were already nearly one year old, and you had not yet been three months in their care. The secret has been well kept; but such is the fact. Your father is unknown, and I say again that I believe him to be the original of the offers I am charged at present to transmit to you.'

It would be impossible to exaggerate the astonishment of Francis Scrymgeour at this unexpected information. He pled this confusion to the lawyer.

'Sir,' said he, 'after a piece of news so startling, you must grant me some hours for thought. You shall know this evening what conclusion I have reached.'

The lawyer commended his prudence; and Francis, excusing himself upon some pretext at the bank, took a long walk into the country, and fully considered the different steps and aspects of the case. A pleasant sense of his own importance rendered him the more deliberate; but the issue was from the first not doubtful. His whole carnal man leaned irresistibly towards the five hundred a year, and the strange conditions with which it was burdened;

he discovered in his heart an invincible repugnance to the name of Scrymgeour, which he had never hitherto disliked; he began to despise the narrow and unromantic interests of his former life; and when once his mind was fairly made up, he walked with a new feeling of strength and freedom, and nourished himself with the gayest anticipations.

He said but a word to the lawyer, and immediately received a cheque for two quarters' arrears; for the allowance was ante-dated from the first of January. With this in his pocket, he walked home. The flat in Scotland Street looked mean in his eyes; his nostrils, for the first time, rebelled against the odour of broth; and he observed little defects of manner in his adoptive father which filled him with surprise and almost with disgust. The next day, he determined, should see him on his way to Paris.

In that city, where he arrived long before the appointed date, he put up at a modest hotel frequented by English and Italians, and devoted himself to improvement in the French tongue; for this purpose he had a master twice a week, entered into conversation with loiterers in the Champs Elysées, and nightly frequented the theatre. He had his whole toilette fashionably renewed; and was shaved and had his hair dressed every morning by a barber in a neighbouring street. This gave him something of a foreign air, and seemed to wipe off the reproach of his past years.

At length, on the Saturday afternoon, he betook himself to the box-office of the theatre in the Rue Richelieu. No sooner had he mentioned his name than the clerk produced the order in an envelope of which the address was scarcely dry.

'It has been taken this moment,' said the clerk.

'Indeed!' said Francis. 'May I ask what the gentleman was like?'

'Your friend is easy to describe,' replied the official.

'He is old and strong and beautiful, with white hair and a sabre-cut across his face. You cannot fail to recognise so marked a person.'

'No, indeed,' returned Francis; 'and I thank you for your politeness.'

'He cannot yet be far distant,' added the clerk. 'If you make haste you might still overtake him.'

Francis did not wait to be twice told; he ran precipitately from the theatre into the middle of the street and looked in all directions. More than one white-haired man was within sight; but though he overtook each of them in succession, all wanted the sabre-cut. For nearly half-an-hour he tried one street after another in the neighbourhood, until at length, recognising the folly of continued search, he started on a walk to compose his agitated feelings; for this proximity of an encounter with him to whom he could not doubt he owed the day had profoundly moved the young man.

It chanced that his way lay up the Rue Drouot and thence up the Rue des Martyrs; and chance, in this case, served him better than all the forethought in the world. For on the outer boulevard he saw two men in earnest colloquy upon a seat. One was dark, young, and handsome, secularly dressed, but with an indelible clerical stamp; the other answered in every particular to the description given him by the clerk. Francis felt his heart beat high in his bosom; he knew he was now about to hear the voice of his father; and, making a wide circuit, he noiselessly took his place behind the couple in question, who were too much interested in their talk to observe much else. As Francis had expected, the conversation was conducted in the English language.

'Your suspicions begin to annoy me, Rolles,' said the older man. 'I tell you I am doing my utmost; a man cannot lay his hand on millions in a moment. Have I not taken you up, a mere stranger, out of pure good-will? Are you not living largely on my bounty?'

'On your advances, Mr Vandeleur,' corrected the other.

'Advances, if you choose; and interest instead of good-will, if you prefer it,' returned Vandeleur angrily. 'I am not here to pick expressions. Business is business: and your business, let me remind you, is too muddy for such airs. Trust me, or leave me alone and find some one else; but let us have an end, for God's sake, of your jeremiads.'

'I am beginning to learn the world,' replied the other, 'and I see that you have every reason to play me false, and not one to deal honestly. I am not here to pick expressions either; you wish the diamond for yourself; you know you do – you dare not deny it. Have you not already forged my name, and searched my lodging in my absence? I understand the cause of your delays; you are lying in wait; you are the diamond hunter, forsooth; and sooner or later, by fair means or foul, you'll lay your hands upon it. I tell you, it must stop; push me much further and I promise you a surprise.'

'It does not become you to use threats,' returned Vandeleur. 'Two can play at that. My brother is here in Paris; the police are on the alert; and if you persist in wearying me with your cater-wauling, I will arrange a little astonishment for you, Mr Rolles. But mine shall be once and for all. Do you understand, or would you prefer me to tell it you in Hebrew? There is an end to all things, and you have come to the end of my patience. Tuesday, at seven; not a day, not an hour sooner, not the least part of a second, if it were to save your life. And if you do not choose to wait, you may go to the bottomless pit for me, and welcome.'

And so saying, the Dictator arose from the bench, and marched off in the direction of Montmartre, shaking his head and swinging his cane with a most furious air; while his companion remained where he was, in an attitude of great rejection.

Francis was at the pitch of surprise and horror; his sentiments had been shocked to the last degree; the hopeful tenderness with which he had taken his place upon the bench was transformed into repulsion and despair; old Mr Scrymgeour, he reflected, was a far more kindly and creditable parent than this dangerous and violent intriguer; but he retained his presence of mind and suffered not a moment to elapse before he was on the trail of the Dictator.

That gentleman's fury carried him forward at a brisk pace, and he was so completely occupied in his angry thoughts that he never so much as cast a look behind him till he reached his own door.

His house stood high up in the Rue Lepic, commanding a view of all Paris and enjoying the pure air of the heights. It was two storeys high, with green blinds and shutters; and all the windows looking on the street were hermetically closed. Tops of trees showed over the high garden wall, and the wall was protected by *chevaux-de-frise*. The Dictator paused a moment while he searched his pocket for a key; and then, opening a gate, disappeared within the enclosure.

Francis looked about him; the neighbourhood was very lonely, the house isolated in its garden. It seemed as if his observation must here come to an abrupt end. A second glance, however, showed him a tall house next door presenting a gable to the garden, and in this gable a single window. He passed to the front and saw a ticket offering unfurnished lodgings by the month; and, on inquiry, the room which commanded the Dictator's garden proved to be one of those to let. Francis did not hesitate a moment; he took the room, paid an advance upon the rent, and returned to his hotel to seek his baggage.

The old man with the sabre-cut might or might not be his father; he might or he might not be upon the true scent; but he was certainly on the edge of an exciting mystery, and he promised himself that he would not relax his observation until he had got to the bottom of the secret.

From the window of his new apartment Francis Scrymgeour commanded a complete view into the garden of the house with the green blinds. Immediately below him a very comely chestnut with wide boughs sheltered a pair of rustic tables where people might dine in the height of summer. On all sides save one a dense vegetation concealed the soil; but there, between the tables and the house, he saw a patch of gravel walk leading from the verandah to the garden-gate. Studying the place from between the boards of the Venetian shutters, which he durst not open for fear of attracting attention, Francis observed but little to indicate the manners of the inhabitants, and that little argued no more than a close reserve and a taste for solitude. The garden was conventual, the house had the air of a prison. The green blinds were all drawn down upon the outside; the door into the verandah was closed; the garden, as far as he could see it, was left entirely to itself in the evening sunshine. A modest curl of smoke from a single chimney alone testified to the presence of living people.

In order that he might not be entirely idle, and to give a certain colour to his way of life, Francis had purchased Euclid's Geometry in French, which he set himself to copy and translate on the top of his portmanteau and seated on the floor against the wall; for he was equally without chair or table. From time to time he would rise and cast a glance into the enclosure of the house with the green blinds; but the windows remained obstinately closed and the garden empty.

Only late in the evening did anything occur to reward his continued attention. Between nine and ten the sharp tinkle of a bell aroused him from a fit of dozing; and he sprang to his observatory in time to hear an important noise of locks being opened and bars removed, and to see Mr Vandeleur, carrying a lantern and clothed in a flowing robe of black velvet with a skull-cap to match, issue from under the verandah and proceed leisurely towards the garden gate. The sound of bolts and bars was then repeated; and a moment after Francis perceived the Dictator escorting into the house, in the mobile light of the lantern, an individual of the lowest and most despicable appearance.

Half-an-hour afterwards the visitor was reconducted to the street; and Mr Vandeleur, setting his light upon one of the rustic tables, finished a cigar with great deliberation under the foliage of the chestnut. Francis, peering through a clear space among the leaves, was able to follow his gestures as he threw away the ash or enjoyed a copious inhalation; and beheld a cloud upon the old man's brow and a forcible action of the lips, which testified to some deep and probably painful train of thought. The cigar was already almost at an end, when the voice of a young girl was heard suddenly crying the hour from the interior of the house.

'In a moment,' replied John Vandeleur.

And, with that, he threw away the stump and, taking up the lantern, sailed away under the verandah for the night. As soon as the door was closed, absolute darkness fell upon the house; Francis might try his eyesight as much as he pleased, he could not detect so much as a single chink of light below a blind; and he concluded, with great good sense, that the bed-chambers were all upon the other side.

Early the next morning (for he was early awake after an uncomfortable night upon the floor), he saw cause to adopt a different explanation. The blinds rose, one after another, by means of a spring in the interior, and disclosed steel shutters such as we see on the front of shops; these in their turns were rolled up by a similar contrivance; and for the space of about an hour, the chambers were left open to the morning air. At the end of that time Mr Vandeleur, with his own hand, once more closed the shutters and replaced the blinds from within.

While Francis was still marvelling at these precautions, the door opened and a young girl came forth to look about her in the garden. It was not two minutes before she re-entered the house, but even in that short time he saw enough to convince him that she possessed the most unusual attractions. His curiosity was not only highly excited by this incident, but his spirits were improved to a still more notable degree. The alarming manners and more than equivocal life of his father ceased from that moment to prey upon his mind; from that moment he embraced his new family with ardour; and whether the young lady should prove his sister or his wife, he felt convinced she was an angel in disguise. So much was this the case that he was seized with a sudden horror when he reflected how little he really knew, and how possible it was that he had followed the wrong person when he followed Mr Vandeleur.

The porter, whom he consulted, could afford him little information; but, such as it was, it had a mysterious and questionable sound. The person next door was an English gentleman of extraordinary wealth, and proportionately eccentric in his tastes and habits. He possessed great collections, which he kept in the house beside him; and it was to protect these that he had fitted the place with steel shutters, elaborate fastenings, and *chevaux-de-frise* along the garden wall. He lived much alone, in spite of some strange visitors with whom, it seemed, he had business to transact; and there was no one else in the house, except Mademoiselle and an old woman servant.

'Is Mademoiselle his daughter?' inquired Francis.

'Certainly,' replied the porter. 'Mademoiselle is the daughter of the house; and strange it is to see how she is made to work. For all his riches, it is she who goes to market; and every day in the week you may see her going by with a basket on her arm.'

'And the collections?' asked the other.

'Sir,' said the man, 'they are immensely valuable. More I cannot tell you. Since M. de Vandeleur's arrival no one in the quarter has so much as passed the door.'

'Suppose not,' returned Francis, 'you must surely have some notion what these famous galleries contain. Is it pictures, silks, statues, jewels, or what?'

'My faith, sir,' said the fellow with a shrug, 'it might be carrots, and still I could not tell you. How should I know? The house is kept like a garrison, as you perceive.'

And then as Francis was returning disappointed to his room, the porter called him back.

'I have just remembered, sir,' said he. 'M. de Vandeleur has been in all parts of the world, and I once heard the old woman declare that he had brought many diamonds back with him. If that be the truth, there must be a fine show behind those shutters.'

By an early hour on Sunday Francis was in his place at the

theatre. The seat which had been taken for him was only two or three numbers from the left-hand side, and directly opposite one of the lower boxes. As the seat had been specially chosen there was doubtless something to be learned from its position; and he judged by an instinct that the box upon his right was, in some way or other, to be connected with the drama in which he ignorantly played a part. Indeed, it was so situated that its occupants could safely observe him from beginning to end of the piece, if they were so minded; while, profiting by the depth, they could screen themselves sufficiently well from any counter-examination on his side. He promised himself not to leave it for a moment out of sight; and whilst he scanned the rest of the theatre, or made a show of attending to the business of the stage, he always kept a corner of an eye upon the empty box.

The second act had been some time in progress, and was even drawing towards a close, when the door opened and two persons entered and ensconced themselves in the darkest of the shade. Francis could hardly control his emotion. It was Mr Vandeleur and his daughter. The blood came and went in his arteries and veins with stunning activity; his ears sang; his head turned. He dared not look lest he should awake suspicion; his play-bill, which he kept reading from end to end and over and over again, turned from white to red before his eyes; and when he cast a glance upon the stage, it seemed incalculably far away, and he found the voices and gestures of the actors to the last degree impertinent and absurd.

From time to time he risked a momentary look in the direction which principally interested him; and once at least he felt certain that his eyes encountered those of the young girl. A shock passed over his body, and he saw all the colours of the rainbow. What would he not have given to overhear what passed between the Vandeleurs? What would he not have given for the courage to take up his opera-glass and steadily inspect their attitude and expression? There, for aught he knew, his whole life was being decided – and he not able to interfere, not able even to follow the debate, but condemned to sit and suffer where he was, in impotent anxiety.

At last the act came to an end. The curtain fell, and the people around him began to leave their places for the interval. It was only natural that he should follow their example; and if he did so, it was not only natural but necessary that he should pass immediately in front of the box in question. Summoning all his courage, but keeping his eyes lowered, Francis drew near the spot. His progress was slow, for the old gentleman before him moved with incredible deliberation, wheezing as he went. What was he to do? Should he address the Vandeleurs by name as he went by? Should he take the flower from his buttonhole and throw it into the box? Should he raise his face and direct one long and affectionate look upon the lady who was either his sister or his betrothed? As he found himself thus struggling among so many alternatives, he had a vision of his old equable existence in the bank, and was assailed by a thought of regret for the past.

By this time he had arrived directly opposite the box; and although he was still undetermined what to do or whether to do anything, he turned his head and lifted his eyes. No sooner had he done so than he uttered a cry of disappointment and remained rooted to the spot. The box was empty. During his slow advance Mr Vandeleur and his daughter had quietly slipped away.

A polite person in his rear reminded him that he was stopping the path; and he moved on again with mechanical footsteps, and suffered the crowd to carry him unresisting out of the theatre. Once in the street, the pressure ceasing, he came to a halt, and the cool night air speedily restored him to the possession of his faculties. He was surprised to find that his head ached violently, and that he remembered not one word of the two acts which he had witnessed. As the excitement wore away, it was succeeded by an overweening appetite for sleep, and he hailed a cab and drove to his lodging in a state of extreme exhaustion and some disgust of life.

Next morning he lay in wait for Miss Vandeleur on her road to market, and by eight o'clock beheld her stepping down a lane. She was simply, and even poorly, attired; but in the carriage of her head and body there was something flexible and noble that would have lent distinction to the meanest toilette. Even her basket, so aptly did she carry it, became her like an ornament. It seemed to Francis, as he slipped into a doorway, that the sunshine followed and the shadows fled before her as she walked; and he was conscious, for the first time, of a bird singing in a cage above the lane.

He suffered her to pass the doorway, and then, coming forth once more, addressed her by name from behind.

'Miss Vandeleur,' said he.

She turned and, when she saw who he was, became deadly pale.

'Pardon me,' he continued: 'Heaven knows I had no will to startle you; and, indeed, there should be nothing startling in the presence of one who wishes you so well as I do. And, believe me, I am acting rather from necessity than choice. We have many things in common, and I am sadly in the dark. There is much that I should be doing, and my hands are tied. I do not know even what to feel, nor who are my friends and enemies.'

She found her voice with an effort.

'I do not know who you are,' she said.

'Ah, yes! Miss Vandeleur, you do,' returned Francis; 'better than I do myself. Indeed, it is on that, above all, that I seek light. Tell me what you know,' he pleaded. 'Tell me who I am, who you are, and how our destinies are intermixed. Give me a little help with my life, Miss Vandeleur – only a word or two to guide me, only the name of my father, if you will – and I shall be grateful and content.'

'I will not attempt to deceive you,' she replied. 'I know who you are, but I am not at liberty to say.'

'Tell me, at least, that you have forgiven my presumption, and I shall wait with all the patience I have,' he said. 'If I am not to know, I must do without. It is cruel, but I can bear more upon a push. Only do not add to my troubles the thought that I have made an enemy of you.'

'You did only what was natural,' she said, 'and I have nothing to forgive you. Farewell.'

'Is it to be *farewell*?' he asked.

'Nay, that I do not know myself,' she answered. 'Farewell for the present, if you like.'

And with these words she was gone.

Francis returned to his lodging in a state of considerable commotion of mind. He made the most trifling progress with his Euclid for that forenoon, and was more often at the window than at his improvised writing-table. But beyond seeing the return of Miss Vandeleur, and the meeting between her and her father, who was smoking a Trichinopoli cigar in the verandah, there was nothing notable in the neighbourhood of the house with the green blinds before the time of the midday meal. The young man hastily allayed his appetite in a neighbouring restaurant, and returned with the speed of unallayed curiosity to the house in the Rue Lepic. A mounted servant was leading a saddle-horse to and fro before the garden wall; and the porter of Francis's lodging was smoking a pipe against the door-post, absorbed in contemplation of the livery and the steeds.

'Look!' he cried to the young man, 'what fine cattle! what an elegant costume! They belong to the brother of M. de Vandeleur, who is now within upon a visit. He is a great man, a general, in your country; and you doubtless know him well by reputation.'

'I confess,' returned Francis, 'that I have never heard of General Vandeleur before. We have many officers of that grade, and my pursuits have been exclusively civil.'

'It is he,' replied the porter, 'who lost the great diamond of the Indies. Of that at least you must have read often in the papers.'

As soon as Francis could disengage himself from the porter he ran upstairs and hurried to the window. Immediately below the clear space in the chestnut leaves, the two gentlemen were seated in conversation over a cigar. The General, a red, military-looking man, offered some traces of a family resemblance to his brother; he had something of the same features, something, although very little, of the same free and powerful carriage; but he was older, smaller, and more common in air; his likeness was that of a caricature, and he seemed altogether a poor and debile being by the side of the Dictator.

They spoke in tones so low, leaning over the table with every appearance of interest, that Francis could catch no more than a word or two on an occasion. For as little as he heard, he was convinced that the conversation turned upon himself and his own career; several times the name of Scrymgeour reached his ear, for it was easy to distinguish, and still more frequently he fancied he could distinguish the name Francis.

At length the General, as if in a hot anger, broke forth into several violent exclamations.

'Francis Vandeleur!' he cried, accentuating the last word. 'Francis Vandeleur, I tell you.'

The Dictator made a movement of his whole body, half affirmative, half contemptuous, but his answer was inaudible to the young man.

Was he the Francis Vandeleur in question? he wondered. Were they discussing the name under which he was to be married? Or was the whole affair a dream and a delusion of his own conceit and self-absorption?

After another interval of inaudible talk, dissension seemed again to arise between the couple underneath the chestnut, and again the General raised his voice angrily so as to be audible to Francis.

'My wife?' he cried. 'I have done with my wife for good. I will not hear her name. I am sick of her very name.'

And he swore aloud and beat the table with his fist.

The Dictator appeared, by his gestures, to pacify him after a paternal fashion; and a little after he conducted him to the garden-gate. The pair shook hands affectionately enough; but as soon as the door had closed behind his visitor, John Vandeleur fell into a fit of laughter which sounded unkindly and even devilish in the ears of Francis Scrymgeour.

So another day had passed, and little more learnt. But the young man remembered that the morrow was Tuesday, and promised himself some curious discoveries; all might be well, or all might be ill; he was sure, at least, to glean some curious information, and, perhaps, by good luck, get at the heart of the mystery which surrounded his father and his family.

As the hour of the dinner drew near many preparations were made in the garden of the house with the green blinds. That table which was partly visible to Francis through the chestnut leaves was destined to serve as a sideboard, and carried relays of plates and the materials for salad: the other, which was almost entirely concealed, had been set apart for the diners, and Francis could catch glimpses of white cloth and silver plate.

Mr Rolles arrived, punctual to the minute; he looked like a man upon his guard, and spoke low and sparingly. The Dictator, on the other hand, appeared to enjoy an unusual flow of spirits; his laugh, which was youthful and pleasant to hear, sounded frequently from the garden; by the modulation and the changes of his voice it was obvious that he told many droll stories and imitated the accents of a variety of different nations; and before he and the young clergyman had finished their vermouth all feeling of distrust was at an end, and they were talking together like a pair of school companions.

At length Miss Vandeleur made her appearance, carrying the soup-tureen. Mr Rolles ran to offer her assistance which she laughingly refused; and there was an interchange of pleasantries among the trio which seemed to have reference to this primitive manner of waiting by one of the company.

'One is more at one's ease,' Mr Vandeleur was heard to declare.

Next moment they were all three in their places, and Francis could see as little as he could hear of what passed. But the dinner seemed to go merrily; there was a perpetual babble of voices and sound of knives and forks below the chestnut; and Francis, who had no more than a roll to gnaw, was affected with envy by the comfort and deliberation of the meal. The party lingered over one dish after another, and then over a delicate dessert, with a bottle of old wine carefully uncorked by the hand of the Dictator himself. As it began to grow dark a lamp was set upon the table and a couple of candles on the sideboard; for the night was perfectly pure, starry, and windless. Light overflowed besides from the door and window in the verandah, so that the garden was fairly illuminated and the leaves twinkled in the darkness.

For perhaps the tenth time Miss Vandeleur entered the house; and on this occasion she returned with the coffee-tray, which she placed upon the sideboard. At the same moment her father rose from his seat.

'The coffee is my province,' Francis heard him say.

And next moment he saw his supposed father standing by the sideboard in the light of the candles.

Talking over his shoulder all the while, Mr Vandeleur poured out two cups of the brown stimulant, and then, by a rapid act of prestidigitation, emptied the contents of a tiny phial into the smaller of the two. The thing was so swiftly done that even Francis, who looked straight into his face, had hardly time to perceive the movement before it was completed. And next instant, and still laughing, Mr Vandeleur had turned again towards the table with a cup in either hand.

'Ere we have done with this,' said he, 'we may expect our famous Hebrew.'

It would be impossible to depict the confusion and distress of Francis Scrymgeour. He saw foul play going forward before his eyes, and he felt bound to interfere, but knew not how. It might be a mere pleasantry, and then how should he look if he were to offer an unnecessary warning? Or again, if it were serious, the criminal might be his own father, and then how should he not lament if he were to bring ruin on the author of his days? For the first time he became conscious of his own position as a spy. To wait inactive at such a juncture and with such a conflict of sentiments in his bosom was to suffer the most acute torture; he clung to the bars of the shutters, his heart beat fast and with irregularity, and he felt a strong sweat break forth upon his body. Several minutes passed.

He seemed to perceive the conversation die away and grow less and less in vivacity and volume; but still no sign of any alarming or even notable event.

Suddenly the ring of a glass breaking was followed by a faint and dull sound, as of a person who should have fallen forward with his head upon the table. At the same moment a piercing scream rose from the garden.

'What have you done?' cried Miss Vandeleur. 'He is dead!'

The Dictator replied in a violent whisper, so strong and sibilant that every word was audible to the watcher at the window.

'Silence!' said Mr Vandeleur; 'the man is as well as I am. Take him by the heels whilst I carry him by the shoulders.'

Francis heard Miss Vandeleur break forth into a passion of tears.

'Do you hear what I say?' resumed the Dictator, in the same tones. 'Or do you wish to quarrel with me? I give you your choice, Miss Vandeleur.'

There was another pause, and the Dictator spoke again.

'Take that man by the heels,' he said. 'I must have him brought into the house. If I were a little younger, I could help myself against the world. But now that years and dangers are upon me and my hands are weakened, I must turn to you for aid.'

'It is a crime,' replied the girl.

'I am your father,' said Mr Vandeleur.

This appeal seemed to produce its effect. A scuffling noise followed upon the gravel, a chair was overset, and then Francis saw the father and daughter stagger across the walk and disappear under the verandah, bearing the inanimate body of Mr Rolles embraced about the knees and shoulders. The young clergyman was limp and pallid, and his head rolled upon his shoulders at every step.

Was he alive or dead? Francis, in spite of the Dictator's declaration, inclined to the latter view. A great crime had been committed; a great calamity had fallen upon the inhabitants of the house with the green blinds. To his surprise, Francis found all horror for the deed swallowed up in sorrow for a girl and an old man whom he judged to be in the height of peril. A tide of generous feeling swept into his heart; he, too, would help his father against man and mankind, against fate and justice; and casting open the shutters he closed his eyes and threw himself with outstretched arms into the foliage of the chestnut.

Branch after branch slipped from his grasp or broke under his weight; then he caught a stalwart bough under his armpit, and hung suspended for a second; and then he let himself drop and fell heavily against the table. A cry of alarm from the house warned him that his entrance had not been effected unobserved. He recovered himself with a stagger, and in three bounds crossed the intervening space and stood before the door in the verandah.

In a small apartment, carpeted with matting and surrounded by glazed cabinets full of rare and costly curios, Mr Vandeleur was stooping over the body of Mr Rolles. He raised himself as Francis entered, and there was an instantaneous passage of hands. It was the business of a second; as fast as an eye can wink the thing was done; the young man had not the time to be sure, but it seemed to him as if the Dictator had taken something from the curate's breast, looked at it for the least fraction of time as it lay in his hand, and then suddenly and swiftly passed it to his daughter.

All this was over while Francis had still one foot upon the threshold, and the other raised in air. The next instant he was on his knees to Mr Vandeleur.

'Father!' he cried. 'Let me too help you. I will do what you wish and ask no questions; I will obey you with my life; treat me as a son, and you will find I have a son's devotion.'

A deplorable explosion of oaths was the Dictator's first reply.

'Son and father?' he cried. 'Father and son? What d—d unnatural comedy is all this? How do you come in my garden? What do you want? And who, in God's name, are you?'

Francis, with a stunned and shamefaced aspect, got upon his feet again, and stood in silence.

Then a light seemed to break upon Mr Vandeleur, and he laughed aloud.

'I see,' cried he. 'It is the Scrymgeour. Very well, Mr Scrymgeour. Let me tell you in a few words how you stand. You have entered my private residence by force, or perhaps by fraud, but certainly with no encouragement from me; and you come at a moment of some annoyance, a guest having fainted at my table, to besiege me with your protestations. You are no son of mine. You are my brother's bastard by a fishwife, if you want to know. I regard you with an indifference closely bordering on aversion; and from what I now see of your conduct, I judge your mind to be exactly suitable to your exterior. I recommend you these mortifying reflections for your leisure; and, in the meantime, let me beseech you to rid us of your presence. If I were not occupied,' added the Dictator, with a terrifying oath, 'I should give you the unholiest drubbing ere you went!'

Francis listened in profound humiliation. He would have fled had it been possible; but as he had no means of leaving the residence into which he had so unfortunately penetrated, he could do no more than stand foolishly where he was.

It was Miss Vandeleur who broke the silence.

'Father,' she said, 'you speak in anger. Mr Scrymgeour may have been mistaken, but he meant well and kindly.'

'Thank you for speaking,' returned the Dictator. 'You remind me of some other observations which I hold it a point of honour to make to Mr Scrymgeour. My brother,' he continued; addressing the young man, 'has been foolish enough to give you an allowance; he was foolish enough and presumptuous enough to propose a match between you and this young lady. You were exhibited to her two nights ago; and I rejoice to tell you that she rejected the idea with disgust. Let me add that I have considerable influence with your father; and it shall not be my fault if you are not beggared of your allowance and sent back to your scrivening ere the week be out.'

The tones of the old man's voice were, if possible, more wounding than his language; Francis felt himself exposed to the most cruel, blighting, and unbearable contempt; his head turned, and he covered his face with his hands, uttering at the same time a tearless sob of agony. But Miss Vandeleur once again interfered in his behalf.

'Mr Scrymgeour,' she said, speaking in clear and even tones, 'you must not be concerned at my father's harsh expressions. I felt no disgust for you; on the contrary, I asked an opportunity to make your better acquaintance. As for what has passed to-night, believe me it has filled my mind with both pity and esteem.'

Just then Mr Rolles made a convulsive movement with his arm, which convinced Francis that he was only drugged, and was beginning to throw off the influence of the opiate. Mr Vandeleur stooped over him and examined his face for an instant.

'Come, come!' cried he, raising his head. 'Let there be an end of this. And since you are so pleased with his conduct, Miss Vandeleur, take a candle and show the bastard out.'

The young lady hastened to obey.

'Thank you,' said Francis, as soon as he was alone with her in the garden. 'I thank you from my soul. This has been the bitterest evening of my life, but it will have always one pleasant recollection.'

'I spoke as I felt,' she replied, 'and in justice to you. It made my heart sorry that you should be so unkindly used.'

By this time they had reached the garden gate; and Miss Vandeleur, having set the candle on the ground, was already unfastening the bolts.

'One word more,' said Francis. 'This is not for the last time – I shall see you again, shall I not?'

'Alas!' she answered. 'You have heard my father. What can I do but obey?'

'Tell me at least that it is not with your consent,' returned Francis; 'tell me that you have no wish to see the last of me.'

'Indeed,' replied she, 'I have none. You seem to me both brave and honest.'

'Then,' said Francis, 'give me a keepsake.'

She paused for a moment, with her hand upon the key; for the various bars and bolts were all undone, and there was nothing left but to open the lock.

'If I agree,' she said, 'will you promise to do as I tell you from point to point?'

'Can you ask?' replied Francis. 'I would do so willingly on your bare word.'

She turned the key and threw open the door.

'Be it so,' said she. 'You do not know what you ask, but be it so. Whatever you hear,' she continued, 'whatever happens, do not return to this house; hurry fast until you reach the lighted and populous quarters of the city; even there be upon your guard. You are in a greater danger than you fancy. Promise me you will not so much as look at my keepsake until you are in a place of safety.'

'I promise,' replied Francis.

She put something loosely wrapped in a handkerchief into the young man's hand; and at the same time with more strength than he could have anticipated, she pushed him into the street.

'Now, run!' she cried.

He heard the door close behind him, and the noise of the bolts being replaced.

'My faith,' said he, 'since I have promised!'

And he took to his heels down the lane that leads into the Rue Ravignan.

He was not fifty paces from the house with the green blinds when the most diabolical outcry suddenly arose out of the stillness of the night. Mechanically he stood still; another passenger followed his example; in the neighbouring floors he saw people crowding to the windows; a conflagration could not have produced more disturbance in this empty quarter. And yet it seemed to be all the work of a single man, roaring between grief and rage, like a lioness robbed of her whelps; and Francis was surprised and alarmed to hear his own name shouted with English imprecations to the wind.

His first movement was to return to the house; his second, as he remembered Miss Vandeleur's advice, to continue his flight with greater expedition than before; and he was in the act of turning to put his thought in action, when the Dictator, bareheaded, bawling aloud, his white hair blowing about his head, shot past him like a ball out of the cannon's mouth, and went careering down the street.

'That was a close shave,' thought Francis to himself. 'What he wants with me, and why he should be so disturbed, I cannot think; but he is plainly not good company for the moment, and I cannot do better than follow Miss Vandeleur's advice.'

So saying, he turned to retrace his steps, thinking to double and descend by the Rue Lepic itself while his pursuer should continue to follow after him on the other line of the street. The plan was ill-devised: as a matter of fact, he should have taken his seat in the nearest café, and waited there until the first heat of the pursuit was over. But besides that Francis had no experience and little natural aptitude for the small war of private life, he was so unconscious of any evil on his part, that he saw nothing to fear beyond a disagreeable interview. And to disagreeable interviews he felt he had already served his apprenticeship that evening; nor could he suppose that Miss Vandeleur had left anything unsaid. Indeed, the young man was sore both in body and mind – the one was all bruised, the other was full of smarting arrows; and he owned to himself that Mr Vandeleur was master of a very deadly tongue.

The thought of his bruises reminded him that he had not only come without a hat, but that his clothes had considerably suffered in his descent through the chestnut. At the first magazine he purchased a cheap wideawake, and had the disorder of his toilet summarily repaired. The keepsake, still rolled in the handkerchief, he thrust in the meanwhile into his trousers pocket.

Not many steps beyond the shop he was conscious of a sudden shock, a hand upon his throat, an infuriated face close to his own, and an open mouth bawling curses in his ear. The Dictator, having found no trace of his quarry, was returning by the other way. Francis was a stalwart young fellow; but he was no match for his adversary whether in strength or skill; and after a few ineffectual struggles he resigned himself entirely to his captor.

'What do you want with me?' said he.

'We will talk of that at home,' returned the Dictator grimly.

And he continued to march the young man up hill in the direction of the house with the green blinds.

But Francis, although he no longer struggled, was only waiting an opportunity to make a bold push for freedom. With a sudden jerk he left the collar of his coat in the hands of Mr Vandeleur, and once more made off at his best speed in the direction of the Boulevards.

The tables were now turned. If the Dictator was the stronger, Francis, in the top of his youth, was the more fleet of foot, and he had soon effected his escape among the crowds. Relieved for a moment, but with a growing sentiment of alarm and wonder in his mind, he walked briskly until he debouched upon the Place de l'Opéra, lit up like day with electric lamps.

'This, at least,' thought he, 'should satisfy Miss Vandeleur.'

And turning to his right along the Boulevards, he entered the Café Americain and ordered some beer. It was both late and early for the majority of the frequenters of the establishment. Only two or three persons, all men, were dotted here and there at separate tables in the hall; and Francis was too much occupied by his own thoughts to observe their presence.

He drew the handkerchief from his pocket. The object wrapped in it proved to be a morocco case, clasped and ornamented in gilt, which opened by means of a spring, and disclosed to the horrified young man a diamond of monstrous bigness and extraordinary brilliancy. The circumstance was so inexplicable, the value of the stone was plainly so enormous, that Francis sat staring into the open casket without movement, without conscious thought, like a man stricken suddenly with idiocy.

A hand was laid upon his shoulder, lightly but firmly, and a quiet voice, which yet had in it the ring of command uttered these words in his ear –

'Close the casket, and compose your face.'

Looking up, he beheld a man, still young, of an urbane and tranquil presence, and dressed with rich simplicity. This personage had risen from a neighbouring table, and, bringing his glass with him, had taken a seat beside Francis.

'Close the casket,' repeated the stranger, 'and put it quietly back into your pocket, where I feel persuaded it should never have been. Try, if you please, to throw off your bewildered air, and act as though I were one of your acquaintances whom you had met by chance. So! Touch glasses with me. That is better. I fear, sir, you must be an amateur.'

And the stranger pronounced these last words with a smile of peculiar meaning, leaned back in his seat and enjoyed a deep inhalation of tobacco.

'For God's sake,' said Francis, 'tell me who you are and what this means? Why I should obey your most unusual suggestions I am sure I know not; but the truth is, I have fallen this evening into so many perplexing adventures, and all I meet conduct themselves so strangely, that I think I must either have gone mad or wandered into another planet. Your face inspires me with confidence; you seem wise, good, and experienced; tell me, for heaven's sake, why you accost me in so odd a fashion?'

'All in due time,' replied the stranger. 'But I have the first hand, and you must begin by telling me how the Rajah's Diamond is in your possession.'

'The Rajah's Diamond!' echoed Francis.

'I would not speak so loud, if I were you,' returned the other. 'But most certainly you have the Rajah's Diamond in your pocket. I have seen and handled it a score of times in Sir Thomas Vandeleur's collection.'

'Sir Thomas Vandeleur! The General! My father!' cried Francis.

The other bowed with gravity. It was a respectful bow, as of a man silently apologising to his equal; and Francis felt relieved and comforted, he scarce knew why. The society of this person did him good; he seemed to touch firm ground; a strong feeling of respect grew up in his bosom, and mechanically he removed his wideawake as though in the presence of a superior.

'I perceive,' said the stranger, 'that your adventures have not all been peaceful. Your collar is torn, your face is scratched, you have a cut upon your temple; you will, perhaps, pardon my curiosity when I ask you to explain how you came by these injuries, and how you happen to have stolen property to an enormous value in your pocket.'

'I must differ from you!' returned Francis hotly. 'I possess no stolen property. And if you refer to the diamond, it was given to me not an hour ago by Miss Vandeleur in the Rue Lepic.'

'By Miss Vandeleur of the Rue Lepic!' repeated the other. 'You interest me more than you suppose. Pray continue.'

'Heavens!' cried Francis.

His memory had made a sudden bound. He had seen Mr. Vandeleur take an article from the breast of his drugged visitor, and that article, he was now persuaded, was a morocco case.

'You have a light?' inquired the stranger.

'Listen,' replied Francis. 'I know not who you are, but I believe you to be worthy of confidence and helpful; I find myself in strange waters; I must have counsel and support, and since you invite me I shall tell you all.'

And he briefly recounted his experiences since the day when he was summoned from the bank by his lawyer.

'Yours is indeed a remarkable history,' said the stranger after the young man had made an end of his narrative; 'and your position is full of difficulty and peril. Many would counsel you to seek out your father, and give the diamond to him; but I have other views. Waiter!' he cried.

The waiter drew near.

'Will you ask the manager to speak with me a moment?' said he; and Francis observed once more, both in his tone and manner, the evidence of a habit of command.

The waiter withdrew, and returned in a moment with the manager, who bowed with obsequious respect.

'What,' said he, 'can I do to serve you?'

'Have the goodness,' replied the stranger, indicating Francis, 'to tell this gentleman my name.'

'You have the honour, sir,' said the functionary, addressing young Scrymgeour, 'to occupy the same table with His Highness Prince Florizel of Bohemia.'

Francis rose with precipitation, and made a grateful reverence to the Prince, who bade him resume his seat.

'I thank you,' said Florizel, once more addressing the functionary; 'I am sorry to have deranged you for so small a matter.'

And he dismissed him with a movement of his hand.

'And now,' added the Prince, turning to Francis, 'give me the diamond.'

Without a word the casket was handed over.

'You have done right,' said Florizel, 'your sentiments have properly inspired you, and you will live to be grateful for the misfortunes of to-night. A man, Mr. Scrymgeour, may fall into a thousand perplexities, but if his heart be upright and his intelligence unclouded, he will issue from them all without dishonour. Let your mind be at rest; your affairs are in my hand; and with the aid of heaven I am strong enough to bring them to a good end. Follow me, if you please, to my carriage.'

So saying the Prince arose and, having left a piece of gold for the waiter, conducted the young man from the café and along the Boulevard to where an unpretentious brougham and a couple of servants out of livery awaited his arrival.

'This carriage,' said he, 'is at your disposal; collect your baggage as rapidly as you can make it convenient, and my servants will conduct you to a villa in the neighbourhood of Paris where you can wait in some degree of comfort until I have had time to arrange your situation. You will find there a pleasant garden, a library of good authors, a cook, a cellar, and some good cigars, which I recommend to your attention. Jérome,' he added, turning to one of the servants, 'you have heard what I say; I leave Mr Scrymgeour in your charge; you will, I know, be careful of my friend.'

Francis uttered some broken phrases of gratitude.

'It will be time enough to thank me,' said the Prince, 'when you are acknowledged by your father and married to Miss Vandeleur.'

And with that the Prince turned away and strolled leisurely in the direction of Montmartre. He hailed the first passing cab, gave an address, and a quarter of an hour afterwards, having discharged the driver some distance lower, he was knocking at Mr Vandeleur's garden gate.

It was opened with singular precautions by the Dictator in person.

'Who are you?' he demanded.

'You must pardon me this late visit, Mr Vandeleur,' replied the Prince.

'Your Highness is always welcome,' returned Mr Vandeleur, stepping back.

The Prince profited by the open space, and without waiting for his host walked right into the house and opened the door of the *salon*. Two people were seated there; one was Miss Vandeleur, who bore the marks of weeping about her eyes, and was still shaken from time to time by a sob; in the other the Prince recognised the young man who had consulted him on literary matters about a month before, in a club smoking-room.

'Good evening, Miss Vandeleur,' said Florizel; 'you look

fatigued. Mr Rolles, I believe? I hope you have profited by the study of Gaboriau, Mr Rolles.'

But the young clergyman's temper was too much embittered for speech; and he contented himself with bowing stiffly, and continued to gnaw his lip.

'To what good wind,' said Mr Vandeleur, following his guest, 'am I to attribute the honour of your Highness's presence?'

'I am come on business,' returned the Prince; 'on business with you; as soon as that is settled I shall request Mr Rolles to accompany me for a walk. Mr Rolles,' he added with severity, 'let me remind you that I have not yet sat down.'

The clergyman sprang to his feet with an apology; whereupon the Prince took an armchair beside the table, handed his hat to Mr Vandeleur, his cane to Mr Rolles, and, leaving them standing and thus menially employed upon his service, spoke as follows:-

'I have come here, as I said, upon business; but, had I come looking for pleasure, I could not have been more displeased with my reception nor more dissatisfied with my company. You, sir,' addressing Mr Rolles, 'you have treated your superior in station with discourtesy; you, Vandeleur, receive me with a smile, but you know right well that your hands are not yet cleansed from misconduct. I do not desire to be interrupted, sir,' he added imperiously; 'I am here to speak, and not to listen; and I have to ask you to hear me with respect, and to obey punctiliously. At the earliest possible date your daughter shall be married at the Embassy to my friend, Francis Scrymgeour, your brother's acknowledged son. You will oblige me by offering not less than ten thousand pounds dowry. For yourself, I will indicate to you in writing a mission of some importance in Siam which I destine to your care. And now, sir, you will answer me in two words whether or not you agree to these conditions.'

'Your Highness will pardon me,' said Mr Vandeleur, 'and permit me, with all respect, to submit to him two queries?'

'The permission is granted,' replied the Prince.

'Your Highness,' resumed the Dictator, 'has called Mr

Scrymgeour his friend. Believe me, had I known he was thus honoured, I should have treated him with proportional respect.'

'You interrogate adroitly,' said the Prince; 'but it will not serve your turn. You have my commands; if I had never seen that gentleman before to-night, it would not render them less absolute.'

'Your Highness interprets my meaning with his usual subtlety,' returned Vandeleur. 'Once more: I have, unfortunately, put the police upon the track of Mr Scrymgeour on a charge of theft; am I to withdraw or to uphold the accusation?'

'You will please yourself,' replied Florizel. 'The question is one between your conscience and the laws of this land. Give me my hat; and you, Mr Rolles, give me my cane and follow me. Miss Vandeleur, I wish you good evening. I judge,' he added to Vandeleur, 'that your silence means unqualified assent.'

'If I can do no better,' replied the old man, 'I shall submit; but I warn you openly it shall not be without a struggle.'

'You are old,' said the Prince; 'but years are disgraceful to the wicked. Your age is more unwise than the youth of others. Do not provoke me, or you may find me harder than you dream. This is the first time that I have fallen across your path in anger; take care that it be the last.'

With these words, motioning the clergyman to follow, Florizel left the apartment and directed his steps towards the garden gate; and the Dictator, following with a candle, gave them light, and once more undid the elaborate fastenings with which he sought to protect himself from intrusion.

'Your daughter is no longer present,' said the Prince, turning to the threshold. 'Let me tell you that I understand your threats; and you have only to lift your hand to bring upon yourself sudden and irremediable ruin.'

The Dictator made no reply; but as the Prince turned his back upon him in the lamplight he made a gesture full of menace and insane fury; and the next moment, slipping round a corner, he was running at full speed for the nearest cab-stand.

III

Prince Florizel walked with Mr Rolles to the door of a small hotel where the latter resided. They spoke much together, and the clergyman was more than once affected to tears by the mingled severity and tenderness of Florizel's reproaches.

'I have made ruin of my life,' he said at last. 'Help me; tell me what I am to do; I have, alas! neither the virtues of a priest nor the dexterity of a rogue.'

'Now that you are humbled,' said the Prince, 'I command no longer; the repentant have to do with God and not with princes. But if you will let me advise you, go to Australia as a colonist, seek menial labour in the open air, and try to forget that you have ever been a clergyman, or that you ever set eyes on that accursed stone.'

'Accurst indeed!' replied Mr Rolles. 'Where is it now? What further hurt is it not working for mankind?'

'It will do no more evil,' returned the Prince. 'It is here in my pocket. And this,' he added kindly, 'will show that I place some faith in your penitence, young as it is.'

'Suffer me to touch your hand,' pleaded Mr Rolles.

'No,' replied Prince Florizel, 'not yet.'

The tone in which he uttered these last words was eloquent in the ears of the young clergyman; and for some minutes after the Prince had turned away he stood on the threshold following with his eyes the retreating figure and invoking the blessing of heaven upon a man so excellent in counsel.

For several hours the Prince walked alone in unfrequented streets. His mind was full of concern; what to do with the diamond, whether to return it to its owner, whom he judged unworthy of this rare possession, or to take some sweeping and courageous measure and put it out of the reach of all mankind at once and for ever, was a problem too grave to be decided in a moment. The manner in which it had come into his hands appeared manifestly providential; and as he took out the jewel and looked at it under the street lamps, its size and surprising brilliancy inclined him more and more to think of it as of an unmixed and dangerous evil for the world.

'God help me!' he thought; 'if I look at it much oftener, I shall begin to grow covetous myself.'

At last, though still uncertain in his mind, he turned his steps towards the small but elegant mansion on the riverside which had belonged for centuries to his royal family.

The Prince made a sudden movement with his hand, and the jewel, describing an arc of light, dived with a splash into the flowing river.

'Amen,' said Florizel with gravity. 'I have slain a cockatrice!'

Not long after, the marriage of Francis Scrymgeour and Miss Vandeleur was celebrated in great privacy; and the Prince acted on that occasion as groom's-man. The two Vandeleurs surprised some rumour of what had happened to the diamond; and their vast diving operations on the River Seine are the wonder and amusement of the idle. It is true that through some miscalculation they have chosen the wrong branch of the river. As for the Prince, that sublime person, having now served his turn, may go, along with the *Arabian Author*, topsy-turvy into space. But if the reader insists on more specific information, I am happy to say that a recent revolution hurled him from the throne of Bohemia, in consequence of his continued absence and edifying neglect of public business; and that his Highness now keeps a cigar store in Rupert Street, much frequented by other foreign refugees. I go there from time to time to smoke and have a chat, and find him as great a creature as in the days of his prosperity; he has an Olympian air behind the counter; and although a sedentary life is beginning to tell upon his waistcoat, he is probably, take him for all in all, the handsomest tobacconist in London.

The Episcopal Seal

J. Maclaren-Ross

Bishop Thurlow looked both bloated and seedy. No disrespect to the Church: he wasn't really a bishop, although this was his Christian name and there had been a bishop somewhere way back in his family, so that his background was episcopal in its general tone and influenced him, no doubt, in choosing the profession he ultimately adopted.

I believe, too, that at one time he had been intended for Holy Orders and had studied for some months at a Theological College; but the bishop seldom spoke of his past: he was a man who lived predominantly in the present.

I first ran across him in the Sink, in Soho. This café, now closed down by the police, had, at the time I'm writing about, something of the status of a club, but without any tiresome regulations. There was a cellar down below where gambling went on for those who could afford it and a room at ground level with coffee and a few chess-sets provided for those who could not.

The bishop was sitting in the upstairs room playing chess when I came in. He sat on a sofa directly underneath the mural, painted by a pacifist, of Christ crucified wearing a gas-mask, which was afterwards daubed over with whitewash by the new proprietor whose way of life caused the police to close the place down.

A cup of tea stood on the table beside him. Tea cost twopence in the Sink; coffee cost sixpence. I also ordered tea, waving aside the stunted grey Greek waiter who rushed threateningly towards me with a cry of 'coffee'.

The usual clientele was present: the bearded man who cast horoscopes, the one-armed ex-Serviceman who recited Shakespeare to theatre queues, a group of Indians talking about post-dated cheques.

Among these was Krishna. He rolled his eyes round in my direction and winked slowly, smiling and smoothing back his hair at the same time with both hands.

I sat down at a table next to the bishop. His opponent, a small man who looked like a betting-clerk, was plainly in difficulties. All his pieces were pinned, and even as I looked across, the bishop discovered check.

'Mate next move,' he murmured; there was no way out; he sat back benevolently, with his hands clasped over his stomach, while the small man peered in desperation down at the board.

'That's foxed it,' he seemed to say. The bishop without replying held out a plump, inexorable palm. Half a crown changed hands: the bishop caused this to vanish, with something of a conjurer's celerity, into his waistcoat pocket.

'Have another?'

The little man paid no attention to this. Cramming on a bowler, he rushed incontinently out of the café. The bishop, smiling gently, set up the pieces again and leant over towards me. 'Care for a game, young man?'

'Not just now, thanks.'

'We could play for a small stake, if you wish. Half a crown?'

'No, really. Not today.'

'Sixpence then. You wouldn't refuse? The humble tanner.'

'No.'

The bishop sighed: 'I'm sorry I can't tempt you.' His stomach shook softly with the sigh; his hands trembled a little over the Staunton men; he said: 'I'll give you pawn and move.'

'Nothing doing.'

'A knight.'

'No. You're too strong a player for me.'

'Nonsense. Nonsense, my dear boy. I talk a good middle game.'

He smiled at me with sparse, discoloured teeth; a rough grey stubble glinted along his distended cheeks over his sagging jowls. He gave me up as a bad job. Something at the next table caught his attention: the Indians were advising the youngest member of their group to write dunning his uncle in Ceylon for twenty quid.

'But how shall I go about it?' the young Indian was saying. 'What shall I say?'

'A cable,' the bishop cut in quickly. The Indians looked round. 'Costs more, but it's quicker. If I may offer the benefit of my experience.'

'Thank you,' the young Indian said.

'And put on it: *Beg assistance*.'

The bishop raised an episcopal forefinger; 'That's all. Short and sweet. It never fails.' He rose to his feet, pushing past the chessboard and the cup of cooling tea: 'Mind you, when it comes off, I shall expect my cut. Ten per cent – for the consultation. This day week.'

He waddled out. All his clothes had been made for a taller man: the black stained jacket hung down well below his hips, the trousers had been turned up twice. I watched him pass through the door into the street, lifting his feet sideways with caution, as a duck walks.

Krishna came over, patting his yellow neck-cloth into place. 'Any news?' he said. He meant: 'Have you any money?' I said: 'No,' and then: 'Who was that?'

'Oh, Thurlow. The bishop. He's a South Kensington man. Rarely up this way.'

'What's he do for a living?'

'Vicars,' Krishna said. 'He does vicars.'

'Vicars?'

'Yes. You know – funds.'

'But is there any money in that?'

245

'Two quid a time, I believe. I've never done it myself, but I know a woman who did six vicars in one day.'

'Twelve quid. Seems incredible.'

'Quite a feat,' Krishna said. 'Of course the bishop put her on to them: he took his ten per cent.'

'We might try that some time.'

'No,' Krishna said.

About a fortnight later I met the bishop again. I found him standing beside me in a pub, at lunch-time.

'How are things in Kensington?' I asked him.

'Terrible, young man; absolutely appalling. I have been obliged to – evacuate.'

'Not bomb damage, I hope?'

'Unfortunately, no. If it were bomb damage I should be able to claim – at some distant date. Have you the price of a bitter on you, young man?'

'I have, but that's about all.'

'Straitened circumstances?' the bishop said. 'Financial necessity?'

'In a nutshell,' I said. 'Did you get your cut from that Indian boy?'

'Of course. My formula never fails. But alas, with the increased cost of living, money goes nowhere these days.'

'Nowhere,' I said.

'Look at the price of drink.'

'Indeed.'

The bishop shook his head: baldness in the exact centre of it gave the effect of a tonsure. He gulped at the glass of bitter and shuddered all over. He was plainly recovering from a bout and in a bad way.

He said: 'But never despair, my boy, I might be able to assist you . . . Let me see . . . have you any living relatives? An uncle? Beg assistance?'

'No.'

'Alone in the world, eh?'

'Yes.'

'Never mind, there are other ways . . . I think that if you could afford a further bitter, I could put you on to something good.'

'It's not vicars?'

'No, no. You wouldn't do for vicars; you're not the type, dear boy. No, I was thinking of the Indigent City Father's Fund.'

'What's that?'

'Another bitter first. To lubricate the workings of the mind.'

'All right.'

The bishop grabbed the glass and took another huge swallow, but this time he did not shudder. He said: 'It's called the City Father's Fund for the Indigent, actually. I think you'd qualify admirably. All you have to say is that at one time you were employed in the City.'

'But I never have been.'

'Come come,' the bishop said sharply. 'A little *nous*, dear boy. You must be prepared to practise a small innocent deception. I'd imagined you to be a young man of resource.'

'Supposing they find out?'

'They won't. What's the time?'

'That clock says a quarter to two.'

'We can just do it,' the bishop said. 'How much ready cash have you?'

'Five bob.'

'That's ample,' swallowing his bitter. 'Come with me.'

We walked out, up Percy Street, the bishop's black jacket flapping round his hips as he trotted along beside me.

'Quick; this taxi!'

We climbed in. I could see my five bob going down the drain. I said: 'Why not a bus?'

'No time. Besides,' the bishop's jowls jolted a little as we jerked past the Negroes in American suitings on the corner by Better Books, round Cambridge Circus and down towards the Strand, 'a taxi is excellent to relax in. Soothes the mind, allows you to prepare in comparative calm for the ordeal ahead.'

'What ordeal?'

'The ordeal of life, dear boy,' the bishop said gently, glancing out through the window at a clock in Trafalgar Square. 'We'll have five minutes in hand.'

'I don't like this at all,' I said.

'Stop fussing, dear boy. Abandon yourself – to blessed peace.'

The bishop closed his eyes and leaned back on the padded seat: he said no more. The taxi wound its way in and out of the labyrinthian purlieus of the City. Suddenly the bishop's eyes flew open; he leaned forward and banged on the glass.

'Stop round this corner.'

We got out and I paid the fare. That left me half a crown. 'This way,' the bishop said. A portal loomed up, with Doric columns on either side. 'In here.' The bishop pushed me ahead of him into a hall full of statuary, up a flight of broad stone steps. On the first landing was a door bearing the name of the Fund; it stood half open on a room full of wooden benches facing an empty magisterial throne raised upon a dais. A few disreputable figures – one of them in actual rags – were huddled dejectedly together on the front bench. Behind these sat the small bowler-hatted man whom the bishop had beaten at chess.

At sight of him the bishop frowned. 'That scrounger Stubbs. What right has he –' But at that moment a clock chimed and a door at the back of the room opened. Everyone stood up: it was like being in court when the magistrate comes in. And, indeed, the man who had just entered had an air almost as magisterial as the throne on to which he now climbed. He wore a gold watch-chain and a wing collar – he might have been the Lord Mayor of London himself. An official in some kind of gown accompanied him, carrying a sheaf of forms which were dished round to all of us.

While we were filling these in, the magisterial man stared up at the ceiling, stroking his chin judicially. He had the look of one about to have his shoes shined; the elevation of his throne and the semi-crouching posture of one of the tramps in the front row contributed to this impression.

The crouching tramp was first man in. A bell rang and his name was called out. He stumbled through an incredibly tall story of one-time employment in the City. The magisterial man cut this short half-way. One or two leading questions deflated the tramp: the official escorted him to the door empty-handed. Then for a time the magisterial man toyed with the other tramps: one in particular he put through a terrific grilling.

I panicked at this and made a move to bolt. But the bishop clutched at my arm. 'Take no notice,' he hissed; 'it's a put-up job. They are all actors!'

'Actors?'

'Paid by the Fund to discourage impostors.'

Meanwhile tramp after tramp had been disposed of: the last one was dismissed in a voice like the crack of a whip. I sweated; it was Stubbs's turn. He stood up. He was sweating too.

'He'll get nothing,' the bishop hissed malignantly into my ear.

He was right. The magisterial man made short work of Stubbs. He shuffled out after the tramps; the bishop pinched my arm with pleasure. He leaned across to see what I'd written on my form. A look of horror came over his face; he pointed to the entry opposite 'Profession'. I'd put down 'Author'. The bishop made frantic signs, but it was too late to change anything; the official in the gown had already taken the form out of my hand and the bishop was on his feet answering questions. He described himself as an auctioneer, which surprised me. A tale of hard luck and wartime unemployment followed. The magisterial man rubbed his chin on the sharp edge of the wing-collar.

'Surely I've seen your face before.'

'Alas, sir,' the bishop said unctuously, 'force of circumstance caused me to apply to you once before. A long time ago.'

'How long?'

'1942. You will find the entry in your records, sir.'

'H'm. All right. Wait there.'

My name was called and I stood up; my knees knocked together. The magisterial man frowned at the form that had been handed up to him.

He said: 'You're an author?'

'Yes, sir.'

'Have you ever been employed in the City of London?'

'Not exactly, sir.'

'How d'you mean, not exactly?'

'Well, I've published a lot in magazines. Their offices are round about the city. Fleet Street and so on.'

'Give me some addresses, please.'

I did. One of them was bang in the City itself, there was no denying that. I had the magisterial man bottled. He hitched at his collar and drummed on the arms of his throne.

'All right. If you'll wait there a moment.'

The official in the gown went out and came back with a bag. It contained pound notes: we signed receipts for three quid apiece, clutching these in our hands we made for the door; the Bishop almost fell downstairs in his hurry.

'Quick!' he said. 'Across the way! While they're still open.'

In the pub he ordered Scotch and, what's more, paid for it himself. 'Well, dear boy, you did it. Congratulations! I'd never have thought up that author stunt. I *said* you were a young man of resource and, mark you, I am rarely wrong.'

'Another drink?'

'That wouldn't come amiss. By the way, before I forget. My cut.'

'Of course.' I hadn't had time to get change: I held out one of my quids.

'Very handsome of you, dear boy.' It vanished seemingly into thin air, or at any rate into his pocket.

'Oh, I say. I didn't mean the whole quid.'

'Now now, dear boy,' the bishop said reproachfully. 'Never go back on a good deed once it's done. After all, we so seldom get the opportunity . . . look, I'll pay for the drinks.'

'Fair enough.'

'Better times!' the bishop raised his glass. 'You wouldn't care to do a vicar with me this afternoon.'

'No, thanks.'

'You're sure?'

'Absolutely.'

'A game of chess then. The Sink.'

'Why not? This pub's shutting.'

At chess the bishop won another five bob off me: he was in fine fettle. Stubbs was there. The bishop gave him a baleful glare.

'I'm glad he got his deserts, the dirty skunk. Sneaking off down there while my back was turned, when it was I who put him on to it . . . the ingratitude . . . you can have no conception.' He craned his neck at the clock. 'But it's late, I must go.'

'A vicar?'

'No no, my wife. One has certain responsibilities . . . the weaker sex . . .'

I had not envisaged him as a married man. I wondered what sort of woman the wife could be. And then one evening I met her; in a pub, naturally. She stood beside the bishop at the bar: she was twice his size. A slattern. Sort of gypsy. Coarse black hair, lot of bangles, and a moustache. And half-seas-over to boot.

The bishop had a clot of dried blood on his cheek; he looked shamefaced and subdued. 'Haven't seen you around lately,' I said to him.

'No; I've been farming.'

I was staggered. 'Farming?'

'Chalk Farm.' He giggled. 'The agricultural life.'

The wife broke in harshly. 'Who the hell's this?'

'A friend. Doris, may I introduce . . .'

'Go to hell. Gimme a cigarette.'

'I'm afraid, my love, you've smoked my last. Perhaps, dear boy, you could oblige . . .'

I produced my packet; and, moreover, having money at the time, bought a round of drinks. The wife's manner immediately

251

softened: she gave me a glittering smile, full of gold. It was a Hampstead pub, and when it closed I went back with them to Chalk Farm.

They lived in a basement. Horrible place, smelling of the wife's stale scent. She changed at once into a kimono and slippers and started to have a row with her husband over some stuff of hers he'd pawned.

'But, my love, we've got to live. Look, I've got a new scheme.'

He opened a drawer and took out a large map of London, with various districts marked in ink, like a vacuum-cleaner salesman's territory-plan. The marked portions represented vicars: the bishop was planning a mass attack all over London.

'This one at Highgate's particularly promising. He goes up to a fiver, I believe. We could all of us try him.'

The wife sniffed. 'It'd better come off.'

'My love, have you ever known me fail?'

I stayed the night. A mattress on the floor in the kitchen. Just as I was dozing off, another row broke out. A scream and a crash of crockery. After that there was a lull, except for the scampering of mice across the kitchen floor.

At seven next morning an alarm-clock went off and hostilities were resumed.

The wife's voice said: 'Wake up, you lazy hound. Where are the cigarettes?'

'My love, I haven't any.'

'Get some then and make it snappy. Do you want to go to prison?'

'Please, my love, have a heart. Give me another five minutes.'

'I've enough on you to hang you.'

'Don't say such things, I implore you.'

'Then get me some cigarettes.'

Of course, he came in to me. 'Why d'you put up with it?' I asked him.

'My dear boy, I couldn't do without Doris. Why, I'd be lost without her. Irrevocably lost.'

He went away with my cigarettes and I went back to sleep again. When I woke there was a council of war going on. The bishop had his map out and was sketching out the day's operations. He was a different man: a general, a leader; even his wife listened meekly and nodded assent at the districts and vicars assigned to her. A thin mousy-looking woman had joined them and was also taking instructions.

'Not a drop to drink, mind you, until after the first two vicars. Then you may indulge in a glass of bitter, but no more. Now, have we enough between us for the first taxi?'

He attempted to enroll me in his canvassing group, but without success. He said: 'Very sad, dear boy; you'd have made a likely recruit. Never mind, however. It's your loss . . .'

I did not see him again for some months. Then he turned up at the Sink, and I was shocked at his appearance. He had never been a man who shaved closely, but now a positive fringe of grey whisker sprouted raggedly round his chin, like the beard of a shrimp, and his eyes looked as though their red rims had been turned inside out. His overcoat came down to his heels and the sleeves covered up his hands. Even his voice had lost its former tone of unctuous authority; it sounded cracked and hoarse as he said: 'Dear boy, I'm on the run.'

'Duns?'

'Worse than that.'

'The police?'

He nodded. 'A hunted man.'

'But what have you done?'

'Get me a cup of coffee and I'll tell you.'

He did. Here is the story.

Doris, his wife, had been married before. The stepson, Gavin, was twenty-one. Suddenly he came home on leave. He wore steel spectacles and was in the Pioneer Corps. A studious type: the bishop enrolled him at once, and the boy proved an enthusiastic pupil. When asked if he could do vicars, he replied: 'Can a duck swim.' And indeed he took to the life like a duck to water. Vicars inaccessible even to the astute bishop coughed up quids wholesale. He did the magisterial man as well. He sent cables to obscure relatives saying Beg Assistance, and received replies in solid cash.

Unfortunately, he was so absorbed in his new profession that he overstayed his leave. Twenty-one days went by and he was posted as a deserter. Pretty soon, while he was on his way to do a vicar in Watford, the police picked him up. He returned to face a court martial.

Doris didn't care for this. She blamed the bishop for leading the boy astray. The bishop had qualms too: he felt he had to get Gavin out of the mess. So he wrote a letter to the commanding officer saying that Gavin had been detained on parish duties for the church, and signed it *The Bishop of Thurlow*. Worse still, he got hold of a bishop's ring from somewhere – he claimed it had belonged to his ancestor – and set the episcopal seal under his signature.

The CO saw through this letter and passed it on to the police. The police now wanted urgently to interview the Bishop of Thurlow. Forced to quit Chalk Farm, he was without beer, boots, or home. Doris had gone to ground with her mother, who hated the bishop and wouldn't allow him inside the house.

The possibility of prison terrified the bishop: he was going to pieces: it was the hold Doris had had over him all these years. 'It'll break me up, I know it will. Can't you do anything to help, dear boy?'

I couldn't; I was passing through one of my moneyless periods. I couldn't even lend him enough to get a bed in a dosshouse.

'Never mind,' the bishop said, pulling himself together with an effort. 'Never despair, dear boy. I will try to get into a Turkish bath – on credit.'

He rose; he gave a ragged smile. He raised one hand, the fingers crossed: it was a benediction. Then he waddled out webfooted, and the door of the Sink closed behind him gently.

The police caught up with him quite soon; he got nine months.

And when I met him in the street a fortnight ago I hardly recognized him. Prison hadn't broken him up, after all; the very reverse. He looked five years younger. His eyes weren't bloodshot, his face was smooth and urbane, his hands no longer trembled, and he seemed on the whole less fat.

'Where have you been all this time?' I asked him tactfully.

'Staying in the country.'

'What was it like?'

'The air was excellent, the food was palatable, but the service was abominable. I shall not go there again.'

The Genuine Tabard

E. C. Bentley

It was quite by chance, at a dinner-party given by the American Naval Attaché, that Philip Trent met the Langleys, who were visiting Europe for the first time. During the cocktail-time, before dinner was served, he had gravitated towards George D. Langley, because he was the finest-looking man in the room – tall, strongly built, carrying his years lightly, pink of face, with vigorous, massive features and thick grey hair.

They had talked about the Tower of London, the Cheshire Cheese, and the Zoo, all of which the Langleys had visited that day. Langley, so the Attaché had told Trent, was a distant relative of his own; he had made a large fortune manufacturing engineers' drawing-office equipment, was a prominent citizen of Cordova, Ohio, the headquarters of his business, and had married a Schuyler. Trent, though not sure what a Schuyler was, gathered that it was an excellent thing to marry, and this impression was confirmed when he found himself placed next to Mrs Langley at dinner.

Mrs Langley always went on the assumption that her own affairs were the most interesting subject of conversation; and as she was a vivacious and humorous talker and a very handsome and good-hearted woman, she usually turned out to be right. She informed Trent that she was crazy about old churches, of which she had seen and photographed she did not know how many in France, Germany, and England. Trent, who loved thirteenth-century stained glass, mentioned Chartres, which Mrs Langley said, truly enough, was too perfect for words. He asked if she had been to Fairford in Gloucestershire. She had; and that was, she declared with emphasis, the greatest day of all their time in Europe; not because of the church, though that was certainly lovely, but because of the treasure they had found that afternoon.

Trent asked to be told about this; and Mrs Langley said that it was quite a story. Mr Gifford had driven them down to Fairford in his car. Did Trent know Mr Gifford – W. N. Gifford, who lived at the Suffolk Hotel? He was visiting Paris just now. Trent ought to meet him, because Mr Gifford knew everything there was to know about stained glass, and church ornaments, and brasses, and antiques in general. They had met him when he was sketching some traceries in Westminster Abbey, and they had become great friends. He had driven them about to quite a few places within reach of London. He knew all about Fairford, of course, and they had a lovely time there.

On the way back to London, after passing through Abingdon, Mr Gifford had said it was time for a cup of coffee, as he always did around five o'clock; he made his own coffee, which was excellent, and carried it in a thermos. They slowed down, looking for a good place to stop, and Mrs Langley's eye was caught by a strange name on a signpost at a turning off the road – something Episcopi. She knew that meant bishops, which was interesting; so she asked Mr Gifford to halt while she made out the weather-beaten lettering. The sign said 'Silcote Episcopi ½ mile.'

Had Trent heard of the place? Neither had Mr Gifford. But that lovely name, Mrs Langley said, was enough for her. There must be a church, and an old one; and anyway she would love to have Silcote Episcopi in her collection. As it was so near, she asked Mr Gifford if they could go there so she could take a few snaps while the light was good, and perhaps have coffee there.

They found the church, with the parsonage near by, and a village in sight some way beyond. The church stood back of the churchyard, and as they were going along the foot-path they noticed a grave with tall railings round it; not a standing-up stone but a flat one, raised on a little foundation. They noticed it because, though it was an old stone, it had not been just left to fall into decay, but had been kept clean of moss and dirt, so you could make out the inscription, and the grass around it was trim and tidy. They read Sir Rowland Verey's epitaph; and Mrs Langley – so she assured Trent – screamed with joy.

There was a man trimming the churchyard boundary hedge with shears, who looked at them, she thought, suspiciously when she screamed. She thought he was probably the sexton; so she assumed a winning manner, and asked him if there was any objection to her taking a photograph of the inscription on the stone. The man said that he didn't know as there was; but maybe she ought to ask vicar, because it was his grave, in a manner of speaking. It was vicar's great-grandfather's grave, that was; and he always had it kep' in good order. He would be in the church now, very like, if they had a mind to see him.

Mr Gifford said that in any case they would have a look at the church, which he thought might be worth the trouble. He observed that it was not very old – about mid-seventeenth century, he would say – a poor little kid church, Mrs Langley commented with gay sarcasm. In a place so named, Mr Gifford said, there had probably been a church for centuries further back; but it might have been burnt down, or fallen into ruin, and replaced by this building. So they went into the church; and at once Mr Gifford had been delighted with it. He pointed out how the pulpit, the screen, the pews, the glass, the organ-case in the west gallery, were all of the same period. Mrs Langley was busy with her camera when a pleasant-faced man of middle age, in clerical attire, emerged from the vestry with a large book under his arm.

Mr Gifford introduced himself and his friends as a party of chance visitors who had been struck by the beauty of the church and had ventured to explore its interior. Could the vicar tell them anything about the armorial glass in the nave windows? The vicar could and did; but Mrs Langley was not just then interested in any family history but the vicar's own, and soon she broached the subject of his great-grandfather's gravestone.

The vicar, smiling, said that he bore Sir Rowland's name, and had felt it his duty to look after the grave properly, as this was the only Verey to be buried in that place. He added that the living was in the gift of the head of the family, and that he was the third Verey to be vicar of Silcote Episcopi in the course of two hundred years. He said that Mrs Langley was most welcome to take a photograph of the stone, but he doubted if it could be done successfully with a hand-camera from over the railings – and of course, said Mrs Langley, he was perfectly right. Then the vicar asked if she would like to have a copy of the epitaph, which he could write for her if they would all come over to his house, and his wife would give them some tea; and at this, as Trent could imagine, they were just tickled to death.

'But what was it, Mrs Langley, that delighted you so much about the epitaph?' Trent asked. 'It seems to have been about a Sir Rowland Verey – that's all I have been told so far.'

'I was going to show it to you,' Mrs Langley said, opening her handbag. 'Maybe you will not think it so precious as we do. I have had a lot of copies made, to send to friends at home.' She unfolded a small typed sheet, on which Trent read what follows:

Within this Vault are interred
the Remains of
Lt.-Gen. Sir Rowland Edmund Verey,
Garter Principal King of Arms,
Gentleman Usher of the Black Rod
and
Clerk of the Hanaper,
who departed this life
on the 2nd May 1795
in the 73rd Year of his Age
calmly relying
on the Merits of the Redeemer
for the salvation of

his Soul.
Also of Lavinia Prudence,
Wife of the Above,
who entered into Rest
on the 12th March 1799
in the 68th Year of her Age.
She was a Woman of fine Sense
genteel Behaviour,
prudent Oeconomy
and
great Integrity.
'This is the Gate of the Lord:
The Righteous shall enter into it.'

'You have certainly got a fine specimen of that style,' Trent observed. 'Nowadays we don't run to much more, as a rule, than "in loving memory;" followed by the essential facts. As for the titles, I don't wonder at your admiring them; they are like the sound of trumpets. There is also a faint jingle of money, I think. In Sir Rowland's time, Black Rod's was probably a job worth having, and though I don't know what a Hanaper is, I do remember that its Clerkship was one of the fat sinecures that made it well worth while being a courtier.'

Mrs Langley put away her treasure, patting the bag with affection. 'Mr Gifford said the Clerk had to collect some sort of legal fees for the Crown, and that he would draw maybe seven or eight thousand pounds a year for it, paying another man two or three hundred for doing the actual work. Well, we found the vicarage just perfect – an old house with everything beautifully mellow and personal about it. There was a long oar hanging on the wall in the hall, and when I asked about it the vicar said he had rowed for All Souls College when he was at Oxford. His wife was charming too. And now listen! While she was giving us tea and her husband was making a copy of the epitaph for me, he was talking about his ancestor, and he said the first duty that

Sir Rowland had to perform after his appointment as King of Arms was to proclaim the Peace of Versailles from the steps of the Palace of St. James's. Imagine that, Mr Trent!'

Trent looked at her uncertainly. 'So they had a Peace of Versailles all that time ago.'

'Yes, they did,' Mrs Langley said, a little tartly. 'And quite an important Peace, at that. We remember it in America, if you don't. It was the first treaty to be signed by the United States, and in that treaty the British Government took a licking, called off the war, and recognised our independence. Now when the vicar said that about his ancestor having proclaimed peace with the United States, I saw George Langley prick up his ears; and I knew why.

'You see, George is a collector of Revolution pieces, and he has some pretty nice things, if I do say it. He began asking questions; and the first thing anybody knew, the vicaress had brought down the old King of Arms' tabard and was showing it off. You know what a tabard is, Mr Trent, of course. Such a lovely garment! I fell for it on the spot, and as for George, his eyes stuck out like a crab's. That wonderful shade of red satin, and the Royal Arms embroidered in those stunning colours, red and gold and blue and silver, as you don't often see them.

'Presently George got talking to Mr Gifford in a corner, and I could see Mr Gifford screwing up his mouth and shaking his head; but George only stuck out his chin, and soon after, when the vicaress was showing off the garden, he got the vicar by himself and talked turkey.

'Mr Verey didn't like it at all, George told me; but George can be a very smooth worker when he likes, and at last the vicar had to allow that he was tempted, what with having his sons to start in the world, and the Income Tax being higher than a cat's back, and the death duties and all. And finally he said yes. I won't tell you or anybody what George offered him, Mr Trent, because George swore me to secrecy; but, as he says, it was no good acting like a piker in this kind of a deal, and he could sense that the vicar wouldn't stand for any bargaining back and forth. And anyway, it was worth every cent of it to George, to have something that no other curio-hunter possessed. He said he would come for the tabard next day and bring the money in notes, and the vicar said very well, then we must all three come to lunch, and he would have a paper ready giving the history of the tabard over his signature. So that was what we did; and the tabard is in our suite at the Greville, locked in a wardrobe, and George has it out and gloats over it first thing in the morning and last thing at night.'

Trent said with sincerity that no story of real life had ever interested him more. 'I wonder,' he said, 'if your husband would let me have a look at his prize. I'm not much of an antiquary, but I am interested in heraldry, and the only tabards I have ever seen were quite modern ones.'

'Why, of course,' Mrs Langley said. 'You make a date with him after dinner. He will be delighted. He has no idea of hiding it under a bushel, believe me!'

The following afternoon, in the Langleys' sitting-room at the Greville, the tabard was displayed on a coat-hanger before the thoughtful gaze of Trent, while its new owner looked on with a pride not untouched with anxiety.

'Well, Mr Trent,' he said. 'How do you like it? You don't doubt this is a genuine tabard, I suppose?'

Trent rubbed his chin. 'Oh, yes, it's a tabard. I have seen a few before, and I have painted one, with a man inside it, when Richmond Herald wanted his portrait done in the complete get-up. Everything about it is right. Such things are hard to come by. Until recent times, I believe, a herald's tabard remained his property, and stayed in the family, and if they got hard up they might perhaps sell it privately, as this was sold to you. It's different now – so Richmond Herald told me. When a herald dies, his tabard goes back to the College of Arms, where he got it from.'

Langley drew a breath of relief. 'I'm glad to hear you say my tabard is genuine. When you asked me if you could see it, I got the impression you thought there might be something phoney about it.'

Mrs Langley, her keen eyes on Trent's face, shook her head. 'He thinks so still, George, I believe. Isn't that so, Mr Trent?'

'Yes, I am sorry to say it is. You see, this was sold to you as a particular tabard, with an interesting history of its own; and when Mrs Langley described it to me, I felt pretty sure that you had been swindled. You see, she had noticed nothing odd about the Royal Arms. I wanted to see it just to make sure. It certainly did not belong to Garter King of Arms in the year 1783.'

A very ugly look wiped all the benevolence from Langley's face, and it grew several shades more pink. 'If what you say is true, Mr Trent, and if that old fraud was playing me for a sucker, I will get him jailed if it's my last act. But it certainly is hard to believe – a preacher – and belonging to one of your best families – settled in that lovely, peaceful old place, with his flock to look after and everything. Are you really sure of what you say?'

'What I know is that the Royal Arms on this tabard are all wrong.'

An exclamation came from the lady. 'Why, Mr Trent, how you talk! We have seen the Royal Arms quite a few times, and they are just the same as this – and you have told us it is a genuine tabard, anyway. I don't get this at all.'

'I must apologise,' Trent said unhappily, 'for the Royal Arms. You see, they have a past. In the fourteenth century Edward II laid claim to the Kingdom of France, and it took a hundred years of war to convince his descendants that the claim wasn't practical politics. All the same, they went on including the lilies of France in the Royal Arms, and they never dropped them until the beginning of the nineteenth century.'

'Mercy!' Mrs Langley's voice was faint.

'Besides that, the first four Georges and the fourth William were Kings of Hanover; so until Queen Victoria came along, and could not inherit Hanover because she was a female, the Arms of the House of Brunswick were jammed in along with our own. In fact, the tabard of the Garter King of Arms in the year when he proclaimed the peace with the United States of America was a horrible mess of the leopards of England, the lion of Scotland, the harp of Ireland, the lilies of France, together with a few more lions, and a white horse, and some hearts, as worn in Hanover. It was a fairly tight fit for one shield, but they managed it somehow – and you can see that the Arms on this tabard of yours are not nearly such a bad dream as that. It is a Victorian tabard – a nice, gentlemanly coat, such as no well-dressed herald should be without.'

Langley thumped the table. 'Well, I intend to be without it, anyway, if I can get my money back.'

'We can but try,' Trent said. 'It may be possible. But the reason why I asked to be allowed to see this thing, Mr Langley, was that I thought I might be able to save you some unpleasantness. You see, if you went home with your treasure, and showed it to people, and talked about its history, and it was mentioned in the newspaper, and then somebody got inquiring into its authenticity, and found out what I have been telling you, and made it public – well, it wouldn't be very nice for you.'

Langley flushed again, and a significant glance passed between him and his wife.

'You're damn right, it wouldn't,' he said. 'And I know the name of the buzzard who would do that to me, too, as soon as I had gone the limit in making a monkey of myself. Why, I would lose the money twenty times over, and then a bundle, rather than have that happen to me. I am grateful to you, Mr Trent – I am indeed. I'll say frankly that at home we aim to be looked up to socially, and we judged that we would certainly figure if we brought this doggoned thing back and had it talked about. Gosh! When I think – but never mind that now. The thing is to go right back to that old crook and make him squeal. I'll have my money out of him, if I have to use a can-opener.'

Trent shook his head. 'I don't feel very sanguine about that,

Mr Langley. But how would you like to run down to his place to-morrow with me and a friend of mine, who takes an interest in affairs of this kind, and who would be able to help you if anyone can?'

Langley said, with emphasis, that that suited him.

The car which called for Langley next morning did not look as if it belonged, but it did belong, to Scotland Yard; and the same could be said of its dapper chauffeur. Inside was Trent, with a black-haired, round-faced man whom he introduced as Superintendent Owen. It was at his request that Langley, during the journey, told with as much detail as he could recall the story of his acquisition of the tabard, which he had hopefully brought with him in a suitcase.

A few miles short of Abingdon the chauffeur was told to go slow. 'You tell me it was not very far this side of Abingdon, Mr Langley, that you turned off the main road,' the superintendent said. 'If you will keep a look-out now, you might be able to point out the spot.'

Langley stared at him. 'Why, doesn't your man have a map?'

'Yes; but there isn't any place called Silcote Episcopi on his map.'

'Nor,' Trent added, 'on any other map. No, I am not suggesting that you dreamed it all; but the fact is so.'

Langley, remarking shortly that this beat him, glared out of the window eagerly; and soon he gave the word to stop. 'I am pretty sure this is the turning,' he said, 'I recognise it by these two haystacks in the meadow, and the pond with osiers over it. But there certainly was a signpost there, and now there isn't one. If I was not dreaming then I guess I must be now.' And as the car ran swiftly down the side-road he went on, 'Yes; that certainly is the church on ahead – and the covered gate, and the graveyard – and there is the vicarage, with the yew trees and the garden and everything. Well, gentlemen, right now is when he gets what is coming to him, I don't care what the name of the darn place is.'

'The name of the darn place on the map,' Trent said, 'is Oakhanger.'

The three men got out and passed through the lych-gate.

'Where is the gravestone?' Trent asked.

Langley pointed. 'Right there.' They went across to the railed-in-grave, and the American put a hand to his head. 'I must be nuts!' he groaned. 'I *know* this is the grave – but it says that here is laid to rest the body of James Roderick Stevens, of this parish.'

'Who seems to have died about thirty years after Sir Rowland Verey,' Trent remarked, studying the inscription; while the superintendent gently smote his thigh in an ecstasy of silent admiration. 'And now let us see if the vicar can throw any light on the subject.'

They went on to the parsonage; and a dark-haired, bright-faced girl, opening the door at Mr Owen's ring, smiled recognisingly at Langley. 'Well, you're genuine, anyway!' he exclaimed. 'Ellen is what they call you, isn't it? And you remember me, I see. Now I feel better. We would like to see the vicar. Is he at home?'

'The canon came home two days ago, sir,' the girl said, with a perceptible stress on the term of rank. 'He is down in the village now; but he may be back any minute. Would you like to wait for him?'

'We surely would,' Langley declared positively; and they were shown into the large room where the tabard had changed hands.

'So he has been away from home?' Trent asked. 'And he is a canon, you say?'

'Canon Maberley, sir; yes, sir, he was in Italy for a month. The lady and gentleman who were here till last week had taken the house furnished while he was away. Me and cook stayed on to do for them.'

'And did that gentleman – Mr Verey – do the canon's duty during his absence?' Trent inquired with a ghost of a smile.

'No, sir; the canon had an arrangement with Mr Giles, the vicar of Cotmore, about that. The canon never knew that Mr

Verey was a clergyman. He never saw him. You see it was Mrs Verey who came to see over the place and settled everything; and it seems she never mentioned it. When we told the canon, after they had gone, he was quite took aback. "I can't make it out at all," he says. "Why should he conceal it?" he says. "Well, sir," I says, "they was very nice people, anyhow, and the friends they had to see them here was very nice, and their chauffeur was a perfectly respectable man," I says.'

Trent nodded. 'Ah! They had friends to see them.'

The girl was thoroughly enjoying this gossip. 'Oh, yes, sir. The gentleman as brought you down, sir' – she turned to Langley – 'he brought down several others before that. They was Americans too, I think.'

'You mean they didn't have an English accent, I suppose,' Langley suggested dryly.

'Yes, sir; and they had such nice manners, like yourself,' the girl said, quite unconscious of Langley's confusion, and of the grins covertly exchanged between Trent and the superintendent, who now took up the running.

'This respectable chauffeur of theirs – was he a small, thin man with a long nose, partly bald, always smoking cigarettes?'

'Oh, yes, sir; just like that. You must know him.'

'I do,' Superintendent Owen said grimly.

'So do I!' Langley exclaimed. 'He was the man we spoke to in the churchyard.'

'Did Mr and Mrs Verey have any – er – ornaments of their own with them?' the superintendent asked.

Ellen's eyes rounded with enthusiasm. 'Oh, yes, sir – some lovely things they had. But they was only put out when they had friends coming. Other times they was kept somewhere in Mr Verey's bedroom, I think. Cook and me thought perhaps they was afraid of burglars.'

The superintendent pressed a hand over his stubby moustache. 'Yes, I expect that was it,' he said gravely. 'But what kind of lovely things do you mean? Silver – china – that sort of thing?'

'No, sir; nothing ordinary, as you might say. One day they had out a beautiful goblet, like, all gold, with little figures and patterns worked on it in colours, and precious stones, blue and green and white, stuck all round it – regular dazzled me to look at, it did.'

'The Debenham Chalice!' exclaimed the superintendent.

'Is it a well-known thing, then, sir?' the girl asked.

'No, not at all,' Mr Owen said. 'It is an heirloom – a private family possession. Only we happen to have heard of it.'

'Fancy taking such things about with them,' Ellen remarked. 'Then there was a big book they had out once, lying open on that table in the window. It was all done in funny gold letters on yellow paper, with lovely little pictures all round the edges, gold and silver and all colours.'

'*The Murrane Psalter*!' said Mr Owen. 'Come, we're getting on.'

'And,' the girl pursued, addressing herself to Langley, 'there was that beautiful red coat with the arms on it, like you see on a half-crown. You remember they got it out for you to look at, sir; and when I brought in the tea it was hanging up in front of the tallboy.'

Langley grimaced. 'I believe I do remember it,' he said, 'now you remind me.'

'There is the canon coming up the path now,' Ellen said, with a glance through the window. 'I will tell him you gentlemen are here.'

She hurried from the room, and soon there entered a tall, stooping old man with a gentle face and the indescribable air of a scholar.

The superintendent went to meet him.

'I am a police officer, Canon Maberley,' he said. 'I and my friends have called to see you in pursuit of an official inquiry in connection with the people to whom your house was let last month. I do not think I shall have to trouble you much, though, because your parlourmaid has given us already most of the information we are likely to get, I suspect.'

'Ah! That girl,' the canon said vaguely. 'She has been talking to you, has she? She will go on talking for ever, if you let her. Please sit down, gentlemen. About the Vereys – ah, yes! But surely there was nothing wrong about the Vereys? Mrs Verey was quite a nice, well-bred person and they left the place in perfectly good order. They paid me in advance, too, because they live in New Zealand, as she explained, and know nobody in London. They were on a visit to England, and they wanted a temporary home in the heart of the country, because that is the real England, as she said. That was so sensible of them, I thought – instead of flying to the grime and turmoil of London, as most of our friends from overseas do. In a way, I was quite touched by it, and I was glad to let them have the vicarage.'

The superintendent shook his head. 'People as clever as they are make things very difficult for us, sir. And the lady never mentioned that her husband was a clergyman, I understand.'

'No, and that puzzled me when I heard of it,' the canon said. 'But it didn't matter, and no doubt there was a reason.'

'The reason was, I think,' Mr Owen said, 'that if she had mentioned it, you might have been too much interested, and asked questions which would have been all right for a genuine parson's wife, but which she couldn't answer without putting her foot in it. Her husband could do a vicar well enough to pass with laymen, especially if they were not English laymen. I am sorry to say, canon, that your tenants were impostors. Their name was certainly not Verey, to begin with. I don't know who they are – I wish I did – they are new to us and they have invented a new method. But I can tell you what they are. They are thieves and swindlers.'

The canon fell back in his chair. 'Thieves and swindlers!' he gasped.

'And very talented performers too,' Trent assured him. 'Why, they have had in this house of yours part of the loot of several country-house burglaries which took place last year, and which puzzled the police because it seemed impossible that some of the things taken could ever be turned into cash. One of them was a herald's tabard, which Superintendent Owen tells me had been worn by the father of Sir Andrew Ritchie. He was Maltravers Herald in his day. It was taken when Sir Andrew's place in Lincolnshire was broken into, and a lot of very valuable jewellery was stolen. It was dangerous to try to sell the tabard in the open market, and it was worth little, anyhow, apart from any associations it might have. What they did was to fake up a story about the tabard which might appeal to an American purchaser, and, having found a victim, to induce him to buy it. I believe he parted with quite a large sum.'

'The poor simp,' growled Langley.

Canon Maberley held up a shaking hand. 'I fear I do not understand,' he said. 'What had their taking my house to do with all this?'

'It was a vital part of the plan. We know exactly how they went to work about the tabard; and no doubt the other things were got rid of in very much the same way. There were four of them in the gang. Besides your tenants, there was an agreeable and cultured person – I should think a man with real knowledge of antiquities and objects of art – whose job was to make the acquaintance of wealthy people visiting London, gain their confidence, take them about the places of interest, exchange hospitality with them, and finally get them down to this vicarage. In this case it was made to appear as if the proposal to look over your church came from the visitors themselves. They could not suspect anything. They were attracted by the romantic name of the place on a signpost up there at the corner of the main road.'

The canon shook his head helplessly. 'But there is no signpost at that corner.'

'No, but there was one at the time when they were due to be passing that corner in the confederate's car. It was a false signpost, you see, with a false name on it – so that if anything went wrong, the place where the swindle was worked would be difficult to trace. Then, when they entered the churchyard their attention was attracted by a certain gravestone with an inscription that interested them. I won't waste your time by giving the whole story – the point is that the gravestone, or rather the top layer which had been fitted on to it, was false too. The sham inscription on it was meant to lead up to the swindle and so it did.'

The canon drew himself up in his chair. 'It was an abominable act of sacrilege!' he exclaimed. 'The man calling himself Verey –'

'I don't think,' Trent said, 'it was the man calling himself Verey who actually did the abominable act. We believe it was the fourth member of the gang, who masqueraded as the Vereys' chauffeur – a very interesting character. Superintendent Owen can tell you about him.'

Mr Owen twisted his moustache thoughtfully. 'Yes; he is the only one of them that we can place. Alfred Coveney, his name is; a man of some education and any amount of talent. He used to be a stage-carpenter and property-maker – a regular artist, he was. Give him a tub of papiermâché, and there was nothing he couldn't model and colour to look exactly like the real thing. That was how the false top to the gravestone was made, I've no doubt. It may have been made to fit on like a lid, to be slipped on and off as required. The inscription was a bit above Alf, though – I expect it was Gifford who drafted that for him, and he copied the lettering from other old stones in the churchyard. Of course the fake signpost was Alf's work too – stuck up when required, and taken down when the show was over.

'Well, Alf got into bad company. They found how clever he was with his hands, and he became an expert burglar. He has served two terms of imprisonment. He is one of a few who have always been under suspicion for the job at Sir Andrew Ritchie's place, and the other two when the chalice was lifted from Eynsham Park and the Psalter from Lord Swanbourne's house. With what they collected in this house and the jewellery that was taken in all three burglaries, they must have done very well indeed for themselves; and by this time they are going to be hard to catch.'

Canon Maberley, who had now recovered himself somewhat, looked at the others with the beginnings of a smile. 'It is a new experience for me,' he said, 'to be made use of by a gang of criminals. But it is highly interesting. I suppose that when these confiding strangers had been got down here, my tenant appeared in the character of the parson, and invited them into the house, where you tell me they were induced to make a purchase of stolen property. I do not see, I must confess, how anything could have been better designed to prevent any possibility of suspicion arising. The vicar of a parish, at home in his own vicarage! Who could imagine anything being wrong? I only hope for the credit of my cloth, that the deception was well carried out.'

'As far as I know,' Trent said, 'he made only one mistake. It was a small one; but the moment I heard of it I knew that he must have been a fraud. You see, he was asked about the oar you have hanging up in the hall. I didn't go to Oxford myself, but I believe when a man is given his oar it means that he rowed in an eight that did something unusually good.'

A light came into the canon's spectacled eyes. 'In the year I got my colours the Wadham boat went up five places on the river. It was the happiest week of my life.'

'Yet you had other triumphs,' Trent suggested. 'For instance, didn't you get a Fellowship at All Souls, after leaving Wadham?'

'Yes, and that did please me, naturally,' the canon said. 'But that is a different sort of happiness, my dear sir, and, believe me, nothing like so keen. And by the way, how did you know about that?'

'I thought it might be so, because of the little mistake your tenant made. When he was asked about the oar, he said he had rowed for All Souls.'

Canon Maberley burst out laughing, while Langley and the superintendent stared at him blankly.

'I think I see what happened,' he said. 'The rascal must have been browsing about in my library, in search of ideas for the part he was to play. I was a resident Fellow for five years, and a number of my books have a bookplate with my name and the name and arms of All Souls. His mistake was natural.' And again the old gentleman laughed delightedly.

Langley exploded. 'I like a joke myself,' he said, 'but I'll be skinned alive if I can see the point of this one.'

'Why, the point is,' Trent told him, 'that nobody ever rowed for All Souls. There never were more than four undergraduates there at one time, all the other members being Fellows.'

The Narrow Way

R. Ellis Roberts

At his confirmation he had annoyed the Bishop of London (at that time it was Frederick Temple) by insisting on taking the additional names of Alfonso Mary Alexander. He had surprised him by the resolute manner in which he had answered his questions about the origin of taking names at confirmation; and enraged him by his explanation that he desired to be called Alexander in memory of that great Pope, the Lord Alexander VI, who had put the whole Christian world under an obligation by his discovery of the devotion of the Angelus. 'This devotion,' the boy murmured to the astounded Bishop, 'as your Lordship no doubt knows, has been from eternity the privilege of the Holy Angels, and was not entrusted to men until the proximity of the horrible heresies of the German deformation rendered the patronage of Mary necessary for the protection of her son.' The Bishop's chaplain had tried to prevent Frank Lascelles' indiscretion; but Temple's abrupt gesture had hindered his efforts. When Lascelles finished the Bishop gazed at him in silence for a minute.

'Well, I hope you'll live to grow out of this foolery. But you know your rights and you shall have 'em.'

Temple was, as his old foes had discovered years before, eminently just.

More than twenty years had passed since that confirmation. Frank Alfonso Mary Alexander Lascelles had gone to Oxford and to Ely, and had been ordained to a small country parish in that diocese. After two years of his curacy, an injudicious layman presented him to the living of S. Uny and S. Petroc in the north of Cornwall. He had been there now for over nineteen years. When he had come he found his church empty; now it was full. It was full of children and boys. Occasionally a few mothers, and, when he was sober, the village drunkard, and, when she was penitent, the prostitute from the Church Town, came to Mass as well; but generally the Church of S. Uny, down by the beach, was filled only by children and boys.

This result Frank Lascelles had been long in attaining. The parish he served was predominantly Methodist. He had found a congregation of three – the publican, the ostler of the hotel, and an old maiden lady who rang the bell, and called herself the pew opener. Lascelles soon shocked the respectability of the publican and the Protestantism of the ostler: but the old lady remained faithful to him. She did not stir when he had the three-decker cut down, and a new altar reared at the East end. She seemed to welcome the great images, Our Lady of the Immaculate Conception, The Sacred Heart, S. Joseph and S. Anthony which Lascelles put up in his church. She did not care whether he said Mass in Latin or English; and incense and holy water both left her tranquil. It was otherwise with the village. Though the Methodists never entered the church, except for a wedding or a funeral, they thought they had a right to control its services and its priest. There were stormy Easter vestries; there was a Protestant church-warden. One horrible day the fishermen broke into the church and took out the images and threw them down the cliff: by next week new ones were in their places. Lascelles was boycotted by his parishioners, except a few would-be bold spirits; and was outlawed, in the genial English way, by his Bishop; but he stuck at his job, went on saying offices to an empty church, and singing Mass to his pew opener and an occasional visitor. Then after five years or so the change began.

It was not along the usual lines of such changes. Generally priests of Lascelles' religion are eager, masculine people who soon win over the more turbulent elements in the parish, and put them, too, in search of the great adventure of Christianity. But Lascelles, though he had grown up, still remained the boy who had chosen Liguori and Alexander for his patrons. He was obsessed with the reality of the spiritual world, of good and evil. His pillow was wet with the tears he shed for the sins of his parish. He was horrified at the evil of the world, and yet constitutionally unable to defy it in any active way. He had only one strong human affection – and that was a great love for children.

At first this was not reciprocated. His odd figure, his shuffling walk, his stoop and his occasional outbursts of anger produced ridicule and fear rather than love. Then one child somehow found how large the heart of him was; and then another, and then another. He had won the children. But this would have availed him little had it not been for the arrival at S. Uny of the Rev. Paul Trengrowse. Mr Trengrowse came to minister to the Primitives about three years after Lascelles' appointment to the parish. He was young, keen, and sincere. He had not been long in the village when the leading members of his congregation told him of the sins of the Parish Priest, and horrors of the parish church. Trengrowse prayed for light. He disliked interfering with the affairs of an alien church; but, if half he was told was true, Lascelles must be fought. So he paid a visit to the church, which was always open, and was duly distressed at the idols he saw there.

As he was gazing at the smirking fatuity of S. Anthony, he heard a footstep. It was Lascelles who was coming from the sacristy to the altar. Fortunately, before he began Mass, Lascelles looked down the church and saw 'a congregation.' So he said Mass in English.

Now Trengrowse was no ordinary minister. He was a man of personal holiness, and of real devotion; and that in his spirit which was sincere and mystical recognised in the Popish-seeming priest muttering his Mass, a kindred soul. Lascelles' absorption in his work, his grave, yet joyful solemnity, his keen sense of the other world made an immense effect on Trengrowse. The Mass proceeded, and when Trengrowse heard 'Therefore with Angels and Archangels and all the Company of Heaven,' he felt that he had had the answer to his prayer. This man was a Christian, however erroneous he might be in details.

So the next Sunday the Primitives, who were hoping for a strong sermon against the Scarlet Woman, were disagreeably surprised. 'Mr Lascelles may be wrong. I think he is wrong, sadly wrong, in many things: but he du love the Lord, and he du worship Him. And, brethren, no man calls Jesus Lord save by the Holy Ghost. Let us pray for Mr Lascelles and the church people of S. Uny; and that we may all be led along the narrow way to everlasting life.'

Had Trengrowse been a man of less character he might have failed in his defence of Lascelles. But he was an acceptable preacher, and a man whose plain love of his religion it was impossible to doubt. So, first with grumbling, later with a ready acquiescence, the villagers of S. Uny followed his lead.

The result was odd. Lascelles attracted the children more and more; and his services attracted them. This worried Trengrowse not a little; but when one of his congregation said scornfully, 'Those bit games to the church be only fit for babes,' he looked gravely at him and replied, 'Ah! Eli, but the book says "Unless ye become as little children." ' This silenced Eli, but it did not silence Trengrowse's own heart. How was it Lascelles could do anything with children, a good deal with boys up to fifteen or so, and nothing with men and women, and little with girls? Lascelles' own explanation was simple. His Bishop would not confirm his children until they were thirteen. Lascelles presented them year after year when they were six or seven. He preached an amazing sermon on the three great aids to the Devil in the parish of S. Uny – and the three heads of his sermon were: Lust, Hypocrisy and the Lord Bishop. The more respectable of the neighbouring clergy were furious, but the Bishop, who was a simple, humble-minded man (quite unlike the ex-headmaster who had inducted Lascelles) refused to take any notice of the attack; but also refused to relax his rule about the age of confirmation candidates. The Archdeacon told Lascelles that his parish was the plague-spot of the diocese, and Lascelles retorted that in a mass of corruption any sign of health looks ominous and unusual. But, although he kept up a brave front to the disapprovers, his failure with his people galled him. He would not have minded if they had still been actively hostile. But that had long ceased. They were now fond of their priest. They liked and shared in his notoriety. They supported him against the officials; and when a malicious Protestant from London attempted to stir up a revolt against Lascelles, he was promptly put into the harbour; and Trengrowse started a petition to the Bishop, expressing the affection 'all we, whether church people or Methodists, feel for Mr Lascelles.'

Lascelles' philosophy refused to permit him to see in his failure evidences of his incapacity for his work. He had the proud humility of the perfect priest. Regarding himself as a mere channel for divine grace, he forgot that his personality was so distinctive that it affected the way in which grace reached his people. Once an old friend had tried to make him see this; but the task was hopeless.

'My dear fellow,' said Lascelles, 'I don't see what you mean. All they want is the Gospel. And that I give them. I say Mass for them. I will hear their confessions. I instruct them. I lead their devotions. All beside is mere human embellishment. No doubt a more competent man would be more pleasing to them, but he could do no more than give them the Gospel, could he?'

II

On All Souls' Day, 1912, Lascelles was depressed. Early that morning he had gone up to the cemetery, and said a Requiem in the little chapel. Then there had been the early Mass at 8.30 in church. The church had been full. Not only were all his children there, but there were a good many fathers and mothers: for the services on the day of the dead appealed to a deep human instinct with a power which not even Lascelles could spoil. The Dies Irae, sung in Latin, had sounded oddly from a congregation so predominantly childish: and Lascelles had preached a short sermon on the 'Significance of Death.'

'We exaggerate the importance of death. It is to us death matters, not to the dead. For them it is a release, for us it is a warning. Death of the body is only a symbol. It is death of the soul we must fear. Believe me, it would be worth while for every one of you in this church to die, if by dying, you could bring a soul to Jesus. God knows, I would die for you, if that would bring you. There are those here to-day – you, Penberthy, and you, Trevose – who have not been to Mass since you were boys. Make a new resolution to-day, and ask the Holy Souls to help you keep it. Come to your duties, and return to your church.'

Lascelles felt at the time that his appeal lacked force. He knew that after Mass, Penberthy would say to Trevose:

'Bootivul service, bean't it, Tom?'

'Iss – it be that. I du like it for once or twice. But for usual give me the chapel. It be more nat'ral like.'

'Iss – it be. Poor Mr Lascelles, I did think he would have a slap at us.'

'Iss – it be his way. My gosh! I don't mind.'

So Lascelles was depressed. He sat among his books, reading a Renascence treatise on 'Death.' He thought a great deal about death. Sometimes he feared it horribly. It seemed the great enemy of faith. It was so disconcerting a thing, so heartless, so unregarding. At other times he felt defiant. But never did he reach the spirit of S. Francis about death. He was too remote from natural life and the events of animal birth and death to understand death as an ordinary thing, something not less usual than the sunset.

'It may be' – he read, 'that there be more deaths than one. For it is evident that some are so hardened in sin that the death of the body comes long after the man has really been dead. Such men are commonly gay and cheerful; for with the death of their soul, has died all godly fear, all apprehension of judgment, all hope of salvation. They become but as brutes. Wherefore the church has always held that heretics, if they be obstinate and beyond recall, may be handed over to the secular arm for the death of the body. It should not trouble us that they display ordinary human virtues: for these be common in the unregenerate, and are but devices of the devil who would persuade men that religion matters naught. They are his children, and may be lawfully treated as such by any godly prince. The church herself kills not: though the Lord Pope, being a Temporal King, has the power of the sword, and may exercise the same.'

Lascelles put the book down and stared at the fire. The words roused a train of thought that almost frightened him. But he was not the man to dismiss any idea because it was terrifying. He believed in giving the devil his due, and always insisted that all temptations should be met boldly, not evaded. He left his chair, and knelt at his prie-dieu, looking at the wounds of the great Crucifix which hung above it.

Half an hour later he rose with a look of resolution on his face.

III

The first case of the plague, as the villagers insisted on calling it, happened just before Epiphany. It attacked Penberthy, who had never been ill before; and in four days he was dead. His disease puzzled the doctor from the market-town, but he put it down as a curious case of infantile paralysis. His colleague from Truro, whom he consulted after the third case had occurred, insisted that the symptoms did not disclose anything more definite than shock following on *status lymphaticus*. The most serious thing was, however, not their incapacity to name, but their inability to cure the mysterious disease which was spreading in S. Uny. Except for a general weariness, a disinclination to move, and a curious 'wambling in the innards,' there were no definite symptoms at all to go on. After the second case they had an inquest, but it yielded no results at all, and Dr Marlowe began to talk of getting an expert from London.

It was not until February, however, that any one came. Then by a fortunate chance Sir Joshua Tomlinson came down to S. Ives for a holiday. The 'plague' at S. Uny had got into the London paper. There had been ten deaths, and two women, the first to be attacked, were lying seriously ill. Dr Marlowe called on Sir Joshua, and the great physician said he would come over and see the patients. Marlowe was glad that chance had sent him a great general physician rather than a surgeon or a specialist. Although he was willing to defy any specialist to find his pet disease in the mysterious sickness that had killed the ten fishermen, he was relieved that no specialist was to be given the opportunity.

'You see, Lascelles,' he said to the priest, 'it's not as if we were in the fifteenth century. We may be in theology, but I'm hanged if we are in medicine. These men are dying like savages: but the savage makes up his mind he has got to die, and dies through sheer hysteria. These fellows want to live. They lust for life.'

'You are right, Marlowe. Their desire for life is a lust. It is scarcely decent in a Christian to cling so to this existence. But there – it's not my business to judge. You know, Marlowe, I have sometimes thought this last month that this mysterious disease is a judgment on S. Uny. It is God's hand held out over our village. Let us pray for those who are dead, and those who are dying, and most of all, dear God, for those who are not yet to die.'

Marlowe, though friendly with Lascelles, was more than a little afraid of him. The vicar had worked like two men during this distress. He had nursed the sick, he had consoled the mourners, he had said Masses and had a service of general humiliation. Somehow he had identified himself with his parish to a degree he had never reached before, and S. Uny was grateful to him. But the little doctor was rather afraid. Lascelles was strained and odd in manner. He spent too long a time in prayer, and not long enough at meals or in bed.

'No, Lascelles. I don't agree with you there. Oh! I'm a good Catholic, I hope, and I know God could intervene; but I don't see why He should.'

'No: you don't see why. No one does, Marlowe, until He speaks, and then they are forced to.'

On the Saturday Sir Joshua came over. He saw Mrs Pentreath and Mrs Whichelo, and he shook his head over both of them. He asked them questions about their diet, and about their way of living, while Marlowe stood by, silent and impatient. Then he said a few kindly, cheerful words, and left them in the big room, which the vicar had had fitted up as a hospital ward; for Marlowe thought the cases were better isolated.

'Well, sir, what do you think?'

'What sort of a man is your vicar? He seems liked.'

'Yes – he is. He's an odd chap – a bit mad, I think. A very keen Catholic, and very depressed at his failure to keep the people.'

'Ah! they don't go to church?'

'Well they *do* now. They have done since this damned illness. He's been awfully good to them. And the children have always gone.'

'It's a funny thing, Dr Marlowe, that no child has been ill.'

'Isn't it? That's what I say to young Jones of Truro. He will insist on his shock theory, following on *status lymphaticus*. I keep on pointing out to him that most of the patients are men who have had shocks every week of their lives since they were twelve. They'd have all been dead long since.'

'Yes. I am sure Jones is wrong. But I don't know what this disease is, Dr Marlowe. I suspect, but I don't know.'

'Here is the vicar coming, Sir Joshua. Shall I introduce you?'

'Please do.'

Lascelles was walking rapidly towards them. He looked ill but eager. His eyes were full of a fanatic pleasure, a kind of holy rapture that appeared to make him even taller than he actually was. He acknowledged the introduction with a bow, and would have passed on, but Sir Joshua stopped him with a question.

'You have come from your sick people, Mr Lascelles?'

'Yes. They are no longer sick. I was just in time to hear their confessions, and give them the viaticum.'

'Good God!' Sir Joshua was evidently shocked. 'It's not ten minutes since we left them.'

'No? The end has always been very sudden, hasn't it, Marlowe?'

'Yes. But this is quicker than usual. Do you think, Sir Joshua' – and he lowered his voice – 'a post-mortem?'

'No. It would be useless. At least it would be no help to me. By the way, Marlowe, how have you entered the cause of death?'

'Well, sir – I've frankly put "Heart failure, cause unknown." There seemed to be nothing between that and "Act of God." '

'Ah! Marlowe, that's what you should have put,' intervened Lascelles. 'It is the hand of God – the hand of God.' Then, with a bow to Sir Joshua, he hurried away.

'So your vicar thinks it is the hand of God. He may be right. God works through human agents. He is an interesting man, Dr Marlowe.'

'Yes: he is. But this trouble has worried him frightfully. I'm rather nervous for him. Have you got any theory, sir. You talked of suspicion.'

'Well, Dr Marlowe, I'll tell you what I think. Your patients have been murdered.'

Marlowe looked at the great physician, as if he was afraid for his sanity.

'No, Dr Marlowe, I'm not mad, though I have no proof of my assertion. All I ask is this, that I may be allowed to see the next patient within at least half an hour of the beginning of the illness.

By the way, can they give me a bed here, do you think? Where do you put up?'

'Oh! I'm staying at the vicar's. I expect he'd be charmed to have you.'

'No. I don't think I will stay with Father Lascelles. I would rather not. I'll find a room somewhere. I think there will be another case tomorrow night.'

IV

That Sunday morning Lascelles preached on the 'Hand of Judgment.' The church was packed. Trengrowse had his service at nine and brought all his congregation to the Mass at eleven. Lascelles seemed wonderfully better. His eye was clearer, his step gayer and his whole figure more buoyant. His tone as he gave out his text was exultant.

'They pierced his hands.

'The symbolism of the Divine Body is strangely arresting. The Jews thought of God as an eye watching, caring for them from heaven. We Christians watch God – here in the Tabernacle, or in the arms of Mary. His care for us we typify by His Hand – the Hand we pierced. This last month God has been with us very wonderfully. He is always with us in the holy Sacrament: but lately He has been with us in the Sacrament of Death. His Hand of Judgment has been over, and under us; it has clasped us – and some of us it has not let go.

'Our natural feeling is one of fear. We are not used to such immediate handling as this of our God's. We have most of us tried to apply religion to our life, now we have to try and apply our life to religion. God will have us think of nothing but Him, speak to none save Him, hope for none save Him. His Hand is still with us. It will bear yet more away from S. Uny before we learn our lesson. Let me help you to learn that lesson right. Let us all take care that we renew our trust in

God, that we recognise His Hand, that we answer His Love.'

Sir Joshua had listened attentively to Lascelles' sermon. He seemed vaguely disappointed, and he was unwilling to discuss it with Marlowe afterwards. There was no doubt that Lascelles' almost fatalist attitude, while it annoyed the doctor, had a strange welcome from the villagers. They turned in a childlike way to the words of this man who spoke as one who knew the ways and the meaning of the Almighty. Never had Lascelles so much real devotion from his people as he secured during the 'plague.' It was not that they shared his feeling of complete abandonment to the Will of God; but the fact that he had such a feeling made their fate seem more tolerable.

On Sunday evening there was a new case, as Sir Joshua had expected. The disease attacked Mrs Bodilly, the wife of the chief grocer in S. Uny. Marlowe was summoned immediately, but he found Sir Joshua already at the poor woman's bedside.

She was frankly terrified; in this her case differed from previous ones, in which the sufferers, though generally resentful, had been not the least afraid. Mrs Bodilly had been at Mass that morning. She had got back and prepared the dinner. At tea-time she had 'felt queer,' but after tea she was better. Then as she was getting ready to go to the special service of Exposition, she fell down and had to be carried up to her room by her husband and sons.

She was, unlike most of the tradesmen's wives, a nominal church woman, but she had never been confirmed and rarely went to church. The fit of external piety roused in her by the 'plague,' was frankly based on nervous alarm. She felt that God was taking it out of S. Uny in this way; and she was anxious to escape.

Her illness found her divided between anger and fear. She was angry that her efforts to placate Divine wrath had not been more successful – she was terrified of dying, terrified still more of death as a punishment. In the most desolate way she sought reassurances from Marlowe and Sir Joshua; but neither could give her any certain consolation. The disease presented no different aspects. It indeed presented no aspect at all, except extreme weakness, astonishing slowness of the pulse, and irregular beating of the heart. Although Sir Joshua was there within five minutes of the seizure, he admitted to Marlowe that he could discover nothing of what he suspected.

'I'll be frank, Dr Marlowe, I suspected poison. I still suspect it. I believe all these people have been poisoned in an extremely subtle way by a man so fanatical as to be almost mad. But I can find no trace of the poison. In this case, I will, if you will permit me, conduct a post-mortem, but I expect I shall fail. If I do, I must take my own line, if you wish me to help you.'

'Really, Sir Joshua, you talk more like a detective than a physician.'

'This is a detective's business, Dr Marlowe. I wish it were not.'

Before they left Lascelles arrived. He had been summoned by Mr Bodilly, and he came prepared to give Mrs Bodilly the last rites. As the boy with the light and the bell approached the stairs, Sir Joshua whispered to Marlowe:

'Your vicar seems very certain of her death.'

Marlowe shrugged his shoulders. 'We haven't saved a case, you know.'

The post-mortem yielded no result. That evening Marlowe dined with Sir Joshua at the village inn, and after dinner the great physician told him of his suspicions. Marlowe listened at first angrily, then with an incredulous horror.

'It can't be. The man lives for his parish, I tell you. Why, he would die for it.'

'Yes: I believe he would. Had I found what I looked for, he certainly would.'

'But, my dear sir, there isn't a trace of any known drug. There's no trace of anything.'

'No. I had expected to find – but never mind. I have a great deal of experience, Dr Marlowe, and I am convinced that your vicar has been murdering his parishioners. And tonight I am coming to tell him so. I will walk home with you. You may be present or not, as you please.'

<h1 style="text-align:center">V</h1>

Lascelles looked up a little wearily when Sir Joshua had finished speaking.

'Is that all?'

Marlowe intervened.

'Look here, old man – I only came because – you'll forgive me Sir Joshua – I didn't want you to be alone under this monstrous, this fantastic accusation of Sir Joshua's. You've only got to contradict him, and we'll go.'

Lascelles looked gratefully at his friend.

'Thank you, Marlowe. But Sir Joshua is right in telling me his suspicions. You have finished, Sir Joshua?'

'Yes. I should like your explanation if you have one, or your admission of my charge, and your promise that this – this – plague shall cease.'

'You use strange words, sir, for a man who has no evidence for what he says.'

'Yes,' – ejaculated Marlowe, 'yes, by Jove, you do –'

'Please, Marlowe. You will not be content with having relieved your mind, Sir Joshua. You wish me to answer you?'

'I do. I require it.'

'You know, sir, you great doctors have one failing. It is one priests have too. You cannot avoid talking to me as if I were your patient – a mental, a nervous case. You can't help believing that your firm tone, your almost – may I say it – discourteous manner will impress me. Well, it doesn't.'

Sir Joshua got red. Lascelles' words too entirely diagnosed his method. He was annoyed that he should seem so transparent to a man whom he regarded as at least half-crazy.

'I beg your pardon. There is something in what you say. Men in all professions have their – ah! tricks.'

'Thank you.'

Lascelles got up and stood by the fireplace looking down on his visitor. In the last month he had changed. He seemed bigger and more masculine – more as if he now had personal responsibilities: he looked less of an official, more of a man. He spoke rather slowly.

'You have accused me of murder, Sir Joshua. You ask me to admit my crime, and to promise to cease. Well, I expected your visit. I have long been familiar with your Treatise on Renascence Toxicology: it is as complete as any published book. And I am glad you and Marlowe came to-night. I have my answer ready. I admit nothing and I promise nothing.'

Sir Joshua looked with a puzzled air at the priest. For a moment his accusation seemed a monstrous thing to himself. Then his common sense surged back.

'Father Lascelles, your answer does not satisfy me. I must take other steps.'

'They will not lead anywhere, Sir Joshua. If *you* find no evidence, no other man can. You say my poor people were poisoned. Well, find the poison. Ah – you know you cannot. It is foolish to threaten me. But I will tell you what I had determined to tell Marlowe to-night. First, I do not expect there will be any more deaths from this plague for a long time.

'Secondly, I have a confession to make. Last All Hallows I was depressed. The work here has not gone as it should. I had the children, but not their parents. I thought much of Death and the Departed at that season of all the dead – and at last I prayed to God that if nothing else would move these people, He would send Death. Send Death mysterious and as a judgment. Death has come, and my people have learnt their lesson. All of those who died were reconciled to Holy Church before death. Of those who remain nearly all have adhered to the Church. This afternoon Mr Trengrowse came and asked to be prepared for Confirmation –'

'Trengrowse, the minister –' cried Marlowe.

'And this evening I had notice that all who are competent intend to make their Communion next Sunday. This parish has been won for God, Sir Joshua, and at the cost of thirteen deaths. Isn't it worth it?'

'Father Lascelles, I cannot regard you as sane. You are not only practically admitting your crime, you are disclosing your motives.'

'I beg your pardon, I admit nothing. I acknowledged I prayed to God to visit this people, if necessary, by His secret Death. That is not a crime. Next Sunday I shall tell my people.'

'And have you *prayed* that the deaths shall cease?' asked Sir Joshua ironically.

'I was doing so when you entered,' replied Lascelles quietly.

'Good God, man, your hypocrisy sickens me. You prate of God's intervention, and all the time you've been sending man after man to death by some foul poison of your own.'

'Sir Joshua – do you believe God commonly works without human intervention?'

'Bah! That is sophistry.'

'You condemn the machinery of justice, the compromise of war, our human evasion of rope and guillotine?'

'Surely, Marlowe,' exclaimed Sir Joshua, 'you can't sit and listen quietly to this damnable nonsense?'

Marlowe had been sitting dazed, looking at Lascelles as if he were fascinated. He replied in a remote voice:

'I don't know. I'm wondering' – he gave a nervous laugh – 'wondering if Lascelles is a saint or a devil.'

Lascelles went on imperturbably:

'You don't answer me. You can't. Why should you think I, an anointed priest, am less fit to be the door-keeper of death than Lord Justice Ommaney? At least I use no case-law. I am the slave of no precedent. I know my people. I know them individually. I love them as persons. And as persons I judge them.'

The tall figure of the man seemed to glow. His face was lit with an unnatural beauty, as he stood looking down on the other two, and dared them to answer him.

Sir Joshua rose. He had lost his somewhat pompous judicial air. He was deeply, humanly moved; and he spoke with an anxiety far more impressive than his previous authoritative tone.

'Father Lascelles, I have nothing more to say. I believe you to have done a very horrible, a very wicked thing. I have heard how you would defend yourself if you were legally brought to book for such an offence. Your defence has, as you are aware, no legal force. I think it has no moral force. You are deceiving yourself strangely. One day you will have a great loneliness of heart. You will realize how terrible a responsibility you have taken. Without the sanction of society, without the approval of your church, you have decided alone, the fate of your fellow-creatures. I am sorry for you. Good-night.'

The light left Lascelles' face. He looked suddenly ill and careworn. Then with a high, frantic gesture he flung his hand towards the Crucifix.

'He, too – He, too – was made sin.'

The Yellow Slugs

H. C. Bailey

The big car closed up behind a florid funeral procession which held the middle of the road. On either side was a noisy congestion of lorries. Mr Fortune sighed and closed his eyes.

When he looked out again he was passing the first carriage of another funeral, and saw beneath the driver's seat the white coffin of a baby. For the road served the popular cemetery of Blaney.

Two slow miles of dingy tall houses and cheap shops slid by, with vistas of meaner streets opening on either side. The car gathered speed across Blaney Common, an expanse of yellow turf and bare sand, turbid pond and scrubwood, and stopped at the brown pile of an old poor law hospital.

Entering its carbolic odour, Mr Fortune was met by Superintendent Bell. 'Here I am,' he moaned. 'Why am I?'

'Well, she's still alive, sir,' said Bell. 'They both are.'

Mr Fortune was taken to a ward in which, secluded by a screen, a little girl lay asleep.

Her face had a babyish fatness, but in its pallor looked bloated and unhealthy. Though the close July air was oppressive and she was covered with heavy bed-clothes, her skin showed no sign of heat and she slept still as death.

Reggie sat down beside her. His hands moved gently within the bed . . . He listened . . . he looked . . .

A nurse followed him to the door. 'How old, do you think?' he murmured.

'That was puzzling me, sir. She's big enough for seven or eight, but all flabby. And when she came to, she was talking almost baby talk. I suppose she may be only about five.'

Reggie nodded. 'Quite good, yes. All right. Carry on.'

From the ward he passed to a small room where a nurse and a doctor stood together watching the one bed.

A boy lay in it, restless and making noises – inarticulate words mixed with moaning and whimpering.

The doctor lifted his eyebrows at Reggie. 'Get that?' he whispered. 'Still talking about hell. He came absolutely unstuck. I had to risk a shot of morphia. I –' He broke off in apprehension as Reggie's round face hardened to a cold severity. But Reggie nodded and moved to the bed . . .

The boy tossed into stertorous sleep, one thin arm flung up above a tousled head. His sunken cheeks were flushed, and drips of sweat stood on the upper lip and the brow. Not a bad brow – not an uncomely face but for its look of hungry misery – not the face of a child – a face which had been the prey of emotions and thwarted desires . . .

Reggie's careful hands worked over him . . . bits of the frail body were laid bare . . . Reggie stood up, and still his face was set in ruthless, passionless determination.

Outside the door the doctor spoke nervously. 'I hope you don't –'

'Morphia's all right,' Reggie interrupted. 'What do you make of him?'

'Well, Mr Fortune, I wish you'd seen him at first.' The doctor was uncomfortable beneath the cold insistence of a questioning stare. 'He was right out of hand – a sort of hysterical fury. I should say he's quite abnormal. Neurotic lad, badly nourished – you can't tell what they won't do, that type.'

'I can't. No. What age do you give him?'

'Now you've got me. To hear him raving, you'd think he was grown up, such a flow of language. Bible phrases and preaching. I'd say he was a twelve-year-old, but he might only be eight or ten. His development is all out of balance. He's unhealthy right through.'

'Yes, that is so,' Reggie murmured. 'However. You ought to save him.'

'Poor little devil,' said the doctor.

In a bare, grim waiting-room Reggie sat down with Superintendent Bell, and Bell looked anxiety. 'Well, sir?'

'Possible. Probable,' Reggie told him. 'On the evidence.'

'Ah. Cruel, isn't it? I hate these child cases.'

'Any more evidence?' Reggie drawled.

Bell stared at his hard calm gloomily. 'I have. Plenty.'

The story began with a small boy on the bank of one of the ponds on Blaney Common. That was some time ago. That was the first time anybody in authority had been aware of the existence of Eddie Hill. One of the keepers of the common made the discovery. The pond was that one which children used for the sailing of toy boats. Eddie Hill had no boat, but he loitered round all the morning, watching the boats of other children. There was little wind, and one boat lay becalmed in the middle of the pond when the children had to go home to dinner.

An hour later the keeper saw Eddie Hill wade into the pond and run away. When the children came back from dinner there was no boat to be seen. Its small owner made weeping complaint to the keeper, who promised to keep his eyes open, and some days later found Eddie Hill and his little sister Bessie lurking among the gorse of the common with the stolen boat.

It was taken from them and their sin reported to their mother, who promised vengeance.

Their mother kept a little general shop. She had been there a dozen years – ever since she married her first husband. She was well liked and looked up to; a religious woman, regular chapelgoer and all that. Her second husband, Brightman, was the same sort – hard-working, respectable man; been at the chapel longer than she had.

The day-school teachers had nothing against Eddie or the little girl. Eddie was rather more than usually bright, but dreamy and careless; the girl a bit stodgy. Both of 'em rather less naughty than most.

'Know a lot, don't you?' Reggie murmured. 'Got all this to-day?'

'No, this was all on record,' Bell said. 'Worked out for another business.'

'Oh. Small boy and small girl already old offenders. Go on.'

The other business was at the chapel Sunday school. Eddie Hill, as the most regular of its pupils, was allowed the privilege of tidying up at the end of the afternoon. On a Sunday in the spring the superintendent came in unexpectedly upon the process and found Eddie holding the money-box in which had been collected the contributions of the school to the chapel missionary society.

Eddie had no need nor right to handle the money-box. More-over, on the bench beside him were pennies and a sixpence. Such wealth could not be his own. Only the teachers ever put in silver. Moreover, he confessed that he had extracted the money by rattling the box upside down, and his small sister wept for the sin.

The superintendent took him to the police-station and charged him with theft.

'Virtuous man,' Reggie murmured.

'It does seem a bit harsh,' Bell said. 'But they'd had suspicions about the money-box before. They'd been watching for something like this. Well, the boy's mother came and tried to beg him off, but of course the case had to go on. The boy came up in the Juvenile Court – you know the way, Mr Fortune; no sort of criminal atmosphere, magistrate talking like a father. He let the kid off with a lecture.'

'Oh, yes. What did he say? Bringin' down mother's grey hairs in sorrow to the grave – wicked boy – goin' to the bad in this world and the next – anything about hell?'

'I couldn't tell you.' Bell was shocked. 'I heard he gave the boy a rare old talking to. I don't wonder. Pretty bad, wasn't it, the Sunday-school money-box? What makes you bring hell into it?'

'I didn't. The boy did. He was raving about hell today. Part of the evidence. I was only tracin' the origin.'

'Ah. I don't like these children's cases,' Bell said gloomily. 'They don't seem really human sometimes. You get a twisted kind of child and he'll talk the most frightful stuff – and do it too. We can only go by acts, can we?'

'Yes. That's the way I'm goin'. Get on.'

The sharp impatience of the tone made Bell look at him with some reproach. 'All right, sir. The next thing is this morning's business. I gave you the outline of that on the phone. I've got the full details now. This is what it comes to. Eddie and his little sister were seen on the common; the keepers have got to keeping an eye on him. He wandered about with her – he has a casual, drifting sort of way, like some of these queer kids do have – and they came to the big pond. That's not a children's place at all; it's too deep; only dog bathing and fishing. There was nobody near; it was pretty early. Eddie and Bessie went along the bank, and a labourer who was scything thistles says the little girl was crying, and Eddie seemed to be scolding her, and then he fair chucked her in and went in with her. That's what it looked like to the keeper who was watchin' 'em. Him and the other chap, they nipped down and chucked the lifebuoy; got it right near, but Eddie didn't take hold of it; he was clutching the girl and sinking and coming up again. So the keeper went in to 'em and had trouble getting 'em out. The little girl was unconscious, and Eddie sort of fought him.' Bell stopped and gave a look of inquiry, but Reggie said nothing, and his face showed neither opinion nor feeling. 'Well, you know how it is with these rescues from the water,' Bell went on. 'People often seem to be fighting to drown themselves and it don't mean anything except fright. And about the boy throwing the girl in – that might have been just a bit of a row or play – it's happened often – not meant vicious at all; and then he'd panic, likely enough.' Again Bell looked an anxious question at the cold, passionless face. 'I mean to say, I wouldn't have bothered you with it, Mr Fortune, but for the way the boy carried on when they got him out. There he was with his little sister unconscious, and the keeper doing artificial respiration, and he called out: 'Don't do it. Bessie's dead. She must be dead.' And the keeper asked him: 'Do you want her dead, you little devil?' And he said: 'Yes, I do. I had to.' Then the labourer chap came back with help and they got hold of Eddie; he was raving, flinging himself about and screaming if she lived she'd only get like him and go to hell, so she must be dead. While they brought him along here he was sort of preaching to 'em bits of the Bible, and mad stuff about the wicked being sent to hell and tortures for 'em.'

'Curious and interestin',' Reggie drawled. 'Any particular torture?'

'I don't know. The whole thing pretty well gave these chaps the horrors. They didn't get all the boy's talk. I don't wonder. There was something about worms not dying, they told me. That almost turned 'em up. Well – there you are, Mr Fortune. What do you make of it?'

'I should say it happened,' Reggie said. 'All of it. As stated.'

'You feel sure he could have thrown that fat little girl in? He seemed to me such a weed.'

'Yes. Quite a sound point. I took that point. Development of both children unhealthy. Girl wrongly nourished. Boy inadequately nourished. Boy's physique frail. However. He could have done it. Lots of nervous energy. Triumph of mind over matter.'

Bell drew in his breath. 'You take it cool.'

'Only way to take it,' Reggie murmured, and Bell shifted uncomfortably. He has remarked since that he had seen Mr Fortune look like that once or twice before – sort of inhuman, heartless, and inquisitive; but there it seemed all wrong, it didn't seem his way at all.

Reggie settled himself in his chair and spoke – so Bell has

reported, and this is the only criticism which annoys Mr Fortune – like a lecturer. 'Several possibilities to be considered. The boy may be merely a precocious rascal. Having committed some iniquity which the little girl knew about, he tried to drown her to stop her giving him away. Common type of crime, committed by children as well as their elders.'

'I know it is,' Bell admitted. 'But what could he have done that was worth murdering his sister?'

'I haven't the slightest idea. However. He did steal. Proved twice by independent evidence. Don't blame if you don't want. "There, but for the grace of God, go I." I agree. Quite rational to admit that consideration. We shall certainly want it. But he knew he was a thief; he knew it got him into trouble – that's fundamental.'

'All right,' said Bell gloomily. 'We have to take it like that.'

'Yes. No help. Attempt to murder sister may be connected with consciousness of sin. I should say it was. However. Other possibilities. He's a poor little mess of nerves; he's unsound, physically, mentally, spiritually. He may not have meant to murder her at all; may have got in a passion and not known what he was doing.'

'Ah. That's more likely.' Bell was relieved.

'You think so? Then why did he tell everybody he did mean to murder her?'

'Well, he was off his head, as you were saying. That's the best explanation of the whole thing. It's really the only explanation. Look at your first idea: he wanted to kill her so she couldn't tell about some crime he'd done. You get just the same question, why did he say he meant murder? He must know killing is worse than stealing. However you take the thing, you work back to his being off his head.'

Reggie's eyelids drooped. 'I was brought here to say he's mad. Yes. I gather that. You're a merciful man, Bell. Sorry not to satisfy your gentle nature. I could swear he's mentally abnormal. If that would do any good. I couldn't say he's mad. I don't know. I can find you mental experts who would give evidence either way.'

'I know which a jury would believe,' Bell grunted.

'Yes. So do I. Merciful people, juries. Like you. Not my job. I'm lookin' for the truth. One more possibility. The boy's motive was just what he said it was – to kill his little sister so she shouldn't get wicked and go to hell. That fits the other facts. He'd got into the way of stealing; it had been rubbed into him that he was doomed to hell. So, if he found her goin' the same way, he might think it best she should die while she was still clean.'

'Well, if that isn't mad!' Bell exclaimed.

'Abnormal, yes. Mad – I wonder,' Reggie murmured.

'But it's sheer crazy, sir. If he believed he was so wicked, the thing for him to do was to pull up and go straight, and see that she did too.'

'Yes. That's common sense, isn't it?' A small, contemptuous smile lingered a moment on Reggie's stern face. 'What's the use of common sense here? If he was like this – sure he was going to hell; sure she was bein' driven there too – kind of virtuous for him to kill her to save her. Kind of rational. Desperately rational. Ever know any children, Bell? Some of 'em do believe what they're taught. Some of 'em take it seriously. Abnormal, as you say. Eddie Hill is abnormal.' He turned and looked full at Bell, his blue eyes dark in the failing light. 'Aged twelve or so – too bad to live – or too good. Pleasant case.'

Bell moved uneasily. 'These things do make you feel queer,' he grunted. 'What it all comes to, though – we mean much the same – the boy ought to be in a home. That can be worked.'

'A home!' Reggie's voice went up, and he laughed. 'Yes. Official home for mentally defective. Yes. We can do that. I dare say we shall.' He stood up and walked to the window and looked out at the dusk. 'These children had a home of their own. And a mother. What's she doing about 'em?'

'She's been here, half off her head, poor thing,' said Bell. 'She wouldn't believe the boy meant any harm. She told me he couldn't, he was so fond of his sister. She said it must have been accident.'

'Quite natural and motherly. Yes. But not adequate. Because it wasn't accident, whatever it was. We'd better go and see mother.'

'If you like,' Bell grunted reluctantly.

'I don't like,' Reggie mumbled. 'I don't like anything. I'm not here to do what I like.' And they went.

People were drifting home from the common. The mean streets of Blaney had already grown quiet in the sultry gloom.

Shutters were up at the little shop which was the home of Eddie Hill, and still bore in faded paint his father's name. No light showed in the windows above. Bell rapped on the door, and they waited in vain. He moved to a house door close beside the shop. 'Try this. This may be theirs too,' he said, and knocked and rang.

After a minute it was opened by a woman who said nothing, but stared at them. From somewhere inside came the sound of a man's voice, talking fervently.

The light of the street lamp showed her of full figure, in neat black, and a face which was still pretty but distressed.

'You remember me, Mrs Brightman,' said Bell. 'I'm Superintendent Bell.'

'I know.' She was breathless. 'What's the matter? Are they – is Eddie – what's happened?'

'They're doing all right. I just want a little talk with you.'

'Oh, they're all right. Praise God!' She turned; she called out: 'Matthew, Matthew dear, they're all right.'

The man's voice went on talking with the same fervour, but not in answer.

'I'll come in, please,' said Bell.

'Yes, do. Thank you kindly. Mr Brightman would like to see you. We were just asking mercy.'

She led the way along a passage, shining clean, to a room behind the shop. There a man was on his knees praying, and most of the prayer was texts: 'And we shall sing of mercy in the morning. Amen. Amen.' He made an end.

He stood up before them, tall and gaunt, a bearded man with melancholy eyes. He turned to his wife. 'What is it, my dear? What do the gentlemen want?'

'It's about the children, Matthew.' His wife came and took his arm. 'It's the police superintendent, I told you. He was so kind.'

The man sucked in his breath. 'Ay, ay. Please sit down. They must sit down, Florrie.' There was a fluster of setting chairs. 'This is kind, sir. What can you tell us to-night?'

'Doin' well. Both of 'em,' Reggie said.

'There's our answer, Florrie,' the man said, and smiled and his sombre eyes glowed. 'There's our prayers answered.'

'Yes. I think they're going to live,' said Reggie. 'But that's not the only thing that matters. We have to ask how it was they were nearly drowned.'

'It was an accident. It must have been,' the woman cried. 'I'm sure Eddie wouldn't – he never would, would he, Matthew?'

'I won't believe it,' Brightman answered quickly.

'Quite natural you should feel like that,' Reggie nodded. 'However. We have to deal with the facts.'

'You must do what you think right, sir, as it is shown you.' Brightman bent his head.

'Yes, I will. Yes. Been rather a naughty boy, hasn't he?'

Brightman looked at his wife's miserable face and turned to them again. 'The police know,' he said. 'He has been a thief – twice he has been a thief – but little things. There is mercy, surely there is mercy for repentance. If his life is spared, he should not be lost; we must believe that.'

'I do,' Reggie murmured. 'Any special reason why he should have been a thief?'

Brightman shook his head. 'He's always had a good home, I'm sure,' the woman moaned. She looked round her room, which was ugly and shabby, but all in the cleanest order.

'What can I say?' Brightman shook his head. 'We've always

done our best for him. There's no telling how temptation comes, sir, and it's strong and the little ones are weak.'

'That is so. Yes. How much pocket-money did they have?'

'Eddie has had his twopence a week since he was ten,' Brightman answered proudly. 'And Bessie has her penny.'

'I see. And was there anything happened this morning which upset Bessie or Eddie?'

'Nothing at all, sir. Nothing that I know.' Brightman turned to his wife. 'They went off quite happy, didn't they?'

'Yes, of course they did,' she said eagerly. 'They always loved to have a day on the common. They took their lunch, and they went running as happy as happy – and then this,' she sobbed.

'My dearie.' Brightman patted her.

'Well, well.' Reggie stood up. 'Oh. By the way. Has Eddie – or Bessie – ever stolen anything at home here – money or what not?'

Brightman started and stared at him. 'That's not fair, sir. That's not a right thing to ask. There isn't stealing between little ones and their mother and father.'

'No. As you say. No,' Reggie murmured. 'Good night. You'll hear how they go on. Good night.'

'Thank you, sir. We shall be anxious to hear. Good night, sir,' said Brightman, and Mrs Brightman showed them out with tearful gratitude. As the door was opened, Brightman called: 'Florrie! Don't bolt it. Mrs Wiven hasn't come back.'

'I know. I know,' she answered, and bade them good night and shut the door.

A few paces away, Reggie stopped and looked back at the shuttered shop and the dark windows. 'Well, well. What does the professional mind make of all that?'

'Just what you'd expect, wasn't it?' Bell grunted.

'Yes. Absolutely. Poor struggling shopkeepers, earnestly religious, keeping the old house like a new pin. All in accordance with the evidence.' He sniffed the night air. 'Dank old house.'

'General shop smell. All sorts of things mixed up.'

'As you say. There were. And there would be. Nothing you couldn't have guessed before we went. Except that Mrs Wiven is expected – whoever Mrs Wiven is.'

'I don't know. Sounds like a lodger.'

'Yes, that is so. Which would make another resident in the home of Eddie and Bessie. However. She's not come back yet. So we can go home. The end of a beastly day. And to-morrow's another one. I'll be out to see the children in the morning. Oh, my Lord! Those children.' His hand gripped Bell's arm . . .

By eight o'clock in the morning he was at the bedside of Bessie Hill – an achievement of stupendous but useless energy, for she did not wake till half-past.

Then he took charge. A responsible position, which he interpreted as administering to her cups of warm milk and bread and butter. She consumed them eagerly; she took his service as a matter of course.

'Good girl.' Reggie wiped her mouth. 'Feelin' better?'

She sighed and snuggled down, and gazed at him with large eyes. 'Umm. Who are you?'

'They call me Mr Fortune. Is it nice here?'

'Umm. Comfy.' The big eyes were puzzled and wondering. 'Where is it?'

'Blaney Hospital. People brought you here after you were in the pond. Do you remember?'

She shook her head. 'Is Eddie here?'

'Oh, yes. Eddie's asleep. He's all right. Were you cross with Eddie?'

Tears came into the brown eyes. 'Eddie was cross wiv me,' the child whimpered. 'I wasn't. I wasn't. Eddie said must go into ve water. I didn't want. But Eddie was so cross. Love Eddie.'

'Yes. Little girl.' Reggie stroked her hair. 'Eddie shouldn't have been cross. Just a little girl. But Eddie isn't often cross, is he?'

'No. Love Eddie. Eddie's dear.'

'Why was he cross yesterday?'

The brown eyes opened wider. 'I was naughty. It was Mrs Wiven. Old Mrs Wiven. I did go up to her room. I didn't fink she was there. Sometimes is sweeties. But she was vere. She scolded me. She said I was little fief. We was all fiefs. And Eddie took me away and oh, he was so cross; he said I would be wicked and must not be. But I aren't. I aren't. Eddie was all funny and angry, and said not to be like him and go to hell, and then he did take me into pond wiv him. I didn't want! I didn't want!'

'No. Of course not. No. Poor little girl. Eddie didn't understand. But it's all right now.'

'Is Eddie still cross wiv me?' she whimpered.

'Oh, no. No. Eddie won't be cross any more. Nobody's cross, little girl.' Reggie bent over her. 'Everybody's going to be kind now. You only have to be quiet and happy. That's all.'

'Oooh.' She gazed up at him. 'Tell Eddie I'm sorry.'

'Yes. I'll tell him.' Reggie kissed her hand and turned away.

The nurse met him at the door. 'Did she wake in the night?' he whispered.

'Yes, sir, asking for Eddie. She's a darling, isn't she? She makes me cry, talking like that of him.'

'That won't do any harm,' Reggie said, and his face hardened. 'But you mustn't talk about him.'

He went to the room where Eddie lay. The doctor was there, and turned from the bedside to confer with him. 'Not too bad. We've put in a long sleep. Quite quiet since we waked. Very thirsty. Taken milk with a dash of coffee nicely. But we're rather flat.'

Reggie sat down by the bed. The boy lay very still. His thin face was white. Only his eyes moved to look at Reggie, so little open, their pupils so small that they seemed all greenish-grey. He gave no sign of recognition, or feeling, or intelligence. Reggie put a hand under the clothes and found him cold and damp, and felt for his pulse.

'Well, young man, does anything hurt you now?'

'I'm tired. I'm awful tired,' the boy said.

'Yes. I know. But that's going away.'

'No, it isn't; it's worse. I didn't ought to have waked up.' The faint voice was drearily peevish. 'I didn't want to. It's no good. I thought I was dead. And it was good being dead.'

'Was it?' Reggie said sharply.

The boy gave a quivering cry. 'Yes, it was!' His face was distorted with fear and wonder. 'I thought it would be so dreadful and it was all quiet and nice, and then I wasn't dead, I was alive and everything's awful again. I've got to go on still.'

'What's awful in going on?' said Reggie. 'Bessie wants you. Bessie sent you her love. She's gettin' well quick.'

'Bessie? Bessie's here in bed like I am?' The unnatural greenish eyes stared.

'Of course she is. Only much happier than you are.'

The boy began to sob.

'Why do you cry about that?' Reggie said. 'She's got to be happy. Boys and girls have to be happy. That's what they're for. You didn't want Bessie to die.'

'I did. You know I did,' the boy sobbed.

'I know you jumped in the pond with her. That was silly. But you'd got rather excited, hadn't you? What was it all about?'

'They'll tell you,' the boy muttered.

'Who will?'

'The keepers, the p'lice, the m-magistrate, everybody. I'm wicked. I'm a thief. I can't help it. And I didn't want Bessie to be wicked too.'

'Of course you didn't. And she isn't. What ever made you think she was?'

'But she was.' The boy's voice was shrill. 'She went to Mrs Wiven's room. She was looking for pennies. I know she was. She'd seen me. And Mrs Wiven said we were all thieves. So I had to.'

'Oh, no, you hadn't. And you didn't. You see? Things don't happen like that.'

'Yes, they do. There's hell. Where their worms don't die.'

The doctor made a muttered exclamation.

Reggie's hand held firm at the boy's as he moved and writhed. 'There's God too,' he murmured. 'God's kind. Bessie's not going to be wicked. You don't have to be wicked. That's what's come of it all. Somebody's holding you up now.' His hand pressed. 'Feel?' The boy's lips parted; he looked up in awe. 'Yes. Like that. You'll see me again and again. Now good-bye. Think about me. I'm thinking about you.' . . . He stayed a while longer before he said another 'Good-bye.'

Outside, in the corridor, the doctor spoke: 'I say, Mr Fortune, you got him then. That was the stuff. I thought you were driving hard before. Sorry I spoke.'

'I was.' Reggie frowned. His round face was again of a ruthless severity. ' "Difficult matter to play with souls," ' he mumbled. 'We've got to.' He looked under drooping eyelids. 'Know the name of the keeper who saw the attempted drowning? Fawkes? Thanks.'

He left the hospital and walked across the common.

The turf was parched and yellow, worn away on either side of paths loosened by the summer drought. Reggie descried the brown coat of a keeper, made for him, and was directed to where Fawkes would be.

Fawkes was a slow-speaking, slow-thinking old soldier, but he knew his own mind.

There was no doubt in it that Eddie had tried to kill Bessie, no indignation, no surprise. Chewing his words, he gave judgment. He had known Eddie's sort, lots of 'em. 'Igh strung, wanting the earth, kicking up behind and before 'cause they couldn't get it. He didn't mind 'em. Rather 'ave 'em than young 'uns like sheep. But you 'ad to dress 'em down proper. They was devils else. Young Eddie would 'ave to be for it.

That business of the boat? Yes, Eddie pinched that all right. Smart kid; you'd got to 'and him that. And yet not so smart. Silly, lying up with it on the common; just the way to get nabbed. Ought to 'ave took it 'ome and sailed it over at Wymond Park.

Never been spotted then. But 'im and 'is sister, they made a regular visit up in the gorse. Always knew where to look for 'em. Silly. Why, they was up there yesterday, loafing round, before 'e did 'is drowning act.

'Take you there? I can, if you like.'

Reggie did like. They went up the brown slopes of the common to a tangle of gorse and bramble over small sand-hills.

'There you are.' The keeper pointed his stick to a patch of loose sand in a hollow. 'That's young Eddie's funk-'ole. That's where we spotted 'em with the blinking boat.'

Reggie came to the place. The sand had been scooped up by small hands into a low wall round a space which was decked out with pebbles, yellow petals of gorse, and white petals of bramble.

'Ain't that just like 'em!' The keeper was angrily triumphant. 'They know they didn't ought to pick the flowers. As well as you and me they do, and they go and do it.'

Reggie did not answer. He surveyed the pretence of a garden and looked beyond. 'Oh, my Lord!' he muttered. On the ground lay a woman's bag.

' 'Allo, 'allo.' The keeper snorted. 'They've been pinching something else.'

Reggie took out his handkerchief, put his hand in it, and thus picked up the bag. He looked about him; he wandered to and fro, going delicately, examining the confusion of small footmarks, further and further away.

'Been all round, ain't they?' the keeper greeted him on his return.

'That is so. Yes.' Reggie mumbled and looked at him with searching eyes. 'Had any notice of a bag lost or stolen?'

'Not as I've 'eard. Better ask the 'ead keeper. 'E'll be up at the top wood about now.'

The wood was a thicket of birch and crab-apple and thorn. As they came near, they saw on its verge the head keeper and two other men who were not in the brown coats of authority. One of these was Superintendent Bell. He came down the slope in a hurry.

'I tried to catch you at the hospital, Mr Fortune,' he said. 'But I suppose you've heard about Mrs Wiven?'

'Oh. The Mrs Wiven who hadn't come back,' Reggie said slowly. 'No. I haven't heard anything.'

'I thought you must have, by your being out here on the common. Well, she didn't come back at all. This morning Brightman turned up at the station very fussy and rattled to ask if they had any news of his lodger, Mrs Wiven. She never came in last night, and he thought she must have had an accident or something. She'd been lodging with them for years. Old lady, fixed in her habits. Never went anywhere, that he knew of, except to chapel and for a cup o' tea with some of her chapel friends, and none of them had seen her. These fine summer days she'd take her food out and sit on the common here all day long. She went off yesterday morning with sandwiches and a vacuum flask of tea and her knitting. Often she wouldn't come home till it was getting dark. They didn't think much of her being late; sometimes she went in and had a bit o' supper with a friend. She had her key, and they left the door unbolted, like we heard, and went to bed, being worn out with the worry of the kids. But when Mrs Brightman took up her cup of tea this morning and found she wasn't in her room, Brightman came running round to the station. Queer business, eh?'

'Yes. Nasty business. Further you go the nastier.'

Bell looked at him curiously and walked him away from the keeper. 'You feel it that way? So do I. Could you tell me what you were looking for out here – as you didn't know she was missing?'

'Oh, yes. I came to verify the reports of Eddie's performances.'

'Ah! Have you found any error?'

'No. I should say everything happened as stated.'

'The boy's going to get well, isn't he?'

'It could be. If he gets the chance.'

'Poor little beggar,' Bell grunted. 'What do you really think about him, Mr Fortune?'

'Clever child, ambitious child, imaginative child. What children ought to be – twisted askew.'

'Kind of perverted, you mean.'

'That is so. Yes. However. Question now is, not what I think of the chances of Eddie's soul, but what's been happening. Evidence inadequate, curious, and nasty. I went up to the private lair of Eddie and Bessie. Same where he was caught with the stolen boat. I found this.' He showed Bell the woman's bag.

'My oath!' Bell muttered, and took it from him gingerly. 'You wrapped it up! Thinkin' there might be fingerprints.'

'Yes. Probably are. They might even be useful.'

'And you went looking for this – not knowing the woman was missing?'

'Wasn't lookin' for it,' Reggie snapped. 'I was lookin' for anything there might be. Found a little pretence of a garden they'd played at – and this.'

'Ah, but you heard last night about Mrs Wiven, and this morning you go up where Eddie hides what he's stolen. Don't that mean you made sure there was something fishy? You see when we're blind, Mr Fortune.'

'Oh, no. I don't see. I knew more than you did. Little Bessie told me this morning she was in Mrs Wiven's room yesterday, privily and by stealth, and Mrs Wiven caught her and called her a thief, and said they were all thieves. I should think little Bessie may have meant to be a thief. Which would agree with Eddie's effort to drown her so she should die good and honest. But I don't see my way.'

'All crazy, isn't it?' Bell grunted.

'Yes. The effort of Eddie is an incalculable factor. However. You'd better look at the bag.'

Bell opened it with cautious fingers. A smell of peppermint came out. Within was a paper bag of peppermint lozenges, two unclean handkerchiefs marked E. W., an empty envelope addressed to Mrs Wiven, a bottle of soda-mint tablets, and some keys.

'Evidence that it is the bag of the missing Mrs Wiven strong,' Reggie murmured. He peered into it. 'But no money. Not a penny.' He looked up at Bell with that cold, ruthless curiosity which Bell always talks about in discussing the case. 'Stealin' is the recurrin' motive. You notice that?'

'I do.' Bell stared at him. 'You take it cool, Mr Fortune. I've got to own it makes me feel queer.'

'No use feelin' feelings,' Reggie drawled. 'We have to go on. We want the truth, whatever it is.'

'Well, all right, I know,' Bell said gloomily. 'They're searching the common for her. That's why I came out here. They knew her. She did sit about here in summer.' He went back to the head keeper and conferred again . . .

Reggie purveyed himself a deck-chair, and therein sat extended and lit a pipe and closed his eyes . . .

'Mr Fortune!' Bell stood over him. His lips emitted a stream of smoke. No other part of him moved. 'They've found her. I suppose you expected that.'

'Yes. Obvious possibility. Probable possibility.' It has been remarked that Mr Fortune has a singular capacity for becoming erect from a supine position. A professor of animal morphology once delivered a lecture upon him – after a hospital dinner – as the highest type of the invertebrates. He stood up from the deck-chair in one undulating motion. 'Well, well. Where is the new fact?' he moaned.

Bell took him into the wood. No grass grew in it. Where the sandy soil was not bare, dead leaves made a carpet. Under the crab-apple trees, between the thornbrakes, were nooks obviously much used by pairs of lovers. By one of these, not far from the whale-back edge of rising ground which was the wood's end, some men stood together.

On the grey sand there lay a woman's body. She was small; she was dressed in a coat and skirt of dark grey cloth and a black and white blouse. The hat on her grey hair was pulled to one side, giving her a look of absurd frivolity in ghastly contrast to the distortion of her pallid face. Her lips were closely compressed and almost white. The dead eyes stared up at the trees with dilated pupils.

Reggie walked round the body, going delicately, rather like a dog in doubt how to deal with another dog.

Beside the body was a raffia bag which held some knitting, a vacuum flask, and an opened packet of sandwiches.

Reggie's discursive eyes looked at them and looked again at the dead face, but not for long. He was more interested in the woman's skirt. He bent over that, examined it from side to side, and turned away and went on prowling further and further away, and as he went he scraped at the dry sand here and there.

When he came back to the body, his lips were curved in a grim, mirthless smile. He looked at Bell. 'Photographer,' he mumbled.

'Sent a man to phone, sir,' Bell grunted.

Reggie continued to look at him. 'Have you? Why have you?'

'Just routine.' Bell was startled.

'Oh. Only that. Well, well.' Reggie knelt down by the body. His hands went to the woman's mouth . . . He took something from his pocket and forced the mouth open and looked in . . . He closed the mouth again, and sat down on his heels and contemplated the dead woman with dreamy curiosity . . . He opened her blouse. Upon the underclothes was a dark stain. He bent over that and smelt it; he drew the clothes from her chest.

'No wound, is there?' Bell muttered.

'Oh, no. No.' Reggie put back the clothes and stood up and went to the flask and the sandwiches. He pulled the bread of an unfinished sandwich apart, looked at it, and put it down. He took the flask and shook it. It was not full. He poured some of the contents into its cup.

'Tea, eh?' said Bell. 'Strong tea.'

'Yes. It would be,' Reggie murmured. He tasted it and spat, and poured what was in the cup back into the flask and corked it again and gave it to Bell.

'There you are. Cause of death, poisoning by oxalic acid or binoxalate of potassium – probably the latter – commonly called salts of lemon. And we shall find some in that awful tea. We shall also find it in the body. Tongue and mouth, white, contracted, eroded. Time of death, probably round about twenty-four hours ago. No certainty.'

'My oath! It's too near certainty for my liking,' Bell muttered.

'Is it?' Reggie's eyelids drooped. 'Wasn't thinkin' about what you'd like. Other interestin' facts converge.'

'They do!' Bell glowered at him. 'One of the commonest kinds of poisoning, isn't it?'

'Oh, yes. Salts of lemon very popular.'

'Anybody can get it.'

'As you say. Removes stains, cleans brass and what not. Also, quickly fatal, with luck. Unfortunate chemical properties.'

'This boy Eddie could have got some easy.'

'That is so. Yes. Lethal dose for a penny or two anywhere.'

'Well, then – look at it!'

'I have,' Reggie murmured. 'Weird case. Ghastly case.'

'Gives me the horrors,' said Bell. 'The old lady comes out here to spend the day as usual, and somebody's put a spot of poison in her drop o' tea and she dies; and her bag's stolen, and found without a farthing where the boy Eddie hides his loot. And, about the time the old lady's dying, Eddie tries to drown his sister. What are you going to make of that? What can you make of it? It was a poison any kid could get hold of. One of 'em must have poisoned her to steal her little bit o' money. But the girl's not much more than a baby. It must have been Eddie that did it – and that goes with the rest of his doings. He's got the habit of stealing. But his little sister saw something of it, knew too much, so he put up this drowning to stop her tongue – and then, when she was saved, made up this tale about killing her to keep her honest. Devilish, isn't it? And when you find a child playing the devil – my oath! But it is devilish clever – his tale would put the stealing and all the rest on the baby. And we can't

311

prove anything else. She's too little to be able to get it clear, and he's made himself out driven wild by her goings on. If a child's really wicked, he beats you.'

'Yes, that is so,' Reggie drawled. 'Rather excited, aren't you? Emotions are not useful in investigation. Prejudice the mind into exaggeratin' facts and ignorin' other facts. Both fallacies exhibited in your argument. You mustn't ignore what Bessie did say – that she went into Mrs Wiven's room yesterday morning and Mrs Wiven caught her. I shouldn't wonder if you found Bessie's fingerprints on that bag.'

'My Lord!' Bell stared at him. 'It's the nastiest case I ever had. When it comes to babies in murder –'

'Not nice, no. Discoverin' the possibilities of corruption of the soul. However. We haven't finished yet. Other interestin' facts have been ignored by Superintendent Bell. Hallo!' Several men were approaching, briskly. 'Is this your photographer and other experts?'

'That's right. Photographer and fingerprint men.'

'Very swift and efficient.' Reggie went to meet them.

'Where did you spring from?'

'By car, sir.' The photographer was surprised. 'On the road up there. We had the location by phone.'

'Splendid. Now then. Give your attention to the lady's skirt. Look.' He indicated a shining streak across the dark stuff. 'Bring that out.'

'Can do, sir,' the photographer said, and fell to work.

Reggie turned to Bell. 'Then they'll go over the whole of her for fingerprints, what? And the sandwich paper. And the flask. Not forgettin' the bag. That's all. I've finished here. She can be taken to the mortuary for me.'

'Very good,' Bell said, and turned away to give the orders, but, having given them, stood still to stare at the thin glistening streak on the skirt.

Reggie came quietly to his elbow. 'You do notice that? Well, well.' Bell looked at him with a puzzled frown and was met for the first time in this case by a small, satisfied smile which further bewildered him. He bent again to pore over the streak. 'It's all right.' Reggie's voice was soothing. 'That's on record now. Come on.' Linking arms, he drew Bell away from the photographers and the fingerprint men. 'Well? What does the higher intelligence make of the line on the skirt?'

'I don't know. I can't make out why you think so much of it.'

'My dear chap! Oh, my dear chap!' Reggie moaned. 'Crucial fact. Decisive fact.' He led Bell on out of the wood and across the common, and at a respectful distance Bell's two personal satellites followed.

'Decisive, eh?' Bell frowned. 'It was just a smear of something to me. You mean salts of lemon would leave a shiny stain?'

'Oh, no. No. Wouldn't shine at all.'

'Had she been sick on her skirt?'

'Not there. No. Smear wasn't human material.'

'Well, I thought it wasn't. What are you thinking of?'

'I did think of what Eddie said – where their worm dieth not.'

'My God!' Bell muttered. 'Worms?' He gave a shudder. 'I don't get you at all, sir. It sounds mad.'

'No. Connection is sort of desperate rational. I told you Eddie was like that. However. Speakin' scientifically, not a worm, but a slug. That streak was a slug's trail.'

'Oh. I see.' Bell was much relieved. 'Now you say so, it did look like that. The sort o' slime a slug leaves behind. It does dry shiny, of course.'

'You have noticed that?' Reggie admired him. 'Splendid!'

Bell was not pleased. 'I have seen slugs before,' he grunted. 'But what is there to make a fuss about? I grant you, it's nasty to think of a slug crawling over the woman as she lay there dead. That don't mean anything, though. Just what you'd expect, with the body being all night in the wood. Slugs come out when it gets dark.'

'My dear chap! Oh, my dear chap!' Reggie moaned. 'You mustn't talk like that. Shakes confidence in the police force.

Distressin' mixture of inadequate observation and fallacious reasonin'.'

'Thank you. I don't know what's wrong with it.' Bell was irritated.

'Oh, my Bell! You shock me. Think again. Your general principle's all right. Slugs do come out at night. Slugs like the dark. That's a general truth which has its particular application. But you fail to observe the conditions. The body was in a wood with no herbage on the ground: and the ground was a light dry sand. These are not conditions which attract the slug. I should have been much surprised if I'd found any slugs there, or their tracks. But I looked for 'em – which you didn't, Bell. I'm always careful. And there wasn't a trace. No. I can't let you off. A slug had crawled over her skirt, leavin' his slime from side to side. And yet his slime didn't go beyond her skirt on to the ground anywhere. How do you suppose he managed that? Miracle – by a slug. I don't believe in miracles if I can help it. I object to your simple faith in the miraculous gasteropod. It's lazy.'

'You go beyond me,' said Bell uneasily. 'You grasp the whole thing while I'm only getting bits. What do you make of it all?'

'Oh, my Bell!' Reggie reproached him. 'Quite clear. When the slug walked over her, she wasn't lying where she was found.'

'Is that all?' Bell grunted. 'I dare say. She might have had her dose, and felt queer and lay down, and then moved on to die where we found her. Nothing queer in that, is there?'

'Yes. Several things very queer. It could be. Oxalic poisoning might lay her out and still let her drag herself somewhere else to die. Not likely she'd take care to bring her flask and her sandwiches with her. Still less likely she'd lie long enough for a slug to walk over her and then recover enough to move somewhere else – and choose to move into the wood, where she wouldn't be seen. Why should she? She'd try for help if she could try for anything. And, finally, most unlikely she'd find any place here with slugs about. Look at it; it's all arid and sandy and burnt up by the summer. No. Quite unconvincin' explanation. The useful slug got on to her somewhere else. The slug is decisive.'

'Then you mean to say she was poisoned some other place, and brought here dead?' Bell frowned. 'It's all very well. You make it sound reasonable. But would you like to try this slug argument on a jury? They'd never stand for it, if you ask me. It's all too clever.'

'You think so?' Reggie murmured. 'Well, well. Then it does give variety to the case. We haven't been very clever so far. However. Study to improve. There is further evidence. She'd been sick. Common symptom of oxalic poisoning. But she'd been sick on her underclothes and not on her outside clothes. That's very difficult. Think about it. Even juries can be made to think sometimes. Even coroners, which is very hard. Even judges. I've done it in my time, simple as I am. I might do it again. Yes, I might. With the aid of the active and intelligent police force. Come on.'

'What do you want to do?'

'Oh, my Bell! I want to call on Mr and Mrs Brightman. We need their collaboration. We can't get on without it.'

'All right. I don't mind trying 'em,' Bell agreed gloomily. 'We've got to find out all about the old woman somehow. We don't really know anything yet.'

'I wouldn't say that. No,' Reggie mumbled. 'However. One moment.'

They had come to the edge of the common by the hospital, where his car waited. He went across to it and spoke to his chauffeur.

'Just calmin' Sam,' he apologized on his return. 'He gets peevish when forgotten. Come on.'

They arrived again at the little general shop. Its unshuttered window now enticed the public with a meagre array of canned goods and cartons which had been there some time. The door was shut but not fastened. Opening it rang a bell. They went in, and found the shop empty, and for a minute or two stood in a mixture of smells through which soap was dominant.

Mrs Brightman came from the room behind, wiping red arms and hands on her apron. Her plump face, which was tired and sweating, quivered alarm at the sight of them. 'Oh, it's you!' she cried. 'What is it? Is there anything?'

'Your children are doing well,' said Reggie. 'Thought I'd better let you know that.'

She stared at him, and tears came into her eyes. 'Praise God!' she gasped. 'Thank you, sir, you're very kind.'

'No. You don't have to thank me. I'm just doin' my job.'

But again she thanked him, and went on nervously: 'Have you heard anything of Mrs Wiven?'

'I want to have a little talk about her. Is Mr Brightman in?'

'No, he isn't, not just now. Have you got any news of her, sir?'

'Yes. There is some news. Sorry Mr Brightman's out. Where's he gone?'

'Down to the yard, sir.'

'Out at the back here?'

'No. No. Down at his own yard.'

'Oh. He has a business of his own?'

'Yes, sir, a little business. Furniture dealing it is. Second-hand furniture.'

'I see. Well, well. We could get one of the neighbours to run down and fetch him, what?' Reggie turned to Bell.

'That's the way,' Bell nodded. 'What's the address, ma'am?'

She swallowed. 'It's just round the corner. Smith's Buildings. Anybody would tell you. But he might be out on a job, you know; I couldn't say.'

Bell strode out, and the messenger he sent was one of his satellites.

'Well, while we're waitin', we might come into your nice little room,' Reggie suggested. 'There's one or two things you can tell me.'

'Yes, sir, I'm sure, anything as I can, I'll be glad. Will you come through, please?' She lifted the flap of the counter for him, she opened the curtained glass door of the room behind. It was still in exact order, but she had to apologize for it. 'I'm sorry we're all in a mess. I'm behindhand with my cleaning, having this dreadful trouble with the children and being so worried I can't get on. I don't half know what I'm doing, and then poor Mrs Wiven being lost –' She stopped, breathless. 'What is it about Mrs Wiven, sir? What have you heard?'

'Not good news,' Reggie said. 'Nobody will see Mrs Wiven alive again.'

The full face grew pale beneath its sweat, the eyes stood out. 'She's dead! Oh, the poor soul! But how do you know? How was it?'

'She's been found dead on the common.'

Mrs Brightman stared at him: her mouth came open and shook: she flung her apron over her head and bent and was convulsed with hysterical sobbing.

'Fond of her, were you?' Reggie sympathized.

A muffled voice informed him that she was a dear old lady – and so good to everybody.

'Was she? Yes. But I wanted to ask you about the children. What time did they go out yesterday?' Still sobbing under her apron, Mrs Brightman seemed not to hear. 'Yesterday morning,' Reggie insisted. 'You must remember. What time was it when Eddie and Bessie went out?'

After a moment the apron was pulled down from a swollen, tearful face. 'What time?' she repeated looking at her lap and wiping her eyes. 'I don't know exactly, sir. Just after breakfast. Might be somewheres about nine o'clock.'

'Yes, it might be,' Reggie murmured. 'They were pulled out of the pond about then.'

'I suppose so,' she whimpered. 'What's it got to do with Mrs Wiven?'

'You don't see any connection?'

She stared at him. 'How could there be?'

The shop-door bell rang, and she started up to answer it. She

317

found Bell in the shop. 'Oh, have you found Mr Brightman?' she cried.

'No, not yet. Where's Mr Fortune?'

Reggie called to him, 'Come on, Bell,' and she brought him into the back room and stood looking from one to the other. 'So Mr Brightman wasn't in his yard?'

'No, sir. Nobody there. At least, they couldn't make anybody hear.'

'Well, well,' Reggie murmured.

'But I told you he might have gone off on a job. He often has to go to price some stuff or make an offer or something.'

'You did say so. Yes,' Reggie murmured. 'However. I was asking about the children. Before they went out yesterday – Bessie got into trouble with Mrs Wiven, didn't she?'

The woman looked down and plucked at her apron.

'You didn't tell us that last night,' Reggie said.

'I didn't want to. I didn't see as it mattered. And I didn't want to say anything against Bessie. She's my baby.' Her eyes were streaming. 'Don't you see?'

'Bessie told me,' said Reggie.

'Bessie confessed! Oh, it's all too dreadful. The baby! I don't know why this was to come on us. I brought 'em up to be good, I have. And she was such a darling baby. But it's God's will.'

'Yes. What did happen?' said Reggie.

'Mrs Wiven was always hard on the children. She never had a child herself, poor thing. Bessie got into her room, and Mrs Wiven caught her and said she was prying and stealing like Eddie. I don't know what Bessie was doing there. Children will do such, whatever you do. And there was Bessie crying and Eddie all wild. He does get so out of himself. I packed 'em off, and I told Mrs Wiven it wasn't nothing to be so cross about, and she got quite nice again. She was always a dear with me and Brightman. A good woman at heart, sir, she was.'

'And when did Mrs Wiven go out?' said Reggie.

'It must have been soon after. She liked her days on the common in summer, she did.'

'Oh, yes. That's clear.' Reggie stood up and looked out at the yard, where some washing was hung out to dry. 'What was Mrs Wiven wearing yesterday?'

'Let me see –' Mrs Brightman was surprised by the turn in the conversation. 'I don't rightly remember – she had on her dark coat and skirt. She always liked to be nicely dressed when she went out.' Under the frown of this mental effort swollen eyes blinked at him. 'But you said she'd been found. You know what she had on.'

'Yes. When she was on the common. Before she got there – what was she wearing?'

Mrs Brightman's mouth opened and shut.

'I mean, when she caught Bessie in her room. What was she wearing then?'

'The same – she wouldn't have her coat on – I don't know as I remember – but the same – she knew she was going out – she'd dress for it – she wouldn't ever dress twice in a morning.'

'Wouldn't she? She didn't have that overall on?' Reggie pointed to a dark garment hanging on the line in the yard which stretched from house to shed.

'No, she didn't, I'm sure. That was in the dirty clothes.'

'But you had to wash it to-day. Well, well. Now we want to have a look at Mrs Wiven's room.'

'If you like. Of course, nothing's been done. It's all untidy.' She led the way upstairs, lamenting that the house was all anyhow, she'd been so put about.

But Mrs Wiven's room was primly neat and as clean as the shining passage and stairs. The paint had been worn thin by much washing, the paper was so faded that its rosebud pattern merged into a uniform pinkish grey. An old fur rug by the bedside, a square of threadbare carpet under the rickety round table in the middle of the room, were the only coverings of the scoured floor. The table had one cane chair beside it, and there was a small basket chair by the empty grate – nothing else in the room but the iron bedstead and a combination of chest of drawers, dressing-table, and washstand, with its mirror all brown spots.

Mrs Brightman passed round the room, pulling this and pushing that. 'I haven't even dusted,' she lamented.

'Is this her own furniture?' Reggie asked.

'No, sir, she hadn't anything. We had to furnish it for her.'

'Quite poor, was she?'

'I don't really know how she managed. And, of course, we didn't ever press her; you couldn't. She had her savings, I suppose. She'd been in good service, by what she used to say.'

'No relations?'

'No, sir. She was left quite alone. That was really why she came to us, she was that lonely. She'd say to me she did so want a home, till we took her. When she was feeling down, she used to cry and tell me she didn't know what would become of her. Of course, we wouldn't ever have let her want, poor dear. But it's my belief her bit of money was running out.'

Reggie gazed about the room. On the walls were many cards with texts.

'Mr Brightman put up the good words for her,' Mrs Brightman explained, and gazed at one of the texts and cried.

' "In My Father's house are many mansions." ' Reggie read it out slowly, and again looked round the bare little room.

Mrs Brightman sobbed. 'Ah, she's gone there now. She's happy.'

Bell was moving from one to other of the cupboards beside the grate. Nothing was in them but clothes. He went on to the dressing-table. 'She don't seem to have any papers. Only this.' He lifted a cash-box, and money rattled in it.

'I couldn't say, I'm sure,' Mrs Brightman whimpered.

Reggie stood by the table. 'Did she have her meals up here?' he asked.

Mrs Brightman thought about that. 'Mostly she didn't. She liked to sit down with us. She used to say it was more homely.'

Reggie fingered the table-cloth, pulled it off, and looked at the cracked veneer beneath. He stooped, felt the strip of old carpet under the table, drew it back. On the boards beneath was a patch of damp.

Mrs Brightman came nearer. 'Well there!' she said. 'That comes of my not doing out the room. She must have had a accident with her slops and never told me. She always would do things for herself.'

Reggie did not answer. He wandered round the room, stopped by the window a moment, and turned to the door.

'I'm taking this cash-box, ma'am,' said Bell.

'If you think right –' Mrs Brightman drew back. 'It's not for me to say – I don't mind, myself.' She looked from one to the other. 'Will that be all, then?'

'Nothing more here.' Reggie opened the door.

As they went downstairs, the shop bell rang again, and she hurried on to answer it. The two men returned to the room behind the shop.

'Poor old woman,' Bell grunted. 'You can see what sort of life she was having – that mingy room and her money running out – I wouldn't wonder if she committed suicide.'

'Wouldn't be wonderful. No,' Reggie murmured. 'Shut up.'

From the shop came a man's voice, lazy and genial. 'Good afternoon, mum. I want a bit o' salts o' lemon. About two penn'orth would do me. 'Ow do you sell it?'

There was a mutter from Mrs Brightman. 'We don't keep it.'

'What? They told me I'd be sure to get it 'ere. Run out of it, 'ave you? Ain't that too bad!'

'We never did keep it,' Mrs Brightman said. 'Whoever told you we did?'

'All right, all right. Keep your hair on, missis. Where can I get it?'

'How should I know? I don't rightly know what it is.'

'Don't you? Sorry I spoke. Used for cleaning, you know.'

Bell glowered at Reggie, for the humorous cockney voice was

321

the voice of his chauffeur. But the cold severity of Reggie's round face gave no sign.

'We don't use it, nor we don't keep it, nor any chemist's stuff,' Mrs Brightman was answering.

'Oh, good day!' The bell rang again as the shop door closed.

Mrs Brightman came back. 'Running in and out of the shop all day with silly people,' she panted. She looked from one to the other, questioning, afraid.

'I was wonderin',' Reggie murmured. 'Did Mrs Wiven have her meals with you yesterday – or in her room?'

'Down here.' The swollen eyes looked at him and looked away. 'She did usual, I told you. She liked to.'

'And which was the last meal she ever had?'

Mrs Brightman suppressed a cry. 'You do say things! Breakfast was the last she had here. She took out a bit o' lunch and tea.'

'Yes. When was that put ready?'

'I had it done first thing, knowing she meant to get out – and she always liked to start early. It was there on the sideboard waiting at breakfast.'

'Then it was ready before the children went out? Before she had her quarrel with Bessie?'

Mrs Brightman swallowed. 'So it was.'

'Oh. Thank you. Rather strong, the tea in her flask,' Reggie mumbled.

'She always had it fairly strong. Couldn't be too strong for her. I'm just the same myself.'

'Convenient,' Reggie said. 'Now you'll take me down into the cellar, Mrs Brightman.'

'What?' She drew back so hastily that she was brought up by the wall. 'The cellar?' Her eyes seemed to stand out more than ever, so they stared at him, the whites of them more widely bloodshot. With an unsteady hand she thrust back the hair from her sweating brow. 'The cellar? Why ever do you want to go there? There's nothing in the cellar.'

'You think not?' Reggie smiled. 'Come down and see.'

She gave a moaning cry; she stumbled away to the door at the back, and opened it, and stood holding by the door-post, looking out to the paved yard.

From the shed in it appeared Brightman's bearded face. 'Were you looking for me, dearie?' he asked, and brought his lank shape into sight, brushing it as it came.

She made a gesture to him; she went to meet him and muttered: 'Matthew! They're asking me to take 'em down to the cellar.'

'Well, to be sure!' Brightman gave Reggie and Bell a glance of melancholy, pitying surprise. 'I don't see any reason in that.' He held her up, he stroked her and gently remonstrated. 'But there's no reason they shouldn't go to the cellar if they want to, Florrie. We ain't to stand in the way of anything as the police think right. We ain't got anything to hide, have we? Come along, dearie.'

An inarticulate quavering sound came from her.

'That's all right, my dearie, that's all right,' Brightman soothed her.

'Is it?' Bell growled. 'So you've been here all the time, Mr Brightman. While she sent us to look for you down at your own place. Why didn't you show up before?'

'I've only just come in, sir,' Brightman said quietly. 'I came in by the back. I was just putting things to rights in the wash-house. The wife's been so pushed. I didn't know you gentlemen were here. You're searching all the premises, are you? I'm agreeable. I'm sure it's in order, if you say so. But I don't know what you're looking for.'

'Mrs Brightman will show us,' said Reggie, and grasped her arm.

'Don't, don't,' she wailed.

'You mustn't be foolish, dearie,' said Brightman. 'You know there's nothing in the cellar. Show the gentlemen if they want. It's all right. I'll go with you.'

'Got a torch, Bell?' said Reggie.

'I have.' Bell went back into the room. 'And here's a lamp, too.' He lit it.

Reggie drew the shaking woman through the room into the passage. 'That's the door to your cellar. Open it. Come on.'

Bell held the lamp overhead behind them. Reggie led her stumbling down the stairs, and Brightman followed close.

A musty, dank smell came about them. The lamp-light showed a large cellar of brick walls and an earth floor. There was in it a small heap of coal, some sacks and packing-cases and barrels, but most of the dim space was empty. The light glistened on damp.

'Clay soil,' Reggie murmured, and smiled at Brightman. 'Yes. That was indicated.'

'I don't understand you, sir,' said Brightman.

'No. You don't. Torch, Bell.' He took it and flashed its beam about the cellar. 'Oh, yes.' He turned to Bell. With a finger he indicated the shining tracks of slugs. 'You see?'

'I do,' Bell muttered.

Mrs Brightman gave a choked, hysterical laugh.

Reggie moved to and fro. He stooped. He took out his pocket-book and from it a piece of paper, and with that scraped something from a barrel side, something from the clay floor, and sighed satisfaction.

Standing up, he moved the ray of the torch from place to place, held it steady at last to make a circle of light on the ground beneath the steps. 'There,' he said, and Mrs Brightman screamed. 'Yes. I know. That's where you put her. Look, Bell.' His finger pointed to a slug's trail which came into the circle of light, stopped, and went on again at another part of the circle. 'It didn't jump. They don't.'

He swung round upon Mrs Brightman. He held out to her the piece of paper cupped in his hand. On it lay two yellow slugs.

She flung herself back, crying loathing and fear.

'Really, gentlemen, really now,' Brightman stammered. 'This

isn't right. This isn't proper. You've no call to frighten a poor woman so. Come away now, Florrie, dearie.' He pulled at her.

'Where are you going?' Reggie murmured. She did not go. Her eyes were set on the two yellow slugs. ' "Where their worm dieth not," ' Reggie said slowly.

She broke out in screams of hysterical laughter; she tore herself from Brightman, and reeled and fell down writhing and yelling.

'So that is that, Mr Brightman.' Reggie turned to him.

'You're a wicked soul!' Brightman whined. 'My poor dearie!' He fell on his knees by her; he began to pray forgiveness for her sins.

'My oath!' Bell muttered, and ran up the steps shouting to his men . . .

Some time afterwards the detective left to keep the little shop ushered Reggie out.

On the other side of the street, aloof from the gaping, gossiping crowd, superior and placid, his chauffeur smoked a cigarette. It was thrown away; the chauffeur followed him, fell into step beside him. 'Did I manage all right, sir?' The chauffeur invited praise.

'You did. Very neat. Very effective. As you know. Side, Sam, side. We are good at destruction. Efficient incinerators. Humble function. Other justification for existence, doubtful. However. Study to improve. What we want now is a toyshop.'

'Sir?' Sam was puzzled.

'I said a toyshop,' Reggie complained. 'A good toyshop. Quick.' . . .

The light of the sunlight was shining into the little room at the hospital where Eddie Hill lay. Upon his bed stood part of a bridge built of strips of metal bolted together, a bridge of grand design. He and Reggie were working on the central span.

There was a tap at the door, a murmur from Reggie, and the nurse brought in Bell. He stood looking at Reggie with reproachful surprise. 'So that's what you're doing,' he protested.

'Yes. Something useful at last.' Reggie sighed. 'Well, well. We'll have to call this a day, young man. You've done enough. Mustn't get yourself tired.'

'I'm not tired,' the boy protested eagerly. 'I'm not really.'

'No. Of course not. Ever so much better. But there's another day to-morrow. And you have a big job. Must keep fit to go on with it.'

'All right.' The boy lay back, looked at his bridge, looked wistfully at Reggie. 'I can keep this here, can I, sir?'

'Rather. On the table by the bed. So it'll be there when you wake. Nice, making things, isn't it? Yes. You're going to make a lot now. Good-bye. Jolly, to-morrow, what? Good-bye.' He went out with Bell. 'Now what's the matter with you?' he complained.

'Well, I had to have a word with you, sir. This isn't going to be so easy. I thought I'd get you at the mortuary doing the post-mortem.'

'Minor matter. Simple matter. Only the dead buryin' their dead. The boy was urgent. Matter of savin' life there.'

'I'm not saying you're not right,' said Bell wearily. 'But it is a tangle of a case. The divisional surgeon reports Mrs Brightman's mad. Clean off her head.'

'Yes. I agree. What about it?'

'Seemed to me you pretty well drove her to it. Those slugs – oh, my Lord!'

'Got you, did it? It rather got me. I'd heard Eddie talk of "the worm that dieth not." I should say he'd seen that cellar. Dreamed of it. However. I didn't drive the woman mad. She'd been mad some time. Not medically mad. Not legally mad. But morally. That was the work of our Mr Brightman. I only clarified the situation. He almost sent the boy the same way. That's been stopped. That isn't going to happen now. That's the main issue. And we win on it. Not too bad. But rather a grim day. Virtue has gone out of me. My dear chap!' He took Bell's arm affectionately. 'You're tucked up too.'

'I don't mind owning I've had enough,' said Bell. 'This sort of thing tells me I'm not as young as I was. And it's all a tangle yet.'

'My dear chap! Oh, my dear chap!' Reggie murmured. 'Empty, aren't we? Come on. Come home with me.'

While Sam drove them back, he declined to talk. He stretched in the corner of the car and closed his eyes, and bade Bell do the same. While they ate a devilled sole and an entrecôte Elise, he discussed the qualities of Elise, his cook, and of the Romanée which they drank, and argued bitterly (though he shared it) that the cheese offered in deference to Bell's taste, a bland Stilton, was an insult to the raspberries, the dish of which he emptied.

But when they were established in big chairs in his library, with brandy for Bell and seltzer for himself, and both pipes were lit, 'Did you say a tangle?' he murmured. 'Oh, no. Not now. The rest is only routine for your young men and the lawyers. It'll work out quite easy. You can see it all. When Mrs Brightman was left a widow with her little shop, the pious Brightman pounced on her and mastered her. The little shop was only a little living. Brightman wanted more. Children were kept very short – they might fade out, they might go to the bad – either way the devout Brightman would be relieved of their keep; and meanwhile it was pleasant making 'em believe they were wicked. Old Mrs Wiven was brought in as a lodger – not out of charity, as the wretched Mrs Brightman was trained to say; she must have had a bit of money. Your young men will be able to trace that. And they'll find Brightman got it out of her and used it to set up his second-hand furniture business. Heard of that sort of thing before, what?'

'I should say I have,' Bell grunted. 'My Lord, how often! The widow that falls for a pious brute – the old woman lodger with a bit of money.'

'Oh, yes. Dreary old game. And then the abnormal variations began. Pious bullyin' and starvin' didn't turn the boy into a criminal idiot. He has a mind. He has an imagination, poor child. Mrs Wiven didn't give herself up to Brightman like his miserable wife. She had a temper. So the old game went wrong. Mrs Wiven took to fussin' about her money. As indicated by Bessie. Mrs Wiven was going to be very awkward. Your young men will have to look about and get evidence she'd been grumbling. Quite easy. Lots of gossip will be goin'. Some of it true. Most of it useful at the trial. Givin' the atmosphere.'

Bell frowned. 'Fighting with the gloves off, aren't you?'

'Oh, no. No. Quite fair. We have to fight the case without the children. I'm not going to have Eddie put in the witness-box, to be tortured about his mad mother helpin' murder. That might break him up for ever. And he's been tortured enough. The brute Brightman isn't going to hurt him any more. The children won't be givin' evidence. I'll get half the College of Physicians to certify they're not fit, if they're asked for. But that's not goin' to leave Mr Brightman any way out. Now then. Things bein' thus, Brightman had his motive to murder Mrs Wiven. If he didn't stop her mouth she'd have him in jail. Being a clever fellow, he saw that Eddie's record of stealin' would be very useful. By the way – notice that queer little incident, Bessie bein' caught pilferin' by Mrs Wiven yesterday morning? Brightman may have fixed that up for another black mark against the children. I wonder. But it didn't go right. He must have had a jolt when Mrs Wiven called out they were all thieves. Kind of compellin' immediate action. His plan would have been all ready, of course – salts of lemon in her favourite strong tea; a man don't think of an efficient way of poisonin' all of a sudden. And then the incalculable Eddie intervened. Reaction of Mrs Wiven's explosion on him, a sort of divine command to save his sister from hell by seeing she died innocent. When Brightman had the news of that effort at drowning, he took it as a godsend. Hear him thanking heaven? Boy who was wicked enough to kill a little sister was wicked enough for anything. Mr Brightman read his title clear to mansions in the skies. And Mrs Wiven was promptly given her cup o' tea. She was sick in her room, sick on her overall and on her underclothes. Evidence for all that conclusive.

Remember the damp floor. I should say Mrs Brightman had another swab at that to-day. She has a craze about cleaning. We saw that. Feels she never can get clean, poor wretch. Well. Mrs Wiven died. Oxalic poisoning generally kills quick. I hope it did. They hid the body in the cellar. Plan was clever. Take the body out in the quiet of the night and dump it on the common with a flask of poisoned tea – put her bag in Eddie's den. All clear for the intelligent police. Devil of a boy poisoned the old lady to steal her money, and was drownin' his little sister so she shouldn't tell on him. That's what you thought, wasn't it? Yes. Well-made plan. It stood up against us last night.'

'You did think there was something queer,' Bell said.

'I did,' Reggie sighed. 'Physical smell. Damp musty smell. Probably the cellar. And the Brightmans didn't smell nice spiritually. However. Lack of confidence in myself. And I have no imagination. I ought to have waited and watched. My error. My grave error. Well. It was a clever plan. But Brightman was rather bustled. That may account for his errors. Fatal errors. Omission to remove the soiled underclothes when the messed-up overall was taken off. Failure to allow for the habits of *Limax flavus*.'

'What's that?' said Bell.

'Official name of yellow slug – cellar slug. The final, damning evidence. I never found any reason for the existence of slugs before. However. To round it off – when you look into Mr Brightman's furniture business, you'll find that he has a van, or the use of one. You must prove it was used last night. That's all. Quite simple now. But a wearin' case.' He gazed at Bell with large, solemn eyes. 'His wife! He'd schooled her thorough. Ever hear anything more miserably appealing than her on her dear babies and poor old Mrs Wiven? Not often? No. Took a lot of breakin' down.'

'Ah. You were fierce,' Bell muttered.

'Oh, no. No.' Reggie sighed. 'I was bein' merciful. She couldn't be saved. My job was to save the children. And she – if that brute hadn't twisted her, she'd have done anything to save

329

'em too. She'd been a decent soul once. No. She won't be giving evidence against me.'

'Why, how should she?' Bell gaped.

'I was thinkin' of the day of judgment,' Reggie murmured. 'Well, well. Post-mortem in the morning. Simple straight job. Then I'll be at the hospital if you want me. Have to finish Eddie's bridge. And then we're going to build a ship. He's keen on ships.'

Churchyard Shadows

Kevin Carolan

It's not that I am inexperienced with women. I lived with Susan
for a year. But being in love with Karen was something else
completely. It was like living on a different plane, like accelerating in a space rocket. I still can't believe that it really happened
to me.

The beginning was commonplace enough. I was eating my
sandwich lunch at my desk as normal. Like most people in the bank
I work through lunch when I'm not in meetings with clients. That
day, however, I felt mentally tired; the research folder swam in front
of my eyes. A short break, with something light to read seemed in
order. Mark, my assistant, gets one of the tabloids. I thought I'd
borrow it to read the football reports. It didn't take long to go through
the lot, given the limited vocabulary of the writer. Bored, I flicked
idly through the rest of the so-called 'newspaper'.

My eyes fell on the classified advertisements. Normally I
refuse to read such rubbish, but today reading through them
seemed the path of least resistance. A lot of them seemed written
in part in code.

'What's GSOH, Mark?'

A voice I wasn't expecting replied.

'Got sense of humour. Not something normally associated
with you, Andrew.' A sarcastic smile spread past Marjorie's face
as she sashayed past.

'Tell me, you aren't reading the classified ads, are you. Not
looking for love, are we?'

Marjorie's voice had the bitchy tone I would have expected from her. I would never have mentioned such a thing if I'd known she was around. She's secretary who's paid to look glamorous at Overend's, but she thinks that that makes her the cat's whiskers. Once she had definitely gone I picked up the paper to throw it back to Mark. As I did so the word 'churches' seemed to leap out at me. Puzzled, I looked again. There it was, at the bottom of the page. '*Attractive, intelligent woman, aged 30, seeks similar man for excitement and maybe more. Interest in country churches a must. Ring Karen on . . .*'

I had thought that most of these ads were just coded messages for prostitution, but this seemed quite different, classier, respectable even. When I was younger, visiting and comparing country churches was a pastime of mine. It seemed sensible to keep the paper and read it again on the Tube going home. In fact I read it and reread it several times. Part of me was keen to ring, curious to find out about this girl, whereas some instinct warned that the whole thing was very dubious and it would be stupid to get involved.

When I got home to the flat I poured myself a long drink, and sat by the phone for almost half an hour debating whether to call or not. Eventually I decided that there was little to lose by just ringing the number to find out more. To tell the truth, life itself was just a little too comfortable, a little too safe, a little too boring. Besides, Susan had left six months ago. We hadn't had a great row, or anything like that, and no one else was involved. We both felt that it was going nowhere – things had just run out of steam.

It was the mention of the word 'churches' which clinched it, though. Ever since I was a child I have been interested in English country churches: the carvings, the decorations, the rood screens, the tombs and ornamental brasses. It seemed obvious to me that any girl with an interest in churches had to be 'different', gentle, traditional. A clear vision of her formed in my mind's eye: classic English rose, tall, fair-haired, girlish. I picked up the phone and dialled. The message on the voice box was brief:

'Hi, this is Karen. Please leave brief details of yourself and a contact number, so I can ring you back.'

The voice was husky, not girlish in the slightest. Southern English, although with no trace of a cockney drawl. There was a slight trace of something exotic in the pronunciation of the letter 'r'.

I left brief details as requested. That was on a Monday. Nothing happened for ten days, and I'd almost forgotten about it when the phone rang on Friday evening about eight o'clock – I had only just got in from work.

'Hello, Andrew?'

'Yes.'

'It's Karen.'

I recognised the voice immediately.

'Would you like to meet tomorrow?'

'Why yes, er – sure.'

'Good. What shall we do? Where shall we go? Andrew, you tell me.'

Before I had a chance to reply the voice continued: 'I've got an idea – let's go and visit a country churchyard somewhere.'

I mentioned the first place which came to mind – a small country town at the eastern end of Berkshire. It was quickly agreed that we would meet at the end of platform eight at Paddington station at ten o'clock the next morning. She rang off before I had time to reflect on what had been arranged. During the week I have to be in the office by 7.30 a.m., so I get up at six. At weekends I like to stay in bed until nine o'clock. Still, up early tomorrow it would have to be.

I got to Paddington by 9.40, and waited by the platform gate. I tried reading the *Financial Times* but my mind was racing and unable to concentrate. Was she going to turn up, or was this some kind of weird hoax? Nobody came and stood by the gate. By 10.20 I'd had enough and stormed off. As I walked briskly towards the Tube entrance a figure in black raced from one of the cafés on the station concourse in my direction. Out of the corner of my eye it looked a bit like a crow flapping towards me.

'Andrew? It's me, Karen. I'm sorry to keep you hanging around. I got here a little while ago, but I suddenly felt very shy, and couldn't bring myself to go up to you.'

I turned and gave her a hard look. She was dressed in a black coat with black trousers and some kind of jersey, with a large black hat covering much of what looked like a thin face. I was about to tell her that I couldn't bear people wasting my time, and that was the end of it, when she took her hat off – and was transformed. A mass of reddish-gold hair flowed around her shoulders making the face seem nicely shaped. The hair colour was perfectly matched by green eyes, and the pale colouring of the skin. You might not call Karen beautiful, but she was certainly stunningly attractive. I felt the blood race through my body, and the words of rebuke died on my lips.

The train for Hendring left in ten minutes. The ticket queue seemed to take ages to move, but we finally got the tickets with just enough time to get on the train. The carriage was fairly empty with just three other people in it. I was desperate to find out more about her.

'Well, Karen, I'm pleased to meet you at last. Do tell me about yourself?'

I cursed myself for the laboured phrasing. Whenever I feel shy or embarrassed I tend to talk in a pompous way. This was the last way I wanted to address this girl, but my old weakness asserted itself.

'Shush, Andrew! I'm not talking about myself so a train full of strangers can hear. Time enough for that later. Let's just sit quietly and read until we get there – please!'

As she said 'please' a curious smile spread across her face. I didn't think that anybody else was in earshot, but shyness was something I understood very well. I got out the *Financial Times* and tried to read it. It only took about forty minutes to get to Hendring. The church, a lovely example of early English perpendicular, is on a slight hill at the end of the high street. I've been there several times. The interior cross-vaulting is impressive, while the rood screen is one of the best examples to survive the Reformation. I took Karen round and explained all the sights in detail; I wanted to demonstrate that I really knew my stuff about churches. She seemed attentive enough, but I was disappointed that she did not ask me any difficult technical questions. Once or twice I thought that it was *me* that she was looking at appraisingly, rather than the architectural features of the church, but it was hard to tell in the gloom. We walked outside.

'Well, what did you think? Interesting, isn't it?'

There was a pause. She smiled that curious, almost painstaking smile again.

'Yes, Andrew, it was. But don't you think that churches lose a lot of their charm, their mystery, when they're so close to all the noise and traffic of modern life?'

'Well, maybe.' I was not convinced.

'What I *really like* are remote country churchyards where I can lose myself in peace and quiet, where you can feel the history. I like churches where you could be the only person in the world, where you feel you could do anything and nobody would know. Take me somewhere like that Andrew – it will be worth it, I promise you. Now I feel tired, so let's go home – please!'

She looked at me beseechingly with that smile fixed on her lips. I got a strange impression of girlish innocence mixed with immense determination. We went home in silence. Again she refused to tell me anything about herself. I consider myself a rational, unemotional sort of chap, but deep down I could feel waves of emotion running through me. Karen looked so soft and vulnerable. I wanted to protect her, get close to her – but she kept me at arm's length. Our train finally arrived back at Paddington, and we got out. Karen spoke quickly.

'Look, I've got to go now. But I really enjoyed today. Let's meet here in a week's time. Same time, same place. I know where to go – it should be good.'

She vanished in the crowd heading for the Tube.

The rest of the week passed in a strange sort of limbo. I had masses of work to do, but my mind kept drifting off to think of Karen. Although my job title is archivist, what I really am at Overend & Gurney is research co-ordinator. The bank makes most of its money from mergers and acquisitions activity. When we're involved in a big takeover, and we normally take part in several each week, my job is to assemble masses of information on the target companies involved. A lot of this is classic financial information, reports and accounts, stockbrokers' reports, and credit ratings and so on, but it also involves trawling through newspaper databases and the Internet. You never know what may be useful until you find it. The investment banking team upstairs will distil it to try and make a strong case why the big investment institutions should accept our offer for their shares, or agree with us that the shares are ridiculously undervalued and reject somebody else's offer if we are the defending bank. Often it is the non-financial aspects which clinch the matter. If the chairman is on the board, say, of various arts charities, we can argue that he has neglected the business, and it's even better if there is something dubious in the past of one of the directors.

Probably the most important part of my job is to prepare summary briefing notes for the team head who is running the account. A bit like a top medical consultant or barrister, they have lots of clients on the go at once. They use my summary to bone up on the situation before they go and see the client – of course their assistants do most of the actual work. Wednesday was bad. I had my misgivings when Marjorie came to see me.

'A little message from upstairs. David wants to see you in his office at 3.00 p.m.'

She turned her head as she walked away.

'I don't think it's good news.'

It wasn't. I could tell that from the way David, who heads up one of the investment banking teams, was perched on the edge of his desk alongside Alan who is his number two.

'Andrew, come in – and shut the door.'

David is late forties, fairly fat with greying hair, has a middle-class accent, and often smells of cigars. He wears what I think are cheap-looking suits with wide pinstripes, although I am sure that they come from the best tailors.

'Andrew, I am not happy. That summary you gave me on Monday on Midlands Industries. You omitted the fact that the earnings are overstated because of capitalisation of research and development. Worse still, you didn't highlight the chairman's flat in Mayfair.'

'Well, that's because it's near the group head office.'

David looked tetchy.

'I *know* that, dear boy. The point is, the chairman's been married three times. The PR boys can use a flat in Mayfair, paid for by the company, to hint at naughty business. It's something I should have known about, and didn't because *you* didn't put it in the summary. I looked a right fool in the meeting with the client. Be careful in future, Andrew. Your work is normally good, but we don't pay you £50,000 a year just to be the librarian. You can go now.'

I went back to my desk, fuming. The trouble was, David was right. I should have highlighted the point about the chairman's flat. It's the sort of thing that in our business should scream out at you when you see it – and I'd missed it because I was thinking of Karen. I resolved to really get stuck into the work, and the rest of the week passed without incident.

Nevertheless, I woke up early on Saturday and leapt out of bed with a spring in my step. As before, I got to Paddington about twenty to ten. I looked around the platform, but there was no sign of Karen. About five minutes later I felt a gentle touch on my shoulder. It was Karen of course, looking much the same as before, except that a tight black skirt had been substituted for the trousers of the previous week. Perhaps it was the effect of meeting her again, but I thought she looked slightly different, the lips brighter, redder, the eyes somehow more visible. There was also a distinct air of perfume that I had not noticed last week. She also carried quite a large rucksack on her back.

'Andrew, you're early.'

'How did you get here? I looked out all over the station for you.'

'Easy, silly. I was on the bridge that connects all the platforms. I saw you coming, and decided to creep up on you and surprise you. Don't look so put out! Look, I've got the tickets – shall we go?'

'Where to?'

'Farringdon – it's a small village outside Oxford. If the weather's half decent it will be glorious. Now come on – the Oxford train leaves in five minutes.'

It turned out to be quite a complicated trip. We got the fast train to Reading, and then a slow 'stopper' that went to Oxford. At Reading I noticed that there was no Farringdon listed. It turned out that we had to get off at a place called Barton Junction, and walk a couple of miles to Farringdon itself. It took about an hour and a half to get to Barton Junction, which seemed just a 'halt' in the middle of nowhere. Fortunately it was one of those nice early summer days where the sky is clear but it is not too hot. We walked along country paths and over stiles for about half an hour until we finally reached Farringdon, not seeing a soul on our journey. I felt so happy to be with Karen, although it niggled that I knew so little about her. Eventually I felt forced to speak out.

'Karen, I can't bear knowing nothing about you. Do tell me about yourself.'

'I will, Andrew, soon – I promise.'

As we walked along, she took my hand and held it there. Again there was that curious smile. Her mouth was fairly small, but I couldn't help noticing how rich, full and red her lips seemed – redder, fuller than they'd looked the week before – and perfect to be kissed. Eventually we reached the church. It looked like a classic English country church. Looking round the external architecture I saw nothing remarkable, so I guessed there had to be something special inside. The spot was fairly deserted. The village had obviously moved down the valley, as there were no houses nearby. I could see quite a large group of houses about three miles away, and what I thought was a pub. On the lychgate a sign was hanging. '*St Ethelburga's Church of England church. Part of the mid-Oxford team ministry. Holy Communion on the first Sunday of each month at 11.00 a.m. Any queries please ring Rev. Jenny Brooks at Barton Green vicarage.*' The churchyard itself looked neglected. I went on to the door and pushed – it was locked.

'Karen, I can't seem to get in. The door seems locked. Where do we get the key?'

'We don't, or rather, you can if you go to Barton Green. But I wouldn't bother – there's nothing worth seeing inside.'

I felt cross.

'Well, why have we come all this way here, then?'

'Simple. It's the perfect place for a picnic, and *there is* something worth seeing in the churchyard. But let's have lunch first. What do you think I have been carrying in this bag?'

So saying she leaned behind her and brought out two glasses and a half-bottle of champagne. We sat down on the grass. In the bag was some French bread, some paté and cheese, fruit and salad. Eating it in the sun in that deserted churchyard was perfection. When we had finished I put my arm round her and kissed her lips. She trembled, and then pushed me away.

'You remember I said that there was something worth seeing in the churchyard? Let's go and find it!'

I followed. At the south-west corner there was a large, curious square tomb, with what looked like reliefs of ships at the top. There was an inscription, but it was too weathered to be intelligible.

'It's the tomb of Admiral Byrne. I think he beat the French in battle in the 1760s.'

'Come round to the side,' she said.

I did and saw metal steps inset into the side of the tomb.

'Climb up to the top and look!'

I mounted the rusty old iron steps. At the top was a glass plate. You could look down into the tomb where an enormous lead coffin was on display. On the floor were fragments of wood of what had clearly once been a crucifix. The whole thing made me feel sad, melancholy. When I got down Karen climbed up. As she climbed her skirt rode up her thighs, and I found myself unconsciously stroking her legs. She came down and turned to me.

'Yes,' she said, falling into my arms.

'But we, we can't make love here in a graveyard!'

'Why not? There's nobody about, and it's wonderfully romantic.'

And we did. Making love to Karen that first time will always stick in my memory. It was quite unlike having sex with other girls. It was like being engulfed. I felt transported out of myself.

We lay, afterwards, on the grass in a close embrace. I felt intensely happy. But in the back of my mind there was a restlessness to know more about Karen. It seemed strange to be so intimate with someone, and yet know so little about them.

'Now, surely you'll tell me about yourself?'

'What do you want to know?'

'Everything about you.'

She laughed.

'Andrew, you're incorrigible! Well, to start with, my name is Karen Francis, I am entering my thirtieth year, and I work at the BBC as a producer.'

'What do you do there? Where do you live? I want to see you as often as possible.'

'As I said I am a producer for BBC Radio. I commission and produce programmes. I suppose production really means managing them until they're finished.'

'Yes, but, Karen, where do you live? I want to see you as much as possible.'

'I share a flat in Islington with two other girls. It's pretty messy and chaotic.'

'When can I see you again?'

'Next Saturday, silly.'

'Why not tomorrow, tonight, every evening next week? Let's meet for dinner tonight. I'll pick you up at your place.'

'Andrew, of course I'd love to see you all the time, but it's not as simple as all that. At the BBC work comes in great masses that all needs to be done urgently. Often I have to work late – I never know in advance when the work will need to be done. I can make sure that I get Saturdays off, but the rest of the time I just have to be available. So you see I can't make dates in the week to see you, much as I'd love to.'

She looked at me again. Her face started to form that curious smile, but it vanished before it fully appeared. She looked very young, vulnerable, in need of protection.

'Look, a lot of what I do at the BBC is grubby, ordinary, even sordid sometimes. When I'm with you I feel romantic, special. I don't want you to get involved in the grimy side of my life. I want us to be special, so Andrew, *please* don't ever try and ring me at work. It's important, Andrew, promise – please!'

'Nothing you do could be grubby, Karen.'

'Andrew, promise you won't.'

'OK.'

The next four weeks passed in the same way. Each Saturday we met in the morning and would go and visit some deserted churchyard. Twice we met at stations and went by train; twice, when it was windy or overcast, Karen picked me up at my flat in Chiswick and drove us to the country. She had one of the large Volvo estates; white, it was one of the older models. I don't know much about cars, but it must have been some fifteen years old. Nevertheless, it went fast. I'm a steady driver – but Karen pushed this old car to go over 80 mph. I was worried that we might get booked by the police, but luckily enough this did not happen.

It almost seemed like living a double life. The quiet, analytical work at the bank during the working week. The wild excitement of Saturday mornings when I would meet Karen. I have never felt so happy, *so alive* in my life. She was everything I wanted in a girl: romantic, trusting, passionately loving. Then the shadows started to come over. The last Saturday in June she picked me up specially early and we went down to a small village in Kent near Faversham. The roads were fairly empty at that time and we made good time. As usual we visited a desolate country church that she knew of, had a picnic, and then made love on a rug in a quiet corner. The weather was overcast, but it was quite warm. We were engrossed in each other when a rough voice boomed out.

'Oy! What's goin' on 'ere then! 'Aven't you got any respect? This is consecrated ground.'

We quickly got dressed. A large man, wearing overalls and boots was looking down at us. I guessed he was some kind of gardener.

'Look, I'm sorry,' I said. 'We didn't think that there was anybody about.'

'I don't care what *you* think. This is our parish church. 'Ow dare you come 'ere and play your filthy games. I've a good mind to report you to the police!'

I felt a touch on my arm. Karen whispered in my ear to let her deal with it.

'We are sorry, we really are,' she said softly.

'My fiancé and I came out here for a drive. It's a beautiful church, and we were overcome by its beauty. I know we shouldn't have done what we did, but we both live with our parents and have nowhere to go – if you know what I mean. It is hard to wait until the wedding day.'

She looked coy, demure even.

'If we have made any mess I am sure we will make a contri-
bution to help you clear it up.'

Another whisper in my ear.

'Andrew, offer him £25!'

The man stopped. A slow light of understanding came into
his eyes.

'All right. I was young meself once.'

He took the £25.

'But clear off now and don't ever come back 'ere. I won't
'ave no disrespect to the church.'

When we had driven on to a pub near Sittingbourne we had a
chance to talk. All sorts of thoughts were buzzing in my mind.

'Karen, what did you mean about us getting married?' I was
not sure how I wanted her to answer the question.

'Well, I had to say something. I could see that you were just
getting his back up. I didn't want him to report us to the police
– he looked just the sort who would have taken down the car
number plate. I thought if I made up some kind of old-fashioned
story he would half buy it, and the offer of cash would do the
rest.'

'But it was all lies. We're not engaged, and we don't live with
our parents. I don't like passing off lies like that.'

She looked testy.

'Well, what would you rather do? Spend the morning in the
police station? Anyway, if you're so virtuous, what are you doing
making love to a girl you're not married to in churchyards?'

I felt that she was right about the last bit, which only made
me more stubborn.

'Karen, I love you. I don't want us to argue. But why do we
keep having to meet in country churches? We could go away for
the weekend, and stay in a nice country inn or something.'

Her face twitched, as if she was thinking very hard.

'Andrew, if I tell you something will you promise not to hold
it against me?'

'Of course not.'

'It's hard to explain. Part of it is that I like to feel romantic, away from the boring mundane part of life. Part of it is history. When I was younger I went to boarding school in the country. When I was sixteen I met an older man. He took me for drives in his car. We often ended up going to a deserted church, where he made love to me. Ever since then I've felt there was something special, exciting about country churches.'

I felt sick, confused, angry.

'You mean that the only reason you want to go out with me is to copy what some old lecher did years ago!'

I felt like punching her.

'No, Andrew, it's not like that. I do love you. You're all that I ever wanted in a man: kind, gentle, honest, thoughtful. Give me time, Andrew, you'll see it's worth it.'

We decided to go home. She drove in silence. I was too confused, too angry with her and with myself to say anything. When we got to Chiswick she dropped me outside the flat. We agreed to meet next Saturday as usual outside the flat at eight o'clock. There was an unspoken understanding that things would be different from now on.

That week we were incredibly busy at work. Three big deals all came to a climax at once. Come Friday I was called into David's office. The atmosphere was electric. I could tell how busy he was by his dishevelled appearance. He came straight to the point.

'Andrew, you know the Internet flotation we're working on?'

'Yes.'

'I hear rumours of a technical problem regarding intellectual copyright. We've got to sort it out by Monday when the markets open. You're the only person who can do it. It'll mean working over the weekend, of course, but I'm afraid there's no alternative. Sort this out and I'll remember it when we work out the bonuses.'

'But . . . but I have things planned for the weekend.'

'Well, you'll have to cancel them, dear boy, won't you! Just make sure the report is on my desk by 7 a.m. on Monday. Oh, and on your way out tell Marjorie to change my flight to Frankfurt tonight from 7.30 to nine o'clock – we're running late. Tell her to tell the Germans that there is some British regulatory problem we need to resolve before we go and see them.'

To have argued further with David in that situation would have meant curtains for my career at Overend's. As soon as I got back to my desk I decided that I would have to call Karen at the BBC. I couldn't take the risk that she wouldn't check her voicemail in time. The main BBC switchboard gave me the number for BBC Radio at Langham Place.

'Hello, can I speak to Karen Francis, please.'

'I'm sorry, can you say the name again?'

'Karen Francis – like in Francis of Assisi.'

The switchboard operator seemed to hesitate for a moment. 'Just a minute.'

The line went dead for a minute or so.

'I'm sorry, there's nobody working here of that name.'

I was not satisfied with the reply.

'I'm sorry to press you, but I got the impression that you did recognise the name.'

The telephonist hesitated.

'Well, actually you gave me a little shock. The name sounded familiar so I checked with the other girls. There used to be a Karen Francis working here, but she died five years ago. Nice girl, got leukaemia, only twenty-five when she died. Still, it's funny how different people have the same names, isn't it? Anyway, there's definitely no Karen Francis working here now.'

'This Karen Francis, what did she do?'

'Er, well, she was a junior producer on documentaries if I remember correctly. Got to go now – the other lines are ringing. Bye!'

I was confused. What the hell was going on? I left a message on Karen's voicemail explaining what had happened, and saying that I couldn't meet her. The rest of the weekend I was working flat out producing this technical report on legal case studies on the

Internet. I didn't have time to think about her much. On Monday David was pleased with the report, which indicated that we didn't appear to have a major problem. I kept hoping to hear from Karen, but there were no messages on my answer phone. I left two messages for her, but the silence was deafening. I hoped that she would turn up at my place the following Saturday, but she didn't. On the next Monday I called in a favour. We use all sorts of information sources. Most of them are above board, but occasionally we use a firm of private detectives. I had occasionally helped them out by doing electronic searches on people they were trying to find. I rang Clive at Executive Information.

'Clive, it's Andrew here. I wonder if you can help me. I'm trying to trace somebody.'

'What information have you got?'

'Not much. A voicebox number at a newspaper, and a car registration number.'

'The voicebox is probably useless. You can rent them under any name you want, and you just ring in from outside and pick up the calls. Assuming the car is owned, and not rented, the police computer will tell you the owner.'

'Is that easy?'

'No, old son. It's illegal to use the police computer for private inquiries.'

'Oh, hell. So there's no way of finding this person.'

'I didn't say that. Most of us here have been on the force, and we have mates still working there. As long as this is likely to stay confidential, nobody will ever know.'

I gave him the number. He rang back ten minutes later.

'*Pas de problem*, old son. The owner of the car is a Kathryn Fields. Two convictions for speeding. If she gets caught one more time, she'll lose her licence. Registered address of the car is 2 Stoneyfields Gardens, Hackney. Hope that's useful. Got to go.'

He rang off.

There's masses of data held on file about everybody – if you know where to look. Within two hours I had compiled a large dossier on Kathryn Fields: National Insurance number, credit rating, job history. She was born in 1963, making her thirty-six rather than the thirty she'd told me. She had a mortgage on a small house in Hackney, and had worked for the BBC for the last ten years, but in the accounting department, rather than as a producer. 'Karen' had certainly told me a pack of lies. Finding out about her had been easy; deciding what to do with it was much harder. Reason told me to ignore such a liar, but I couldn't forget the excitement and euphoria of our time together.

I rang BBC Radio, asking for Kathryn Fields. This time I was put through without question.

'Hello, accounts. Can I help you?'

It was Karen's voice all right.

'Yes, please. I'm looking for a Karen Francis.'

There was a pause.

'Oh, very clever, Andrew. Tracked me down, huh?'

'Look, Kathryn . . .'

'If you're going to speak to me, call me Karen.'

'OK, Karen. I'm very keen to see you. Can we meet at my place this week?'

An even longer pause.

'Andrew, I'm not sure that this is a good idea.'

'Please, Karen. Don't you think that you owe me an explanation?'

After more urging from me, she finally agreed to come round that evening. I'm not a bad cook, and prepared a light supper of chicken and rice, pesto and sun-dried tomatoes. She came round about eight. Over supper we talked about general things for a while, then I got to the point.

'Karen, I feel angry, abused. Why did you tell me such a pack of lies? Why give me a false name? Why, Karen, why?'

'Andrew, things aren't always as simple, as black or white, as you seem to think. I hate my job at the BBC – if you really want to know, I am an accounts clerk. My family are quite prosperous, and I should have gone to university, but I dropped out of school, and ended up in this dead-end job. I hate this mediocre job, this crummy house I live in, the stupid friends I have.'

She began to cry.

'Can't you see that I wanted a bit of romance and excitement, something strange, different? I wanted to get away from myself, and my dull, petty little life, and be somebody else.'

'But why use an assumed name?'

'A few years ago someone pointed that I looked quite like the real Karen Francis. *She* was a high-flier, glamorous, determined, an assistant producer in her mid-twenties. I used to think that if I had gone to university, I could have been like her. When she died, I thought, well, why not become her? The fact that our initials were the same seemed to hint that this was meant to happen.'

She stayed the night, but things seemed dull, the excitement had vanished. She was passive, going through the motions. It was like looking at a lovely painting with all the beautiful colours washed out. Only a depressing greyness was left.

She left in the morning without kissing me.

'You see, Andrew, what a dull mouse Kathryn Fields is. I don't want us to meet again. I have fond memories of our trips to country churches. If we meet like this again, those memories will be wasted, become dirty.'

Her mouth twisted in disgust. She began to cry again. At that moment I just wanted her to get out of my house. One last question demanded to be asked.

'Can't you become Karen Francis again?'

'No. She died five years ago. That would just be poor little Kathryn pretending to be glamorous Karen – and failing.'

She sobbed, and left the house.

'Goodbye, Andrew.'

During the next few weeks I tried furiously to get Karen out of my mind, but the memory of our time together would not go away. By late July things became very quiet in the office as everyone went away on holiday. A brilliant idea occurred to me

– I would find some perfect country churchyard, take Karen to it, and we could begin again. I started to trawl though the Internet, looking for all mentions of country churches. I eventually found just what I was looking for: Axford Newton in Dorset, a perfect late-medieval church that had been abandoned during the war when the surrounding land had been commandeered by the Army. Most of the year the church was out of bounds owing to Army manoeuvres, but it was open to the public in the first half of August. It seemed the perfect place to take Karen.

I kept looking on the Internet for other places to go. There was nothing special in the data over the last three years. Four years back a disturbing headline hit me: '*Man found dead in churchyard.*' I downloaded the full story. In September 1995 a man's body had been found in the grounds of the little church of Hallington in Norfolk. He had head injuries, which might have been consistent with falling and hitting his head on a gravestone. The police were puzzled that he had got to such a remote location with no obvious means of transport. He had been drinking heavily, and had eaten recently, but no signs of food or drink were found on the spot.

Fascinated, I looked further. In May 1992 a man had been found hanging from a rope in a remote church in Cumbria. He too had been drinking heavily. The police suspected that it was some kind of sex act which had gone wrong, as he was naked except for a pair of woman's stockings. Police inquiries found no evidence that he had got there by public transport, and they mentioned sightings of a large white car, but no further details were forthcoming, and the inquest decided it was misadventure.

I kept looking. I thought the trail had petered out, that it was nothing but coincidence thrown together by my own sense of guilt. But I kept searching further back just to be sure. In 1987 I found more evidence, and sure proof of the sickening suspicion growing within me. In June of that year Leon Harris, a leading barrister, had been found stabbed to death in a gardener's shed attached to the Magdalen church of Endsbury, near Salisbury. A police statement suggested that he had surprised a tramp committing a crime, and was attacked to keep him quiet. The reasons for Harris being in the churchyard had never been established. The press suggested that Harris might have gone to the shed with a tramp for gay sex, but police discounted this as he was a happily married man with no known homosexual links. Despite an extensive murder hunt no culprit was ever found.

I continued looking further and further back. It took a long time, but eventually I found what I knew had to be there. It was in the *West of England Gazette*, 18 March 1979:

> *Man Killed outside Yerby Church*
> *James Wilson, 43, a businessman from Bristol was found stabbed to death in the grounds of Holy Trinity church at Yerby yesterday. Police are questioning a 16-year-old girl who was with him at the time. No further details were made available.*

Three days later there was more:

> *Schoolgirl Charged with Yerby Death*
> *Kathryn (Kate) Fields, a pupil at the exclusive St Bennet's School for Girls, was today charged with the murder of businessman James Wilson at Yerby church on 17 March. She was remanded in custody. Miss Alexandra Hamilton, headmistress of St Bennet's, said that this had come as a terrible shock to the school. She added that she was sure that Kate was innocent of any wrongdoing. She confirmed that the family had commissioned a solicitor to represent her, and that he would be applying for bail.*

The trial took place in November. There was no argument that Kate Fields had gone with James Wilson to Yerby churchyard, that they had had a picnic there, and that she had stabbed him to death with a kitchen knife belonging to St Bennet's school. The prosecution argued that this was deliberate murder, planned with a cold deliberation beyond her years by the defendant. The defence case was based on self-defence, and the argument that this was a young, innocent schoolgirl manipulated by an older man. They stated that Wilson had flattered Fields, taken her out to concerts and restaurants in the Bristol area, with the sole aim of seducing her. He had aimed to do this in Yerby churchyard. When she resisted, he tried to rape her. In self-defence she picked up a knife she had used to cut cheese and bread, and stabbed him with it. The defence's closing speech made much of her youth and innocence. The prosecution had tried to allege that she was notoriously promiscuous, but Miss Hamilton had destroyed that idea in the witness box: 'St Bennet's girls do not behave like that.' After a brief wait, the jury found her not guilty. Miss Hamilton then explained that in view of the publicity it had been decided it would not be appropriate for Kate to go back to St Bennet's. The newspaper writer thought that she was going to lose herself in the anonymity of London.

I had now been trawling though the Internet for about six hours. My eyes ached, and it was about ten o'clock at night. We were not supposed to use the office computer systems for our own purposes, and this was something I respected. I had not done this before, and felt guilty about it, but knew that nobody was likely to check. One trader had been sacked for downloading computer pornography at his desk, but you had to be pretty stupid to do something like that. I decided to ring Clive, knowing he worked irregular hours. I was in luck, as he was there.

'Working late, Andrew. Got nothing, or nobody, better to go home to?'

'Just working late, Clive. A question, how do the police normally catch a serial killer?'

There was a strained silence.

'What a strange question! Overend's aren't going to start bumping off their rivals, are they?'

'No, seriously.'

'Well, I was never on a murder enquiry. Fraud and vice was my line, but from what I remember most repeat killers have a pattern they stick to, it makes them feel safe. In the force we call it the *modus operandi*, or M.O. You know the police often talk of distinctive details they won't release, well, that's partly to rule out the cranks that call in, and partly it's to identify the M.O. One case I heard, this guy got prostitutes to go in his car, he gave them drugs in a drink, and strangled them. He always tied their wrists with a certain type of twine. So, when you found a naked whore's body, tied with that kind of twine, and drugged in a certain way, you were pretty sure it was our boy. It took four years, but they got him in the end. He's on the Isle of Wight, and he ain't ever going to come out.'

'But what if a killer changed their M.O.?'

'It would be much harder to track them down. When you set up a murder inquiry, you have this period of intense activity. You check all the obvious suspects, like all the local paedophiles if a child is killed, and see if there are any obvious similarities of cases over the last, say, five years. If nothing turns up – and for most murders it's obvious who's done it – after a couple of months you wind down the murder team. There's too much other crime that needs sorting out.'

I rang off. I thought for a while, and then went home. I rang Karen from a phone box on the way home. It was about midnight. Her phone rang for ages before she answered it. She sounded sleepy.

'Who is it?'

'It's me, Andrew. We must meet, tomorrow. My place, eight o'clock. Bring your car.'

'Andrew, I don't want ever to see you again. It's for your own good, believe me. It's over, Andrew, can't you accept that?'

'Karen, I want to see you for the last time. I want to blot out the memory of when you came to my flat. I've found a wonderful church in Dorset we could go to. Let's end it on a high, OK?'

There was a long pause. Finally she spoke:

'Yes, Andrew, that would be perfect! See you tomorrow, then.'

She arrived at eight o'clock on the dot, and drove like the wind. We were in Hampshire by nine, and reached Axford by ten thirty. It was one of those August days that promised to be blisteringly hot later in the day, but early in the morning it was perfect. In the car there was the excitement and mystery of our first meetings. As usual we had a picnic, stretched a rug, and made love in the open. She was even more passionate than usual, but there was a lingering tenderness there which had not been present before. We both knew that this was the end.

Later, lying close together, I spoke to her.

'Karen, last night I was searching databases for places to go. I discovered all about you. I found out about the Wilson trial, the guy in Norfolk, and the one in Cumbria. It was you, wasn't it?'

To my surprise she didn't murmur or appear shocked.

'Of course it was. I guessed you'd tumbled.'

It was me that looked surprised.

'Andrew, you're so obvious sometimes. That mysterious phone call last night – "meet me tomorrow". The way you've been watching me all the time today, as if I'm going to stick a knife in you. Well, what are you going to do – hand me over the police?'

I had been thinking about that.

'No, I'm not going to do that. I just want you to promise me that you'll stop doing this. I couldn't bear to see you in police custody. Just promise me that you'll stop. I'll keep an eye out for strange deaths in churchyards, and if I see any, I will tell the police what I know, I swear I will.'

'And what's the payoff for not telling the police – want me to be your sex slave, do you?'

She wrapped her body provocatively around mine.

'No, Karen, nothing like that. We shouldn't ever meet again. In different circumstances we could have been very good together, but not now, not with me knowing what I know.'

'And what's to stop me knocking you on the head to shut you up for ever?'

'I know it's corny, but I have written up all the stuff about you and sent it to my brother. If I suddenly disappear, or come to a sticky end, he has instructions to read it and send it to the police.'

I hadn't, in fact, done that. The idea that I might actually be in danger had only occurred to me on the drive down. She looked hard at me. That curious smile returned to her lips.

'Yeah, that's the sort of thing you would just do.'

She kissed me gently on the lips.

'Well, Andrew, I guess it's goodbye.'

She picked up the bottle of champagne we had been drinking.

'Let's tidy up before we go.'

I leant forward to pack. I faintly heard a swish in the air, and felt a hard blow on the back of the head. There was no pain, just a sense of shock. I blacked out. When I woke up, it was about twelve thirty. I managed to wrap a handkerchief around my head which was bleeding a little, and stagger to the main road about a mile and a half away. Lots of cars went past, but nobody seemed to want to give me a lift. After about an hour an old man stopped in a battered pick-up. He took me to Dorchester Hospital. I told the doctor I had fallen over while climbing rocks.

'It's not too bad. There is lots of bruising and minor damage to the scalp, but no sign of a break in the skull. We'll need to take more X-rays to make sure, and to keep you in overnight in case of delayed concussion, but you should be able to go home tomorrow.'

I did.

Tuesday I got a letter, stamped Heever Service Station.

Dearest Andrew

You came close to the truth. James Wilson ruined my life. He seduced me. We had been to bed several times, but when he tried to force me in the churchyard I stabbed him. I didn't mean to kill him. After the trial I got thrown out of St Bennet's. Instead of going to university I ended up in rubbish jobs in London.

I didn't mind. I thought that was my fate. Then Leo came

along. He reminded me of James. He took me out for drives in his big car, and boasted of the top restaurants he took me to. One fine autumn day we went for a drive in the country, and he wanted to have sex in the open. I didn't want to. He took me to this shed. I knew what was coming. When I stabbed him I meant to kill him. You were right about the others. There were three more you didn't discover. Two I threw their bodies into the sea, one I buried in a half-open vault.

You know I really loved you, Andrew, don't you? You're nice and gentle and kind. I could never have managed to kill you. I did think of it, of hitting you with the bottle and running over your unconscious body, but decided that I couldn't do it. (And I didn't believe your stupid story about 'details left with my brother'.) If things had been different, you know we might have made a good couple.

Thanks for the offer of keeping silent, but Kathryn's dull little life is not worth living. If Karen has to die again, then so be it.

Love,
Karen

I checked the police bulletins. A white Volvo had been involved in a chase with a police car on the M3 on Saturday when checked for speeding. It had tried to leave the police car behind by accelerating to over 100 miles per hour, but the female driver had lost control and crashed into a concrete roadside post. The unconscious driver was taken by ambulance to Winchester Hospital, but died before getting there.

I said a little prayer for Karen. It was just like her to kill herself by crashing her car in a duel with the traffic cops. I shall never forget her. Once a year, on the anniversary of our first date, I visit the quiet Somerset churchyard where she is buried to lay flowers. So in a way our meetings in country churches go on.

Also edited by Kevin Carolan:

CELTIC MYSTERIES
Classic Ghost Stories for Today's Readers

Wales, Ireland, Scotland and Cornwall. Great places to go on holiday and relax in the summer – in daylight. In the long nights of winter it's a different story. Bleak moors; bare, frozen mountains; rough seas. And that's just the natural world. What about the ancient stone circles, ruined churches and dark castles which litter the landscape of the Celtic lands? It's not surprising that many of the greatest ghost stories ever written came out of this background.

CELTIC MYSTERIES gathers them together for the first time in one volume, many of them little known even to lovers of supernatural fiction. There are horrific tales by such masters of the macabre as Bram Stoker, J. S. LeFanu and William Hope Hodgson, as well as spine chillers such as 'Thrawn Janet' by R. L. Stevenson and 'The Open Door' by Margaret Oliphant. Tales of children stolen by the 'little people', of banshees and devil worship, and of malignant, brooding revenge. Pick up the book, and you'll find yourself in a world where mists descend upon mountains without warning, and the sea harbours unimaginable horrors.

Hodder & Stoughton
0 340 74667 3